Space, Structures, in a Post-Pandemic World

MW01257394

Pandemics have long-term effects on how we live and work, and the COVID-19 pandemic was no exception, accelerating us into a digital economy, in which people increasingly work, shop, and learn online, transforming how we use space in-person and remotely. *Space, Structures, and Design in a Post-Pandemic World* explores the rebalancing of our physical and digital interactions and what it means for the built environment going forward.

This book examines the effect of the pandemic on our use of land, interior space, energy, and transportation, as well as on our approach to design, wealth, work, and practice. Author Thomas Fisher also discusses the plagues of institutional racism and climate change that coincided with the COVID-19 pandemic and how these were inter-related. At the same time as all of this, the automation of all or part of many jobs continued unabated, eliminating much of the work that people did before COVID-19 arrived. This text discusses how we might leverage the under-utilized human talent and material assets all around us to rebuild our communities and our economy in more creative ways for a more equitable, resilient future.

Space, Structures, and Design in a Post-Pandemic World will influence anyone interested in how design thinking can transform how we see the world and those looking for new ways to understand what the COVID-19 pandemic means and what opportunities it creates for our environments.

Thomas Fisher is a Professor in the School of Architecture, Director of the Minnesota Design Center, and former Dean of the College of Design at the University of Minnesota. A former President of ACSA, he is also the former Editorial Director of *Progressive Architecture* magazine, recognized in 2005 as the fifth most published architecture writer in the United States. He has written or edited 11 books, 70 book chapters or introductions, and over 450 articles in professional journals and major publications.

Space, Structures, and Design in a Post-Pandemic World

Thomas Fisher

Routledge
Taylor & Francis Group

NEW YORK AND LONDON

Cover image: Oregon Sky Eye. SoulRider.222/Eric Rider © 2021, Flickr CC BY-2.0.

First published 2022
by Routledge
605 Third Avenue, New York, NY 10158

and by Routledge
4 Park Square, Milton Park, Abingdon, Oxon, OX14 4RN

Routledge is an imprint of the Taylor & Francis Group, an informa business

© 2022 Thomas Fisher

Library of Congress Cataloging-in-Publication Data
A catalog record for this title has been requested

ISBN: 978-1-032-05580-0 (hbk)
ISBN: 978-1-032-05581-7 (pbk)
ISBN: 978-1-003-19819-2 (ebk)

DOI: 10.4324/9781003198192

Typeset in Times New Roman
by codeMantra

I dedicate this book to the family compound, which showed me how to endure the pandemic with patience and perseverance.

CONTENTS

FIGURES

PREFACE

This book began as a blog, which I started writing as the COVID-19 pandemic unfolded in early 2020.[1] But I have long been interested in the impact that pandemics have had on cities, having published an early article on that topic in 2010.[2] Pandemics may not seem like events that have systemic impacts, but they very much do. Pandemics also accelerate trends already under way, revealing dysfunctions long ignored, and pushing us past various tipping points.

During and immediately after pandemics, we understandably focus on the scarcity of equipment and vaccines, the lack of knowledge and preparedness, and the gap in healthcare access and public-health understanding. But pandemics also highlight the under-appreciated abundances and excess capacities in societies: the abundance of mutual aid that arises in response to unmet needs, the abundance of unleveraged assets that we can use in creative ways, and the abundance of human capacity that sits idle, awaiting employment. That paradox of abundance in the midst of scarcity highlights another important aspect of a pandemic: It forces us to think and act in new ways as it lays waste to old assumptions, out-of-date practices, and obsolete policies.

This book has three parts, each reflecting a different aspect of our post-pandemic future. The first part looks at the impact of pandemics on the use of space and the design of systems, as well as on our politics, economics, and employment. Those five chapters explore the implications of the COVID-19 pandemic's rebalancing of the digital and physical worlds. While that rebalancing had begun prior to the pandemic, COVID-19 accelerated us in that direction in ways that have profound implications for how many of us will live, work, learn, and interact long into the future.

The second part of the book explores those implications in greater detail. Its four chapters examine how particular building types – homes and offices, stores and restaurants, schools and colleges, and museums and libraries – will be transformed by the greater choice that many people will have between doing something in-person or remotely, physically or digitally. Past pandemics also expanded people's choices and in that sense, the COVID-19 pandemic was no different.

The third part of the book steps back to consider the impact of the COVID-19 pandemic on cities and infrastructure. Pandemics have often triggered anti-urban sentiments as people flee cities out of a fear of infection, but pandemics do not kill cities so much as transform them, especially in terms of their form and function. The third part of the book ends with a thought experiment in how to redefine our relationship with the natural world, from which the zoonotic virus of COVID-19 emerged.

There is much in the book that is somewhat speculative and necessarily journalistic, since it deals with the future, as much as the present and past, and it reports on a situation that was unfolding as I wrote about it. But I hope the book offers some useful perspective based on the lessons of past pandemics and some helpful guidance given what we already know is happening.

While pandemics are profoundly disruptive events that can be disorienting for those who go through them, they also open up abundant opportunities for those who are open to creating a new and more equitable and sustainable future. Pandemics are among the worst experiences any of us will ever endure and among the best things that could happen to any of us willing to re-imagine the possibilities of a better life for all.

Notes

1 Thomas Fisher, "A Journal of the Pandemic Year." https://pandemicyear. wordpress.com/
2 Thomas Fisher, "Viral Cities," *Places*, October 2010. https://placesjournal.org/ article/viral-cities/

PART 1

POST-PANDEMIC CHALLENGES AND OPPORTUNITIES

1

SPACE

Every pandemic affects how we use – and view – physical space. In the wake of the Black Death in Europe, cities developed a new appreciation of the spatial location of dead bodies and with that came the emergence of cemeteries, often at the outskirts of the city, and the eventual end of the practice of burying people in backyards or under the floor of churches in cities.[1] During that medieval plague, there also arose a new-found appreciation of social distancing. The quarantine island – Poveglia – in the Venice lagoon, for example, was a place where sailors and their goods had to stay for weeks to ensure they were not carrying disease, before they were allowed into the city itself.[2]

A different set of spatial practices emerged in the mid-19th century in the wake of the cholera pandemics that occurred around the world at various times during that era. Prior to that pandemic, people often viewed cities as large versions of small towns and rural villages, with outhouses in backyards and slop sinks emptied into the streets. But the large number of deaths that resulted from waterborne cholera bacteria led cities to change their spatial and infrastructural practices.[3] Sanitary sewers and indoor plumbing became a pervasive part of urban life, with later zoning and building codes requiring them in all new developments. That shift, in part because of cholera, enabled

DOI: 10.4324/9781003198192-2

Figure 1.1 "Poveglia," a quarantine island in Venice, Italy.

cities to become larger and denser as more people could live more safely, closer together and in taller buildings, without having to use backyard latrines.

That water infrastructure especially benefited poorer people, who more often lived in housing that lacked indoor plumbing. With it came a host of other benefits related to urban density, such as more employment opportunities, higher productivity, and greater access to services, as well as downsides, such as higher housing costs, more congestion, and greater pollution.[4] Pandemics, in other words, have both good and bad long-term consequences. These events rapidly accelerate us into the future as technologies and systems that may have been present but marginal before the infection become dominant afterward, permanently altering our lives.

That acceleration happened again after the 1918 flu pandemic. The influenza virus spread so widely and so fast, in part, because of the crowded housing, streets, and trolleys of large cities, whose density had been at least partly enabled by the water infrastructure put in place after the previous pandemic. As a respiratory illness, the post-World-War-I flu pandemic prompted people to wear masks, avoid

Figure 1.2 St. Louis Red Cross emergency corps, 1918 influenza epidemic.

public places, and remain socially distanced, akin to what happened during the COVID-19 pandemic.[5] But the spatial impact of that after 1918 differed from what we recently experienced.

The 1918 flu pandemic helped spur a desire on the part of many people to socially distance permanently and move away from dense cities, accelerating the suburbanization that would dominate the rest of the century.[6] While the automobile and single-family housing existed prior to the 1918 pandemic, what had been largely the privilege of the well-to-do before World War I – automobiles and large-lot houses – became much more widespread after the pandemic. Banking reforms and new financing mechanisms that arose in the 1920s and 1930s further fueled the ability of many people to afford cars and stand-alone houses.

Meanwhile zoning codes became far more prescriptive, especially after the 1926 Supreme Court decision – *Village of Euclid versus Ambler Realty* – that supported the right of local governments to determine land use in their communities.[7] Zoning codes that initially focused on building setbacks to ensure that streets received sufficient daylight, in the case of New York City, or on separating industrial uses from all other activities, in the case of Los Angeles, evolved into regulatory documents that specified land uses, building locations, and unit sizes. The common practice of requiring six-foot-wide side yard setbacks even recalled the social distancing recommendations of the 1918 pandemic.

As happened after the 19th-century cholera pandemics, this shift in the 20th century toward lower-density, socially distanced living had both good and bad effects. On one hand, home ownership, especially after World War II, became more affordable to a much larger portion of the population. On the other hand, it led to white flight, racial covenants, red lining, and other means of segregating the American population by race, religion, income, and class.[8] The change in our use and perception of physical space after a pandemic seems to depend, in part, upon the nature and cause of the illness. Bacterial infections tend to prompt shifts in the nature and location of buried infrastructure, while viral infections appear to affect our behavior in social spaces more.

It may be too early to know precisely how our use of space will change in the wake of the COVID-19 pandemic, but we can already see some of its impact, following a similar course to the previous pandemics. For example, mobile digital technology and the Internet existed prior to 2020, as did their use in enabling growing numbers of people to work from home, shop online, and learn at a distance. But the recent pandemic made that technology and those practices a dominant way in which many people worked, shopped, and learned during the pandemic.[9] COVID-19, in other words, forced a rebalancing of the digital and physical environment in a matter of days or weeks, accelerating us rapidly into a future that otherwise might have taken years or even decades to evolve.

Not everyone benefited from that acceleration. Less affluent families, unable to afford wide-bandwidth access to the Internet, and households in remote locations, where such connectivity is not even available, found it difficult to access classrooms, workplaces, or goods and services.[10] We often see the gaps between urban and remote rural locations as somehow different from those that exist between the white population and communities of color in cities, but the inequities that arose during the COVID-19 pandemic showed how much those otherwise quite diverse communities, in very different locations, have in common. Pandemics do not just accelerate us into the future; they exacerbate inequalities and also highlight opportunities and potential alliances in the present.

The COVID-19 pandemic broke us of old spatial practices as well. Prior to the pandemic, most of us thought that to do something, we had to go somewhere: to an office or factory in order to work, to a store or mall in order to shop, or to a classroom or lecture hall in order to learn. Ironically, that reflected assumptions established during the previous post-pandemic era, when, after 1918, we began to organize cities, suburbs, and small towns into single-use zoning districts that required us to drive from one to the other over the course of a day. Although the digital technology existed to free us from such constant commuting for at least a couple of decades prior to 2020, it took the pandemic to reveal that potential.

Still, old habits take a long time to die and the assumptions that shaped our built environment may take a long time to change, in part because of the sunk cost we have in the way things are. We saw this happen in previous pandemics as well. Despite the widespread embrace of sanitary sewers and indoor plumbing after the 19th-century cholera pandemics, parts of cities and especially more remote rural locations continued to have outdoor latrines for some time.[11] And despite the desire to socially distance after the 1918 flu pandemic, many people continued to live, not out of choice, in overcrowded tenements for much of the last century. In hindsight, we might wonder why we continue to hold on to such old spatial practices, but prior to the change in thinking that comes with pandemics, it can seem hard to imagine the world any other way.

Pandemics, though, do not just disrupt our previous assumptions: they also give us greater choice in how to live our lives. That greater choice does not necessarily eliminate what existed before: we can still find outhouses in remote locations in the U.S., for instance, despite the prevalence of indoor plumbing, and we still have high-density housing and heavily used transit despite the prevalence of car-oriented suburbs. The same will no doubt happen in the wake of the COVID-19 pandemic. Workers have already returned to offices, shoppers to stores, and students and teachers to classrooms, but the ability to telework, shop online, and distantly learn will, from now on, remain a viable, and for some, a more desirable option. Most of us – and rightfully, all of us – now have a choice in terms of what we do in physical or digital space.

The Built Environment's Digital Challenge

That presents a challenge – and an opportunity – for the built environment. Offices, stores, and schools as well as myriad other building types – factories, malls, theaters, stadiums, and the like – still have important roles to play, but owners of and tenants in those facilities will have to compete for our attention and our attendance, as we learned how to do almost everything remotely during the pandemic. Having the choice of whether or not to appear in person or via a digital platform means that those responsible for the built environment – from the owners of buildings to those who design, finance, construct, and operate them – will have to think in terms of what physical space can do that the online world cannot, what interactions and experiences can only happen in person, and for what reasons. While pandemics affect the health of the human population in the short term, they affect the built environment for decades afterward.

The sorting out of what gets done in person or remotely will certainly affect the amount and type of built space we need, something that was also an issue in previous pandemics. In the wake of the Black Death, with its dramatic toll on urban populations, cities had an excessive amount of empty buildings, which were eventually demolished, creating large open spaces in cities that anticipated the idea that green space could exist not just outside cities but within them as well.[12] The public-health implications of pandemics, in other words, go beyond epidemiology to include a renewed attention to the quality of our lives and the health-related aspects of the physical environment.

Likewise, the 19th-century cholera pandemics forced governments to confront the large number of outhouses and massive amount of horse manure in the streets, all of which could contaminate water

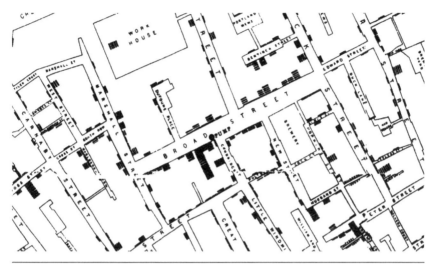

Figure 1.3 John Snow's Broad Street Pump map.

supplies, a connection first recognized by Dr. John Snow in his famous mapping of the cholera cases caused by the Broad Street pump during London's 1854 outbreak.[13] In addition to the water-related infra-structure that this prompted in cities around the world starting in the latter half of the 19th century, cholera led to the paving of streets to allow for easier cleaning of them, and the provision of public baths, for those who did not have access to indoor plumbing.[14]

The amount and density of built space also became an issue af-ter the 20th-century flu pandemic. In industrial cities, with people living near where they worked, densely packed apartment buildings and trolley cars enabled the rapid spread of airborne viruses.[15] That experience helped prompt building codes that prescribed health-related regulations, such as occupant numbers, ventilation rates, and fire-egress routes. The period after the 1918 flu pandemic also saw a significant expansion in the frequency and size of single-family res-idential districts and in the accommodation of private automobiles, which became the default transportation mode in the most developed countries.

In the wake of the COVID-19 pandemic, we face such issues again. As in previous pandemics, people fled cities to more isolated rural locations as the COVID-19 virus spread, constituting a form of geographical distancing.[16] But despite such initial urban flight, people in the past have always returned to cities because of the role such settlements play both economically and culturally.[17] The question we now face is: Will our acceleration into the digital age still follow that history? Will the fact that many people can now work, shop, and learn from almost anywhere affect the rapid urbanization that has been happening around the world? When offered more choice in where we can now live, in other words, what will we decide?

It will undoubtedly take decades before we know the answer to that question. But in terms of physical space, one response to it already seems clear. Whether people occupy smaller cities and towns as remote workers or continue to occupy cities and suburbs as metropolitan residents, all will have the benefit of an extraordinary abundance of excess built space. Communities that have suffered from decline and depopulation over the last several decades already have empty storefronts and vacant land, but in the wake of the COVID-19 pandemic, once-thriving cities and suburbs now face the same dilemma. How we deal with that excess space will determine how well we recover from the pandemic and what direction our built environment takes.

Offices will still exist, for example, but many organizations may seek smaller footprints as employees do some amount of their work at home or in other remote locations. Stores will still exist, but many retailers may need less square footage as more goods are delivered to people's doorsteps. And schools will still exist, but many may need fewer seats as some students learn remotely or educators teach remotely at least part of the time. How we such facilities will be one of the major tasks of those who are responsible for creating and managing the built environment for decades to come.

The recent pandemic forced that re-imaging from the start. In a matter of weeks, once COVID-19 arrived, employees and parents had to convert their homes into workplaces and classrooms; restauranteurs had to transform their businesses into take-out operations, with curbside or door-to-door delivery; and retailers had to convert their stores to distribution centers for their customers, many of whom became online shoppers. Those responses showed how creative people can be in the use of space when pushed to do so. The changing use of

Figure 1.4 "Empty office building," a common sight after the pandemic.

space, however, also challenged one of the bedrock assumptions of the modern built environment: that it contains specialized buildings, designed to accommodate the singular uses that the different parts of our lives seem to demand.

As the architectural historian Nikolas Pevsner has shown in his history of building types, many specialized structures – hotels, offices, warehouses – arose in the 19th century in parallel with the industrial revolution and during and after of the cholera epidemics of that era.[18] Prior to industrialization, many human activities occurred in multi-use buildings, often in houses and farmsteads, where people worked as well as lived, in a highly flexible built environment whose functions changed with the time of day or season. What makes that history newly significant is that, as happened in the pre-industrial economy, large numbers of people now work from home again, accounting by some estimates for over two-thirds of U.S. economic activity.[19] That suggests that we may have entered a high-tech, digitally enabled, internet-reliant version of a pre-19th century, homestead economy, in which goods and services increasingly are delivered by us and to us in our homes, rather than requiring that we go out to get them.

This does not mean the end of buildings, of course. But the post-COVID-19 reality represents a profound shift in how we think about the built environment, how we occupy it, and how much of it we need – all of which will have a major impact on human settlements. Most municipalities, for example, garner a sizable percentage of their tax revenues from commercial and industrial property owners, in an effort to keep the tax burden on the constituents living – and voting – in their communities as low as possible.[20] As the amount of commercial and industrial space we need shrinks and as property foreclosures becomes a likely possibility in many places where the demand for leased space has decreased dramatically, municipalities will have to rethink how they fund government services, what services they can still afford to provide, and where they can increase density to raise more revenues without increasing taxes.

Viral Tipping Points

Pandemics, in other words, rapidly and sometimes radically change the rules that govern our policies and spatial practices. Malcolm Gladwell's idea of "tipping points" helps explain how this happens.[21] He wrote about the Law of the Few, the Stickiness Factor, and the Power of Context as ways to understand how epidemics occur. His Law of the Few states that it doesn't take much to start an epidemic, only a few Connectors, as Gladwell called them: people with a lot of acquaintances, who are also Mavens, who like to spread information in persuasive ways. We may never know the few people who unintentionally spread COVID-19 beyond Wuhan, China, but they may have had connections to those places where the virus began to spread early on, in countries like South Korea, Iran, and Italy.[22] And it probably took only a few handshakes among a few infected people, who then got on planes or trains, to turn a localized outbreak of a novel disease into a global pandemic.

The same Law of the Few also applies to built space. Some companies, able to operate effectively and efficiently with their staff working remotely, decided that they would not return to their leased space or require as many buildings as they previously occupied, representing a tipping point in the real estate markets in many cities. Once a few large employers, who also serve as major Connectors and Mavens in their hometowns, make such a move, that gives other employers allowance to think the same, who in turn spread the idea to their suppliers. The real estate meme of remote work then goes viral.

Gladwell reminded us that Connectors and Mavens, alone, cannot create an epidemic. What they transmit also has to have a Stickiness Factor, which makes something stick after it has begun to spread. "There is a simple way to package information," wrote Gladwell, "that, under the right circumstances, can make it irresistible. All you have to do is find it."[23] Gladwell refers here to the stickiness of ideas or information, but his observation applies to zoonotic viruses as well. They not only jump from animals to humans, as happened with COVID-19, but they can also resist our immune systems by tinkering on the margin, as Gladwell described it. And they can prove irresistible to us, in the sense that they are very contagious and easily transmitted from person to person, as again we discovered with this novel coronavirus.

The idea of remote work also had a Stickiness Factor that many people have found irresistible. The COVID-19 pandemic showed how much money owners and tenants spend on real estate that sits unused for much of the time – the offices that sit mostly empty overnight and on weekends, the houses and apartments that sit mostly empty during the workday, and the school buildings that sit mostly empty on holidays and over the summer break. With the rapid increase in the number of people working and learning from home during the pandemic came a recognition that many of us could use the space we already have more thoroughly and in many different ways as well as use less space in order to do what we had been doing. The idea attributed to the architect Mies van der Rohe of "less is more" took on new meaning in the post-pandemic world.[24] While people with too little need more, people with too much probably need less, and all of us might do better if we did more with less.

Finally, there is the Power of Context as Gladwell phrased it, where "epidemics are strongly influenced by their situation."[25] The context has to be right for a virus to spread, be it because of government secrecy suppressing the scope of the situation, as happened initially in

China with COVID-19, or because of a government's dismissal of the seriousness of the problem, as happened with the Trump administration in the U.S. and the leaders of other countries, like the Bolsonaro administration in Brazil. While viruses ignore political boundaries, their spatial dispersion very much depends upon the political decisions of leaders.

The Power of Context in the post-pandemic world could be rephrased as the power of computing. Well before COVID-19 arrived, we had the digital tools that allowed us to use space differently than we had in the past, setting the context for the rapid shift to doing almost everything remotely during the pandemic. That never could have happened had we not already had the means to make that change, and it certainly saved lives. Many more people would have become infected and died from COVID-19 if mobile digital and smartphone technology had not already become pervasive, allowing most people to meet their needs without having to venture out into the surrounding context.

But when it comes to a tipping point, as Gladwell argued, the size of a population also matters. He wrote about the Rule of 150, in which research has shown that groups of people at or below 150 in number work well together as a community, while groups larger than that tend not to. The Rule of 150 suggests that in a global community such as ours, where we spend most of our lives moving among strangers or at best, acquaintances, it becomes very difficult to get consensus or agreement, which makes it all the easier for a virus to spread because of the different beliefs and practices of various groups. The politicization of the COVID-19 pandemic that occurred in the U.S. showed the Rule of 150 at work, raising the question: Has the country become so big and diverse that it cannot effectively fight a common enemy like COVID-19?

The Rule of 150 may apply to how we use space differently in the post-pandemic era as well. During the pandemic, we became accustomed to living in bubbles, with family members or close acquaintances whose daily habits and health status we knew. Most if not all of those bubbles were no larger – and probably a lot smaller – than 150 people, which may be the maximum number of people any of us need to have frequent contact with, at least in face-to-face interactions in physical space. For interactions with more than those 150, the digital environment has given us the ability and the choice to connect to any number of people, anywhere in the world, using various communications platforms.

Gladwell drew upon ample social science research to come up with the number 150 as the upper limit of what he called a Clan, the people with whom any of us can maintain close or stable relationships. And as he points out in his book, some companies have used that number as the upper limit in the size of its units, learning that units any larger become difficult to manage. It may be that, while most workers can connect to an almost infinite number of people through global, digital platforms, there is a limit to how many colleagues any of us can productively work with, and how large a workplace any of us needs.

Pandemics and the Ponzi Scheme

As the subtitle to Gladwell's book says: little things can make a big difference. We saw that with COVID-19, when a tiny virus jumped

Figure 1.5 "LED Billboard, #George Floyd".

from an animal to a person in Wuhan, China, making all the difference in virtually everyone's life across the entire globe. Within weeks of that initial infection, the virus hit Gladwell's tipping point and our world was not – and will never be – quite the same. What set the COVID-19 pandemic apart from previous ones, though, were the multiple pandemics that came to a head all at once. It's as if that novel coronavirus tipped over an entire order that had appeared stable and strong, until it all started to fall apart and collapse before our eyes in 2020.

In that year, three crises happened almost simultaneously. Soon after COVID-19 prompted the lockdown of national economies, George Floyd was killed in Minneapolis, where I work, triggering Black-Lives-Matter protests around the world.[26] Meanwhile, record-breaking wildfires erupted in California, as they had earlier in the year in Australia, all fueled by the extreme droughts brought on by climate change.[27] The simultaneity of those events was no coincidence. They all had a common origin in what we might think of as our Ponzi Scheme with the planet, a scheme that has been at least four centuries in the making.[28]

A Ponzi Scheme is a type of fraud in which its perpetrators get others to invest in it with the promise of enrichment, while exploiting them in order to guarantee profits for those at the top of what is essentially a financial pyramid. While the name derives from the work of the famous 1920 swindler, Charles Ponzi, the most notorious recent example was the 2009 financial Ponzi Scheme of Bernard Madoff, who died in prison.[29] Madoff conned 4,800 people by fraudulently claiming that he had invested their money, when he really used their money to pay handsome returns to his initial clients.

While Ponzi Schemes are fraudulent and illegal, we learned from Madoff's scheme that if it gets large enough, people do not – or do not want to – see it. Madoff had many supporters up to the moment his whole financial house-of-card's collapsed, as Ponzi Schemes always do. Such schemes require exponential growth in order to satisfy those who have invested in them, and eventually the perpetrators of the fraud run out of people to exploit and run out of money to return to investors once the latter understand that they have been swindled.

Nor do such schemes end slowly; Madoff's scheme fell apart in a matter of days. And while Madoff's Ponzi Scheme was the largest such scheme in human history, his fraud pales in comparison to the one that the Global North has perpetrated on the people and places of the Global South for several centuries now.

The Global North's Ponzi Scheme began some 500 years ago. As European nations like France, England, and Spain grew increasingly crowded and in need of more space and more resources to fund their militaries and leaders, they launched what has since been called the Age of Exploration.[30] But the term "exploration" puts too fine a point on what was really a series of campaigns aimed at exploiting indigenous populations through slavery or other forms of servitude, extracting resources ranging from gold to sugar to furs, and expanding into territory long settled by native people. This history is well known, but we have yet to connect it to the three pandemics that came to a head in 2020.

Consider the COVID-19 pandemic. It arose from the continued spatial expansion of human settlements into wilderness areas, with people coming into contact with wildlife whose diseases can jump to humans. The recent pandemic continued the long history of people coming in contact with previously isolated populations and then contracting illnesses that then become epidemic, such as the measles and smallpox that extinguished 70% or more of the Native American population after contact with European settlers.[31] COVID-19 simply flipped the usual narrative, with a virus from the Global South that became epidemic, initially, in the Global North, which paid for it in millions of deaths.

Or consider the pandemic of police violence against black and brown people, reflected in the Black Lives Matters movement. Police brutality also has a long history in the Ponzi Scheme, as the perpetrators of the scheme have oppressed communities of color in order to secure cheap labor to extract the resources needed to maintain the guaranteed returns. Indeed the very term "race" shifted in meaning near the start of the Ponzi Scheme, no longer just referring to a competition – a race – but also to the categorization of people as superior or inferior based on their skin color, their "race."[32] That

semantic shift reflected the Ponzi Scheme's devaluation of some people in order to justify their exploitation.

The pandemic of climate change also came to a head in 2020 as the
result of a different kind of violence, one focused on the planet itself.
Humanity has inflicted carnage on other species, killing off species
at such a rate that biologists now define our era as the earth's Sixth
Extinction as we extract finite resources and unleash carbon into our
atmosphere, disrupting weather patterns across the globe.[33] Our rapidly changing climate suggests that the planet has tolerated our abuse
of it for long enough, pushing back on us with ever increasing force
until we cease and desist our exploiting, extracting, and extinguishing
behavior.

The planetary Ponzi Scheme took a long time to develop and it did
not suddenly end in 2020. Human exploitation still thrives around
the world, having taken new forms, like sex trafficking. Resource extraction still happens across the planet, now more focused on oil and
natural gas rather than gold. And biological and cultural extinctions
continue apace, as record numbers of animals and languages are dis-
appearing from the earth. Meanwhile, the pyramid scheme continues
to concentrate wealth at the top, with 1% of the world's population
now controlling nearly half of the globe's wealth.[34]

As happened with Madoff's scheme, those who have benefited the most from this several-centuries-long Ponzi Scheme do not
want to admit to it. The U.S., for example, has benefited enormously
from the scheme, and it also has one of the highest percentages of
climate-change deniers, white nationalists, and COVID-19 skeptics
in the world.[35] Those who have benefited the most from this Ponzi
Scheme have been the most committed to it and the greatest enablers
of it, perhaps because they have the most to lose when the scheme
collapses. The scheme has also become so spatially dispersed into
every corner of the planet that it has become, paradoxically, more
difficult to see. Such schemes fall apart, though, not only when they
run out of people and resources to exploit, but also when the existing
investors and greatest beneficiaries start calling the bluff.

We saw that in the wake of George Floyd's killing, when Black
Lives Matter protests in cities around the world involved as many –

or more – white people than people of color. And we saw it, as well, in the protests against climate change, often led by the youth who recognize that they will bear the costs of the damage that pollution has done. We will likely look back on the year 2020 as the point where even those who have profited the most from the Ponzi Scheme have begun to say no. People – like the planet itself – have finally had enough.

Post-Ponzi-Scheme Life

The question now is how we deal with the collapse and reorganization that seems likely to characterize the years and decades ahead. As the planetary Ponzi Scheme crumbles, what might a post-pandemic, post-Ponzi-Scheme look like for all of us – black, brown, or white; rich or poor; humans and other species – as we try to occupy the planet in more equitable, sustainable, and resilient ways? One answer might be to redefine what constitutes a good life. That does not mean simply returning to the way things were prior to the Ponzi Scheme, to a feudal world in which a few oligarchs controlled much of the material wealth and kept most of the population in various forms of servitude. While that type of human organization, overall, might have had less of a negative impact on the natural environment than the subsequent Ponzi Scheme, it certainly wasn't equitable and it was, as Steven Pinker has shown, even more violent and dangerous than the world today.[36]

Instead, we might imagine a world in which we retain the knowledge accrued during the Ponzi Scheme that can benefit people and the planet enormously, such as our knowledge of how to improve human and environmental health, our understanding of the importance of universal education, and our recognition of the value of creativity and innovation to our future. At the same time, we need to create a world that provides equal opportunity for every person, indeed every sentient being, to achieve their full potential and to thrive. This sounds utopian and even pollyannish. But the events of 2020 give us some insight into how we might go about achieving such goals.

One step might involve rethinking the materialism that has been a driving force behind the Ponzi Scheme from the very beginning.

Religions like Buddhism and philosophies like Stoicism have long recognized how much suffering occurs when we become attached to and attempt to dominate that which we cannot control, be it people, possessions, or the planet itself. Freeing ourselves of such attachments has benefits not only in terms of personal happiness, but also in terms of social harmony as the ownership of property and possessions becomes something to avoid rather than to desire and have to protect. The pandemic gave us all a taste of this life. Most of us gave up attachments that might have seemed inconceivable prior to that event, be it connections to acquaintances who we could not interact with face-to-face, workplaces or other destinations we could no longer visit, and possessions we could no longer access or use.[37] Which may help explain why individual well-being, at least in the U.S., improved in 2020.[38]

The COVID-19 pandemic, in other words, showed that we can distance ourselves from attachments and accept situations over which we have no control. And while that may have seemed like a loss, it also revealed the sense of freedom that can come from becoming less dependent. The psychological experience of the pandemic suggested a way of getting past the Ponzi Scheme, which was all about possessing more things, controlling more space, and treating other people and places as possessions. A post-Ponzi-Scheme existence might mean imagining a future in which we measure our wealth, gauge our happiness, and assess our freedom not in terms of how much we have, but rather according to how much we can do without.

That suggests another step we might take in the post-Ponzi-Scheme world: growing up as a species.[39] We humans like to think of ourselves as smarter than all the other species on the planet, and in some respects we are, but in other respects we are a highly immature species that, like an immature person, does stupid and sometimes self-destructive things. Some indigenous cultures rightly view humanity as a baby species that, like a newborn, depends upon other species to feed and nurture it and yet throws tantrums or cries when our needs are not immediately met. We might also think of ourselves as an adolescent species, not only because we have not been on this planet nearly as long as many others, but also because we use the

power that technology allows to do dumb things, as adolescents often do, like over-consuming finite resources that we will need in the
future or extinguishing at an increasingly rapid rate other species that
we depend on for our own health and sustenance.

Here, too, the pandemic provided a glimpse of what it might mean
to become an adult species. During the pandemic, most of us led more
low-carbon lives, with lockdowns making it almost impossible to travel
and with remote working, shopping, and learning making it less necessary to do so. Like adolescents learning to curtail activities that had
negative consequences for themselves and others, we found ourselves
forced by the pandemic to cease the incessant moving about that demands so much of our energy, wastes so much of our time, and en-
dangers us and others in the process. Becoming a more mature species
might entail following other species that rarely travel as much or as far
we do and that are more a part of the places in which they have evolved.

Which brings us to another step we might take: giving more auton-
omy to local places and cultures.[40] The Ponzi Scheme created a global economy in which those in positions of power in faraway places
made decisions – and exploited people and resources – that destroyed
local cultures and their locations. And once they ran off the planet
in terms of a resource base, the perpetrators of the Ponzi Scheme –
the nations of the Global North and eventually countries across the
planet – began to borrow heavily from future generations, damaging
their ability to meet their needs. With the collapse of that Scheme
comes a reckoning with the spatial and temporal scale at which we
need to live: moving from global to more local economies that, instead of borrowing from the future, husband current resources, and
steward existing ecosystems so that our progeny can thrive.

The pandemic, again, showed us what living a more local life might
be like. Having to stay close to home, in the neighborhoods in which
we lived, we began to reconnect with the people and places around
us, getting to know neighbors, perhaps for the first time, and supporting local businesses in hopes that they would not go out of business.
We saw this with a movement to reform policing and to put public
safety more under civilian control. And we saw it in myriad other
ways as well, from gardens popping up in people's yards to gatherings

popping up in public parks to take out cuisine and outdoor dining popping up along sidewalks or in former parking lots. All of these speak to our capacity to thrive locally in places we care about and in communities that can also care about us.

Living a post-Ponzi-Scheme life may seem daunting, if not outright scary. But most of us managed to survive and even thrive during the pandemic, discovering that, despite the deaths and deprivations it wrought, it also brought some real advantages in terms of the quality of our lives and of the environments and communities in which we live. And we can prosper in the post-Ponzi-Scheme era as well, for many of the same reasons. We might travel less, consume less, and own less than we did with the Ponzi Scheme, but we also might realize, as we do when leaving our adolescence behind, that there are benefits to being an adult, whether it be as a person or as a species.

Just as we should not fear this transition in our place on this planet, neither should we delay in making the change. Martin Luther King spoke about "the fierce urgency of now" in his search for social justice in America, and in many respects his call to action has come true.[41] We have seen how quickly our work lives and family lives can change in the face of a pandemic. So why can't we transform other things just as quickly? Challenges like racial injustice or climate change once looked like they would take decades to change in slow, incremental steps, but that now seems like an excuse for inaction. That may help explain the impatience, especially among younger people, with the slow pace of social and environmental change and a desire to address, head on, chronic problems that we should have resolved a long time ago. If we can change so many other aspects of our lives in a matter of days and weeks, why can't we finally address the seemingly intractable problems of racism and climate change?

The questions we need to ask going forward include: What does an abundant future look like that does not involve exploiting other people, extracting finite resources, and exposing the world to virulent disease? And what does a reorganized future look like in which we live within our ecological footprint, lead healthier lives, and offer equitable opportunity for all? These are some of the questions that we will explore in this book, all with "the fierce urgency of now."

Notes

1 Vanessa Harding, "Burial of the Plague Dead in Early Modern London," *Epidemic Disease in London*, ed. J.A.I. Champion (Centre for Metropolitan History Working Papers Series, No. 1, 1993), 53–64. https://archives.history.ac.uk/cmh/epiharding.html
2 Tim Stickings, "Inside the Abandoned Plague Island Where Sick Sailors Were Left to Die at the Gateway to Venice – Home of the World's First Quarantine," *The Daily Mail*, October 26, 2020. www.dailymail.co.uk/news/article-8880273/Venetian-plague-island-home-worlds-quarantines.html
3 David Rosner, "'Spanish Flu, or Whatever It Is …': The Paradox of Public Health in a Time of Crisis," *Public Health Reports*, 2010; 125 (Suppl 3): 38–47. www.ncbi.nlm.nih.gov/pmc/articles/PMC2862333/
4 Jonathan R. Olsen et al., "Are Urban Landscapes Associated with Reported Life Satisfaction and Inequalities in Life Satisfaction at the City Level? A Cross-sectional Study of 66 European Cities," *Social Science & Medicine* (2019). https://phys.org/news/2019-03-urban-landscapes-life-satisfaction-inequalities.html
5 Patrick Sisson, "What the 1918 Pandemic Can Teach Cities about Public Spaces Today," *Curbed*, March 18, 2020. https://archive.curbed.com/2020/3/18/21178053/coronavirus-pandemic-public-space-influenza-history
6 "American Planning History since 1900," American Planning Association. www.planning.org/timeline/
7 "*Village of Euclid v. Ambler Realty Co.* 272 U.S. 365 (1926)" U.S. Supreme Court. https://supreme.justia.com/cases/federal/us/272/365/
8 Richard Rothstein, *The Color of Law: A Forgotten History of How Our Government Segregated America* (New York: Liveright, 2017).
9 "How the COVID-19 Crisis Affects Our Everyday Life," Deloitte. www2.deloitte.com/ch/en/pages/about-deloitte/articles/how-covid19-affects-everyday-life.html
10 John R. Allen, Darrell M. West, "How to Address Inequality Exposed by the COVID-19 Pandemic," Brookings, November 4, 2020. www.brookings.edu/president/how-to-address-inequality-exposed-by-the-covid-19-pandemic/
11 James D. Lutz, "Lest We Forget, a Short History of Housing in the United States," Lawrence Berkeley National Laboratory. www.aceee.org/files/proceedings/2004/data/papers/SS04_Panel1_Paper17.pdf
12 Keith D. Lilley, "Urban Planning after the Black Death: Townscape Transformation in Later Medieval England (1350–1530)," *Urban History*, 42(1), 2014, 1–21. www.researchgate.net/publication/271652851_Urban_planning_after_the_Black_Death_Townscape_transformation_in_later_medieval_England_1350–1530
13 Steven Johnson, *The Ghost Map: The Story of London's Most Terrifying Epidemic – and How It Changed Science, Cities, and the Modern World* (London: Penguin, 2006).
14 Lee Flannery, "Design in the Time of Cholera: How Pandemics Reshaped the Built Environment," *Planetizen*, May 8, 2020. www.planetizen.com/news/2020/05/109286-design-time-cholera-how-pandemics-reshaped-built-environment
15 Brian Beach, Karen Clay, Martin H. Saavedra, "The 1918 Influenza Pandemic and Its Lessons for COVID-19," National Bureau of Economic Research, August 2020. www.nber.org/system/files/working_papers/w27673/w27673.pdf
16 Cynthia Paez Bowman, "Coronavirus Moving Study: People Left Big Cities, Temporary Moves Spiked in First 6 Months of COVID-19 Pandemic," Mymove, June 1, 2021. www.mymove.com/moving/covid-19/coronavirus-moving-trends/
17 Richard Florida, "This is Not the End of Cities," Bloomberg CityLab, June 19, 2020. www.bloomberg.com/news/features/2020–06–19/cities-will-survive-pandemics-and-protests

18 Nikolaus Pevsner, *A History of Building Types* (Princeton: Princeton University Press, 1976).
19 May Wong, "Stanford Research Provides a Snapshot of a New Working-from-Home Economy," *Stanford News*, June 29, 2020. https://news.stanford. edu/2020/06/29/snapshot-new-working-home-economy/
20 Sage Belz, Louise Sheiner, "How Will the Coronavirus Affect State and Local Government Budgets?" Brookings, March 23, 2020. www.brookings.edu/blog/up-front/2020/03/23/how-will-the-coronavirus-affect-state-and-local-government-budgets/
21 Malcolm Gladwell, *The Tipping Point, How Little Thinks Can Make a Big Difference* (Boston: Little, Brown & Company, 2000).
22 Derrick Bryson Taylor, "A Timeline of the Coronavirus Pandemic," *The New York Times*, March 17, 2021. www.nytimes.com/article/coronavirus-timeline.html
23 Gladwell, *The Tipping Point*, 132.
24 Detlef Mertins, "What Did Mies van der Rohe Mean by Less Is More?" Phaidon. www.phaidon.com/agenda/architecture/articles/2014/april/02/what-did-mies-van-der-rohe-mean-by-less-is-more/
25 Gladwell, *The Tipping Point*, 26.
26 Mary Blankenship, Richard V. Reeves, "From the George Floyd moment to a Black Lives Matter movement, in tweets," Brookings, July 10, 2020. www. brookings.edu/blog/up-front/2020/07/10/from-the-george-floyd-moment-to-a-black-lives-matter-movement-in-tweets/
27 Jeff Master, "Reviewing the Horrid Global 2020 Wildfire Season," *Yale Climate Connection*, January 4, 2021. https://yaleclimateconnections.org/2021/01/reviewing-the-horrid-global-2020-wildfire-season/
28 Thomas Fisher, *Designing to Avoid Disaster* (New York: Routledge, 2013), 9–14.
29 Diana B. Henriques, "Bernard Madoff, Architect of Largest Ponzi Scheme in History, Is Deas at 82," *New York Times*, April 14, 2021. www.nytimes. com/2021/04/14/business/bernie-madoff-dead.html
30 Amanda Briney, "A Brief History of the Age of Exploration," ThoughtCo, January 24, 2020. www.thoughtco.com/age-of-exploration-1435006
31 Michael S. Rosenwald, "Columbus Brought Measles to the New World. It Was a Disaster for Native Americans," *Washington Post*, May 5, 2019. www. washingtonpost.com/history/2019/05/05/columbus-brought-measles-new-world-it-was-disaster-native-americans/
32 "Race," Online Etymology Dictionary. www.etymonline.com/word/race
33 Elizabeth Kolbert, *The Sixth Extinction: An Unnatural History* (New York: Henry Holt & Company, 2014).
34 Camilo Maldonado, "Credit Suisse: Top 1% Own Nearly 50% of Global Wealth and China's Wealthy Now Outnumber America's," Forbes, October 23, 2019. www.forbes.com/sites/camilomaldonado/2019/10/23/credit-suisse-top-1-own-nearly-50-of-global-wealth-and-chinas-wealthy-now-outnumber-ameri-cas/?sh=37bfcfd92ede
35 Jérôme Viala-Gaudefroy, "Why Is Climate Skepticism So Successful in the United States?" *The Conversation*, January 21, 2020. https://theconversation.com/why-is-climate-scepticism-so-successful-in-the-united-states-129826
36 Steven Pinker, *The Better Angels of our Nature* (New York: Viking, 2011).
37 Jeff Howanek, "COVID-19 Sparks a Shift Away from American Materialism," *Monitor*, January 27, 2021. www.kantar.com/north-america/inspiration/society/covid-sparks-a-shift-away-from-american-materialism

38 "Americans Say Their Individual Well-Being Improved in 2020," *The Economist*, July 21, 2021. www.economist.com/graphic-detail/2021/07/21/americans-say-their-individual-well-being-improved-in-2020

39 Thomas Fisher, "The Adulthood of the Species," Foreword in *New Directions in Sustainable Design*, Adrian Parr, Michael Zaretsky, editors (New York: Routledge, 2011), xv–xvii.

40 Vaughn Ericson, "The Post-Pandemic Trend Toward Localism," True Media, May 21, 2020. www.truemediaservices.com/2020/05/21/the-post-pandemic-trend-toward-localism/

41 Randolph Walters, "MLK Reflection: The Fierce Urgency of Now," Eastern University, January 15, 2021. www.eastern.edu/news/mlk

2
DESIGN

Pandemics represent a design failure. The very fact a pandemic occurs points to a failure on the part of governments to prevent the emergence of a novel disease, to prepare for the possibility that one might spread, and to protect their citizens if it does. Governments tend to design systems that have a strong utilitarian bent, trying to achieve the greatest good for the greatest number, but that focus on the greatest number tends to ignore outlier phenomena and minority perspectives.

We saw that play out during the pandemic. Experts warned of a possible pandemic decades ago and were dismissed or ignored,[1] epidemiologists recognized health inequities to little avail,[2] and the Chinese doctor who first sounded the alarm about COVID-19 was silenced and then died of the illness it caused.[3] They all had the greatest good for the greatest number in mind, but they did not have the clout to get governments to act or, in the case of the Chinese doctor, to act in a way that would actually achieve the greatest good.

Anti-fragile Systems

To avoid such a catastrophe in the future, we need systems that are not simply a calculus of how many people will benefit. That calculus is too easily misused, depending upon how one defines the good and

                    DOI: 10.4324/9781003198192-3

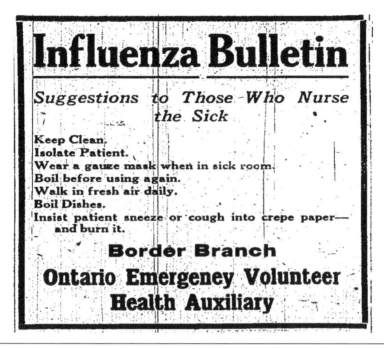

Figure 2.1 Emergency Volunteer Health Auxiliary, Influenza Bulletin, 1918.

who gets counted in the equation. Instead, we need to design systems that are what Nassim Nicholas Taleb calls "anti-fragile," able to deal with – and grow from – unexpected, "black-swan" events like a pandemic.[4] Unlike rigid, overly determined systems that can break down under stress, anti-fragile systems "gain from disorder," as Taleb writes. At the same time, they can adapt and respond to uncertainty and change in flexible and even improvisational ways.

When rightly done, design produces anti-fragile systems. Design follows a process that continually tries to produce results that not only improve upon what exists, but also seek transformative solutions in response to particular and often unique situations. At the scale of designed products, for example, the design process can lead to highly ordered and nicely integrated outcomes that function well and have an appealing form.

But with large-scale systems, the design process needs to follow a different course. It requires a more bottom-up approach that engages diverse people, welcomes different perspectives, and attends to minority opinions. That more inclusive process is, itself, anti-fragile in that its solutions grow stronger under the stress of differing ideas and conflicting agendas. And it tends to produce more anti-fragile solutions as a result, remaining open to unexpected events and unanticipated changes.

Anti-fragile systems do not exclude utilitarianism. But they also embrace other ethics, like the categorical imperatives of Kant that urge us to treat others as ends in themselves rather than means to our ends and to act in ways that would have universal validity. And they demand that we construct new social contracts that embrace diverse perspectives and that prioritize virtues such as equity, justice, and fairness.

System Design

What does such an approach to design look like when applied on the ground, to actual situations? The work done at the center that I direct, the Minnesota Design Center at the University of Minnesota, offers some examples that might help answer that question.[5] While we work mainly at the scale of neighborhoods, cities, and regions, we also do a lot of system design that addresses policies and processes as much as the physical aspects of a place. And we take an anti-fragile design approach in search of solutions that do not just extend past practices and respond to current trends, but that also anticipate black-swan events, unexpected changes, and uncertain futures.

In that way, design complements planning, two fields that often get confused, in part because the two have a lot in common. Both fields have a focus on possible futures as well as present and past situations. Both seek to improve the human condition and the environments in which we live. And both are as old as humanity itself: we would not have survived as a species without the ability to plan or design when confronted with changing circumstances. But planners and designers differ in their methods and mindsets, and that matters.

Planning has deeper roots in the social sciences and stronger ties to the inductive methods of science: gathering and assessing data about a situation, drawing generalizable conclusions from that data, and implementing strategies and putting the relevant systems in place. Design typically involves a different logic than planning, a logic that the philosopher Charles Sanders Peirce called abduction.[6] Unlike induction, which develops general theories or approaches from accumulated evidence, abduction makes connections among disparate and seemingly unrelated phenomena in a pragmatic search for a new way of understanding a situation and a better solution to a problem.

Planners also make such abductive leaps every time they see connections among things that others have missed, just as designers often use inductive methods every time they work from data in the process of creating something new. The difference lies more in the emphasis each places on one logic or the other, reflecting the different weight each puts on reason versus imagination. While both planning and design focus on the unmet needs of people and, increasingly, other species as well, the two fields differ in the roles they often play. Planners are often involved in creating the rules within which designers work: the codes, regulations, and policies that set boundaries on designers, whose abductive logic often leads to their bending the rules and creatively interpreting the codes.

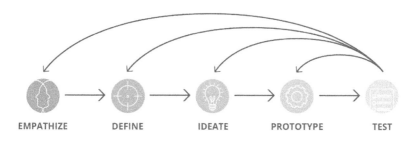

Figure 2.2 The design thinking process.

Design Thinking

As a form of logic, abduction involves a rigorous process, now commonly called "design thinking."[7] Design thinking typically involves five steps:

1   A research phase that entails looking at a situation from as many different perspectives as possible;
2   A reframing phase in which the common ways of seeing the situation are defined in new terms;
3   An ideation phase that includes generating as many possible solutions to the reframed problem as possible;
4   A prototyping phase in which the most promising ideas get implemented in a low-cost, low-risk way;
5   A testing and iteration phase in which the prototypes are evaluated and either refined or rejected, which may then lead to a revisiting of one or more of the previous phases.

That work takes time and by the time the COVID-19 pandemic arrived, it was too late for leaders to respond in creative ways to the spreading infection. Instead, some of the most influential leaders denied the seriousness of the disease or came up with crazy ways of dealing with it.[8] The abductive process often generates a lot of ideas, as designers know, but design thinking also involves repeated and quite rigorous rounds of criticism of those ideas, winnowing out those that do not work or align with the facts of a situation.

Designers do this by running through many possible scenarios and anticipating the likely effects, good and bad, that might occur. When engineers design a structure or architects an exterior wall, they imagine all the possible forces acting on it or conditions confronting it, to ensure that it can withstand them. The same should happen when designing a system, although that rarely occurs, especially at a global scale. As the COVID-19 pandemic showed, we had systems that were not only poorly designed to deal with a novel and deadly disease, but also perversely well suited to spread it, from lax health screenings at airports to insufficient and uncoordinated responses across borders.

The pandemic tested the design of our political as well as our public health systems, and they failed us.

Which means that we need better system design, especially when dealing with wicked problems like a pandemic. Design is particularly useful with such problems: those that are undefined, unprecedented, and unresponsive to established ways of working. In such situations, the abductive leaps of design can open up new ways of seeing a problem and new approaches to addressing it. Everyone is capable of making such leaps, but most of us have had that capacity, inherent in how the human brain works, drummed out of us by an educational system that has largely ignored abductive logic and often dismissed design as a matter of personal preference or the product of a few creative geniuses.

Design thinking represents a rebellion against such views. It makes the claim that everyone has the ability to design, to imagine a future preferable to what currently exists. And it focuses on the design process rather than the appearance of things, moving away from personal preferences and toward building the capacity of communities to engage in the design process themselves in order to address the challenges they face in creative ways. In that way, design thinking flips the old idea of the designer as a visionary individual who has all the answers, to one in which the designer serves as a facilitator of the ideas generated by those who have the lived experience and the most at stake in improving a situation.

Mistaken ideas about design thinking, nevertheless, remain.[9] Some have a superficial understanding of it and act as if it can solve every problem, which it cannot, while others assume that it only involves thinking, overlooking its action orientation. At the same time, skeptics sometimes dismiss design thinking as just common sense or worse, a way of reinforcing the status quo and existing inequities.[10] Although some designers too readily accept prevailing power relations, the design process, done well, challenges current structures and questions common assumptions.

Among the power structures that design thinking challenges is that of the professional expert who presumes to know what is best in a situation and who imposes that assumption on others. Expert advice matters, of course, especially during a pandemic, and we saw in the U.S. what happens when non-experts push untested ideas or claim that what experts are engaged in is a hoax.[11] But it also matters how experts engage and communicate with the broader public, as we discovered during the pandemic. Overly reassuring statements or overly panicked ones from experts can confuse people, as can conflicting advice or contradictory statements.[12] Design thinking asks us to see a situation from the point of view of others; had that happened prior to the pandemic, we might have seen less misinformation and distrust of the experts.

Co-Design

At the center of design thinking, then, lies the notion that the best ideas come from a co-design process, benefiting from a diversity of perspectives and involving people who may not think of themselves as designers, but who have a lot to contribute to the process. As one of my colleagues, Jess Roberts, has observed, community-based planning processes can often be extractive, gathering the ideas of community members in order to justify planning decisions. Instead, community members need to be treated as co-participants in the design, deeply involved in its development.

That is especially relevant to public health and to anticipating black-swan events like a pandemic. Roberts, along with the staff of the Destination Medical Center's Economic Development Agency in Rochester, Minnesota, wrote a job description for community co-designers.[13] With the help of diverse community partners, they then identified people who had the time and interest to work as paid members of the planning team for a new, four-block-long, public-health-focused street called "Discovery Walk."

The diversity of the co-design cohort was key, since part of their role was to have conversations with and to represent the interests of communities that rarely have a role in the planning process. Also, that diversity led to more creativity. Over the course of a few months, the team engaged in a series of design sprints, in which the co-designers collectively explored ideas, alternating with a number of design studios, in which they pursued those ideas in greater depth.

Out of this process came a number of insights about the character of Discovery Walk. It needed to provide places for contemplation as well as conversation, for people to be alone as well as together as they face potentially life-changing decisions from the nearby Mayo Clinic. At the same time, the co-design process pointed to the need for respite from such challenges, with places for physical activity and connections to nature. The design professionals responsible for creating Discovery Walk brought the co-designers on as part of their project team to ensure that those insights continued to guide the design and implementation of the street, and the co-design process will likely become standard practice in the work of Rochester's Destination Medical Center going forward.

Appreciative Inquiry

While the co-design process involves "empathy," that term can sound condescending; most people don't want empathy, they want agency. The design process goes better when it begins with what David Cooperrider, professor of organizational behavior, calls "appreciative inquiry," a process that involves understanding what is working well in a community, what it has to work with, and what sets it apart.[14] My center used that process on a pilot project, funded by the State of Minnesota through its Department of Employment and Economic Development, working with a number of small, rural communities on how to improve their social and economic health and how to become more anti-fragile in response to the stresses on them.

My colleague, Mary Vogel, and I began by observing how those communities represented themselves on their websites, and almost all of them had the same pitch: affordable communities with friendly people leading a slower-paced lifestyle. While no doubt true, those claims did little to differentiate one community from another or to attract or retain businesses and new residents, which these communities desperately want and need. So we began working with three communities interested in taking a new approach to economic development, recognizing that the old way had not worked for them. We had residents identify the assets that mattered to them and those that they thought were often overlooked.

Based on that appreciative-inquiry process, we helped these communities identify what unique qualities they had to offer and what existing assets they had to work with. In Wabasha, for example, we reflected back to the city's inhabitants what we had heard from them as they spoke about being a small community on the Mississippi River and about the visitors who come there to boat, bird watch, and mountain bike. Out of those conversations came a new sense of identity as an active-living river town, with an economic development strategy that targeted people interested in birding, boating, and biking. It also led the city to focus on the physical features of the place that would reinforce that identity, including an undeveloped inlet as a place for bird watching and recreational boating and biking. And it helped the city see how it could attract new residents with businesses and housing that would appeal to people interested in such activities.

In another town, Grand Meadow, we learned from community conversations how many people commuted to the nearby cities of Rochester and Austin to work, often at odd hours of the day, and how many families struggled to find childcare as a result. At the same time, we heard how many residents valued living there because of the quality of its schools and how they described it as a family friendly place. Based on that self-identity and the conflict between its being family friendly, with few childcare options, we worked with the com-

Wabasha: An Active Living River Town
James Pettinari, Pettinari Design

Figure 2.3 Wabasha, Minnesota.

munity to improve pedestrian access to the school and safer pedestrian crossings at the state road through town. And we explored the idea of a community-based childcare strategy, proposing a babysitting network in which older residents would watch the children of working parents. While that idea ran aground because of bureaucratic hurdles, it showed how a community can address its needs in creative ways when making new connections among its existing assets.

The design process, though, doesn't always work in every situation. A core principle of design involves failing often and failing fast in order to learn from those failures, and my colleagues and I are the first to admit that some communities are not ready to participate in this abductive process. In one small town we worked with, the community played up its identity as an early Norwegian settlement, even though the population of the town and surrounding area had become much more diverse in recent decades. Indeed, our conversations with and observations in the community made it clear that it had become a center for artisanal agriculture, producing crops of value to the beverage companies in the area, with a diverse workforce from the entire region.

We tried to make the case that the future of the town lay in building upon that strength rather than in focusing on a past that no longer had much meaning to most people there. And we showed how the town might leverage assets like its many parks, the old hospital, and its largely intact commercial main street for events related to its growing artisanal food and beverage community. But changing the identity of a place can take time and the ideas that emerged from our work with the community have yet to move forward; design thinking sometimes fails by moving faster than leaders are willing to go.

Another cause of failure can be divisions within a community that can crush any creative ideas. In a community that we worked with in the opposite corner of the state, the town encompassed a large nature preserve that it hoped to use to attract new businesses and residents. Different members of the community, however, had very different ideas for the preserve: some wanted to use it for active recreation like all-terrain vehicles and dirt-bike racing, others wanted to preserve it for ecological restoration, and some leaders in town thought that they should prioritize getting a nursing home built first, for which there was an immediate need.

Design generally seeks win–win solutions to problems, and we worked with the diverse members of that community to help them resolve those different perspectives, noting that the nursing home could get built without neglecting the nature preserve, and that the latter could accommodate both recreation and restoration if done thoughtfully and carefully. But too many residents seemed more intent on blocking each other than in working together in a mutually beneficial way, and as a result, nothing happened.

Such failures show that design thinking does not suit every problem. Design involves creative change and if a community isn't ready for change or doesn't want to change – however much it may need to – no amount of abductive logic will make much of a difference. In the case of the pandemic, the hesitancy of so many people to get vaccinated showed how the data in support of the vaccine could not overcome the stories casting doubt upon it. Some people refuse to change their thinking even if refusing to do so might prove deadly.

Design versus Ideology

The reframing of problems at the center of design thinking can also run counter to ideological thinking, which tends to frame problems, like vaccine resistance during the pandemic, in terms of a single set of answers and an unshakeable set of beliefs. If people believe that they already know the solution to a problem or that there is only one right answer and they know what it is, then design can do little to help. I once led a workshop on design thinking at a political conference where the two political parties sat on opposite sides of the room, with little or no interaction. So the first thing I did was to have participants sit with someone from the other party before we got to work, since the best way to overcome polarization is to work together on something that transcends ideological differences.

Design thinking can also help us get past resistance to change by reframing problems as unrecognized opportunities, which even the most die-hard skeptic or ideologue may find of interest. Design does that through a set of strategies common to almost all creative endeavors. Designers will frequently:

- use analogies or metaphors to understand a situation in a new way;
- alter the scale or size of something to see it from another perspective;
- juxtapose or rearrange things to look for more productive ways forward;
- reinterpret or re-imagine a situation in search of creative alternatives.

Analogies and metaphors are useful in helping us understand a new or unprecedented situation in terms of what we already know, as when we talked about COVID-19 as the enemy that we all need to fight, as in a war, or when we likened its spread to second-hand smoke.[15] A new idea that may seem strange to many people can become more acceptable by making an analogy to something that is familiar. Analogous thinking is also useful when seeking solutions in other areas of human activity that work well and to then applying those lessons to the problem at hand. While we typically associate analogies and metaphors with literature and language, designers will often have participants in the process make diagrams or pictograms to describe their ideas, which gets them thinking in more lateral ways.

An example of the latter arose in the work that my colleague, Emily Stover, and I, along with Sook Jin Ong of the Future Services Institute, did with four Minnesota counties looking for creative ways to respond to the 1999 *Olmstead* Supreme Court decision, which prohibits segregation of people with disabilities.[16] The leaders of the four counties acknowledged that the existing group-home system did segregate adults with mental and physical disabilities and that the system needed to change.

The first thing we did was to involve in the design process adults living in group homes and to have them describe their experiences and visualize how they felt about their living situations. Many of them drew images of prisons or highways with only on-ramps and no off-ramps. We then put together working teams – each of which included at least one group-home resident or family member, a group-home provider, and county and state staff responsible for overseeing the system – and asked them to develop as many ideas as possible about how to improve the situation by drawing analogies from other things in their lives that they thought worked well.

The process itself represented an abductive leap, in that none of the residents, providers, or regulators had ever engaged in conversations with each other in this way. But most striking were the ideas that came out of the process. Many people see design as an expensive luxury for the wealthy and powerful and miss the fact that the ultimate goal of the design process is to not only do more with less, but also to do the most for those who have the least. That clearly happened in this case.

The diverse teams winnowed down their many ideas to those that were not only doable, but also affordable and even less expensive than the process as it currently existed. One group advocated for a revised placement process that housed people with similar interests – cooking, music, sports – in the same homes, something that hadn't happened before. Another group proposed establishing a coffee house that group-home residents would run so that they could have an income and an opportunity to interact with people outside of the system. The prototyping of those and other ideas is currently under way.

Not all of our design thinking work has been this successful. A local nonprofit asked us to work with a county to reduce the number of housing evictions occurring there. As we talked with a range of people who had faced eviction as well as those working in the housing courts and in the emergency services area, we saw a range of challenges and the need to bring together diverse groups of people to come up with new approaches. The participants did come up with a number of innovative ideas that were framed in terms of short-, medium-, and long-term solutions, some of which required very little money to implement.

It turned out, though, that the nonprofit that had asked us to do this work in the first place wanted us to justify their belief that the emergency services system was the problem and needed to be reformed. When we presented them with a range of ideas, none of which conformed to their agenda, they dismissed the work and

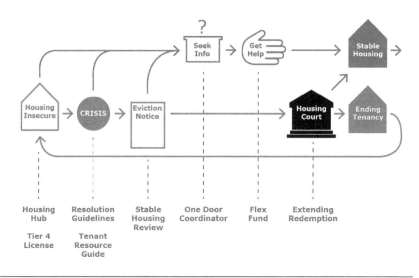

Figure 2.4 Design interventions in the eviction process.

accused us of wasting time, as they certainly wasted ours and all of the people who put creative energy into the effort. If those in control do not want new ideas, better to not start the design process than to dash the hopes of the people involved.

Engaging Leaders

Design thinking requires a mix of optimism and pragmatism, seeing every institutional barrier or dismissive bureaucrat as an opportunity to move in a new direction in order to see what else might work. We saw this happen when working with the Centers for Disease Control and Prevention. The CDC asked us to lead a series of workshops in which we would teach emerging leaders how to approach their work in more creative ways. What, we wondered, could we teach some of the top global health experts, and so we began by listening to and learning from them as we hoped they would us. We asked them to describe the work they did and to diagram what they saw as the biggest challenges they faced in doing that work.

We then had each team describe their work to other teams, out of which came a reframing of the challenges and a realization that, of the eight teams in the room, there were actually four major challenges that pairs of teams had in common. As those pairs started to work together on their reframed problem, we asked them to start generating as many ideas as possible about how to address it from as many different perspectives as possible. At first, that idea generation proved difficult for some unaccustomed to producing a great quantity of ideas. But after several rounds of idea generation, the success of which was measured, in part, by the amount of laughter in the room, there emerged some truly inspired and innovative ideas that no one had thought of before, with immediate benefits in their work.

Creative ideas rarely come out of nowhere; most result from seeing what we already know in new ways. I once led a design-thinking workshop with city and county managers, representing governments of very different sizes, with very different capacities. In such settings, I try to talk about design as little as possible, not only because it often carries with it a reputation of elitism, but also because doing design is much more effective than talking about it. So in this workshop, where a previous speaker had talked about the budget challenges these managers face, I decided to flip the conversation and have the audience members list all the underutilized assets they had at their disposal, as many as possible, as fast as possible.

For a group that had just heard about all that they lacked, my request caught most people off guard. Many did not know where to begin or what I meant, so I gave them possible examples: the school that sits empty most nights and weekends, the outdoor ice rink that sits empty all summer, the golf course that sits unused all winter. And with that prompt, they were off, making long lists of assets in their communities that remained unused or underused at various times of the week, month, or year. What had been a room of many gloomy faces became, in the process, an animated place, with people comparing their lists and coming up with new ideas together. Design represents an abundance mindset, and for the managers, that involved switching from a deficit to an asset approach to their challenges.

The Design Mindset

Design thinking is as much a mindset as it is a method, which means that every field can apply its lessons, whether related to design or not. And it is never too early to start thinking about the next great global disruption – whether epidemiological, economic, or environmental – and how more creative and pragmatic approaches can help us avoid another disaster such as the one we lived through with COVID-19. This will require governments to start integrating design thinking into their practices in some of the following ways:

Research Phase

- Look for opportunities to apply design thinking in situations where other approaches to problem-solving have not been effective, since design thinking is most helpful when addressing wicked problems and chronic challenges.
- Create as many opportunities as possible to have as many diverse stakeholders as possible; map, sketch, and talk about the human, social, cultural, historical, natural and physical assets they have to work with.
- Attend to what people do as much as what they say, and to what they don't say as much as what they do. Such things often hold keys to what is actually going on in a situation and where new ideas might emerge.

Reframing Phase

- Reflect back to participants not just what you have heard them say and observe them do, but also how they might think about problems and opportunities in new ways and what connections might exist among different aspects of them.
- Engage diverse communities in that reframing conversation, emphasizing that they are co-creators of their futures and that the reframing process is an on-going activity in response to new and changing circumstances.
- Use analogies and metaphors to characterize the new ways of seeing problems and ask for suggestions about what to call the various reframing ideas to capture the essential concepts and to make them easier to remember.

Ideation Phase

- Encourage participants in the process to generate as many ideas as possible, as quickly as possible. All ideas at this stage are potentially good ones and often the best ideas seem, at first, the craziest or silliest ones.

- Ask people to diagram or doodle each idea, since a visual representation can add greatly to their descriptions, and look for connections among ideas that might suggest areas of consensus or future exploration.
- Have participants present their ideas and have breakout groups select the most promising ideas to present to the entire group, which can further winnow down the ideas to those that might get prototyped.

Prototyping Phase

- Develop low-cost and low-risk ways to test the ideas that have emerged from the above process, using strategies of temporary installations and short-term experiments.
- Involve as many different stakeholders as possible to gather a diversity of perspectives on the prototypes and to ensure that policy makers are involved in the process and less likely to oppose any change.

Testing and Iteration Phase

- Get feedback on the prototypes from a variety of people, ranging from those involved in their development to those who are most skeptical of the innovations, in order to get the fullest idea of their effects.
- Look at the scalability and replicability of the best ideas, recognizing that strategies that might work well at one spatial or temporal scale may have different consequences at others.
- Be prepared for failures and to return to earlier phases of the process, which can include reconsidering the research results, reframing the problems again, or revisiting other ideas from the ideation phase.

There is no one way to do design thinking. The process demands listening to diverse voices, observing what people do as much as what they say, reframing problems as opportunities in disguise, generating an abundance of ideas to come up with some valuable new ones, and prototyping and testing the best of them to see which work well within the constraints of a situation. But design also requires a degree of improvisation, with a lot of judgment in terms of what to do when, combined with a willingness to fail and to learn from those failures.

Design thinking isn't right for every problem or community, especially those in which failure is not an option, nor change a desirable outcome. But the abductive logic that underpins design is, as Charles Sanders Peirce wrote, "the only logical operation which introduces any new idea," and where new ideas are needed and welcome, there is no better way to achieve them than by design.[17]

Notes

1 Robin Marantz Henig, "Experts Warned of a Pandemic Decades Ago. Why Weren't We Ready?" *National Geographic*, April 8, 2020. www.nationalgeographic. com/science/article/experts-warned-pandemic-decades-ago-why-not-ready-for-coronavirus
2 Isaac Chotiner, "The Interwoven Threads of Inequality and Health," *New Yorker*, April 13, 2020. www.newyorker.com/news/q-and-a/the-coronavirus-and-the-interwoven-threads-of-inequality-and-health
3 Chris Buckley, "Chinese Doctor, Silenced after Warning of Outbreak, Dies From Coronavirus," *New York Times*, February 7, 2020. www.nytimes.com/2020/02/06/world/asia/chinese-doctor-Li-Wenliang-coronavirus.html
4 Nassim Nicholas Taleb, *Antifragile: Things That Gain from Disorder* (New York: Random House, 2012).
5 Minnesota Design Center, University of Minnesota. https://design.umn.edu/minnesota-design-center
6 Igor Dourven, "Peirce on Abduction," *Stanford Encyclopedia of Philosophy*, 2021. https://plato.stanford.edu/entries/abduction/peirce.htmlhttps://plato.stanford.edu/entries/abduction/peirce.html
7 Tim Brown, "Design Thinking Defined," *IDEO*. https://designthinking.ideo.com/
8 Christian Paz, "All the President's Lies about the Coronavirus," *Atlantic*, November 2, 2020. www.theatlantic.com/politics/archive/2020/11/trumps-lies-about-coronavirus/608647/
9 Thomas Fisher, "Rethinking Design Thinking," *Huffington Post*, February 8, 2017. www.huffpost.com/entry/rethinking-design-thinking_b_589b504ce4b061551b3e066a
10 Natasha Iskander, "Design Thinking Is Fundamentally Conservative and Preserves the Status Quo," *Harvard Business Review*, September 5, 2018. https://hbr.org/2018/09/design-thinking-is-fundamentally-conservative-and-preserves-the-status-quo
11 Reuters Staff, "Fact Check: COVID-19 Is Not a Hoax to Eliminate Trump," Reuters, June 29, 2021. www.reuters.com/article/uk-factcheck-covid-hoax-eliminate-trump/fact-check-covid-19-is-not-a-hoax-to-eliminate-trump-idUSK-BN27S31E

12 Peter M. Sandman, "Public Health's Share of the Blame: US COVID-19 Risk Communication Failures," Center for Infectious Disease Research and Policy, August 24, 2020. www.cidrap.umn.edu/news-perspective/2020/08/commentary-public-healths-share-blame-us-covid-19-risk-communication
13 "Destination Medical Center Creates Equitable Design Process for Public Spaces," *Destination Medical Center*, September 18, 2020. https://dmc.mn/destination-medical-center-creates-equitable-design-process-for-public-spaces/
14 David Cooperrider, "What is Appreciative Inquiry?" David Cooperrider and Associates. www.davidcooperrider.com/ai-process/
15 Erick Anderson, "Prominent San Diego Scientists Argue COVID-19 Spreads Like Secondhand Smoke," KPBS, April 19, 2021. www.kpbs.org/news/2021/apr/19/prominent-scientists-argue-covid-spreads-faster-in/
16 Future Services Institute, "How Can We Help Minnesotans Living with Disabilities Lead More Independent Lives?" http://futureservicesinstitute.org/pathways-to-fuller-lives
17 Igor Dourven, "Peirce on Abduction."

3
POLITICS

For all of the terrible aspects of pandemics, they also bring out the best in many people. The COVID-19 pandemic, for example, prompted an abundance of giving: people donating to hospitals the medical supplies they had at home, delivering food to elderly neighbors who should not go out, and making financial contributions to relief organizations or other non-profits helping families in need.[1] That giving largely occurred voluntarily, as organizations put out calls for help. And that aid mostly occurred without compensation or even recognition, showing a degree of self-sacrifice that has been relatively rare in recent years.

Such selflessness brings to mind the argument of the historian, Arthur Schlesinger Jr., that the U.S. has cycled between phases that emphasize individualism and competition and those that emphasize cooperation and collaboration.[2] He believed that one phase prompts the other and he also acknowledged that several factors could shorten or lengthen these phases. The U.S. has been in a very long competitive, individualistic phase, one of the longest in American history since 1980 and Ronald Reagan's presidency. The only phases that have come close to this, wrote Schlesinger, were the 32-year-long highly competitive phase of the Gilded Age in the late 19th century,

DOI: 10.4324/9781003198192-4

and the 18-year-long cooperative phase of the Progressive Era in the early 20th century.

Given the length of time competitive individualism has reigned in the U.S., I have wondered if Schlesinger's theory still held, and the pandemic convinced me that it did, showing how quickly the political pendulum can swing in America, as it has in many other countries as well. In a matter of a few weeks, we saw the national conversation in the U.S. turn from reducing taxes and shrinking government – classic individualistic ideas – to massive government spending and collaborative community participation – classic cooperative ones. Nearly 40 years after Ronald Reagan, it took a pandemic to loosen the grip of the idea that greed is good, and to push Americans back toward the self-sacrificing cooperation that has characterized people's response to collective crises in the past.

The political pendulum swings that Schlesinger described do not eliminate the opposing viewpoints; the latter simply become less compelling and more of a minority position. And we have already begun to see that in U.S. politics, as the Republican party – once a bastion of the believers in free-market competition – became the minority party in both houses of the U.S. Congress in 2021.[3] That party still talks as if it will regain power soon and that their political losses were the exception in what they see as the ascendency of conservative values, whatever that means after the Trump administration shredded almost all of them. But if Schlesinger was right, they are wrong. The pandemic has likely thrust the U.S. and many other countries into a more cooperative phase that will probably continue for at least 8 years, which is the shortest phase we have ever had in the cycles of American history, and more likely 16 years, the average length of time for each phase.

The politics of pandemics, of course, differs from country to country. Compare how the Chinese reacted to COVID-19 versus many Americans. When I asked a colleague of mine in China how they had fared during the pandemic, especially since his country had been the likely source of the coronavirus, he said that they had largely gotten the disease under control. Everyone in his city wore masks every time their left their house or apartment, without exception – a level of obedience to authority rarely seen in the U.S. While the U.S. lacked national leadership in the initial phase of the pandemic when it came to the wearing of masks, some Americans also showed little regard for the recommendations of experts if that advice appeared to reduce their individual freedoms. Would Patrick Henry have ever imagined, in 1775, that his phrase "give me liberty or give me death" would become a both–and proposition, with liberty from public-health restrictions bringing, if not death, then almost certain infection?

Negative and Positive Freedom

A lot of the political polarization around this topic stems for how people define freedom. The historian Isaiah Berlin made a distinction between what he called negative and positive freedom, a difference that seems particularly relevant to the COVID-19 pandemic.[4] Negative freedom means freedom from restriction, an interpretation of the word that those who object to wearing masks clearly hold. Of all the nations, Americans may be one of the most extreme in their adherence to negative freedom, a reflection of our equally extreme emphasis, in various phases of our history, on individualism and competition. While negative freedom has some advantages – cultivating a lot of cultural creativity and technical innovation, for example – it has definite disadvantages during a pandemic, as the U.S. learned with infection and death rates far higher than most other countries.

Positive freedom sees liberty, instead, arising not from few restrictions, but from the embrace of a cause, adherence to a belief, or cooperation with a larger crowd of like-minded people. This, too, has deep roots in countries like the U.S. Indigenous communities, for example, often viewed freedom in this way, as an integral part of being a member of a family, a tribe, and a culture, all of which restrict some individual actions in order to achieve a greater good. The same seems true of societies like that of China, rooted in Confucian and Taoist worldviews that emphasize respect for authority and acceptance of the paradoxes that, to get what we need, we sometimes need to give up what we want.

The divide between negative and positive freedom is rarely so clear-cut, however. I suspect that many of the people in the U.S. who

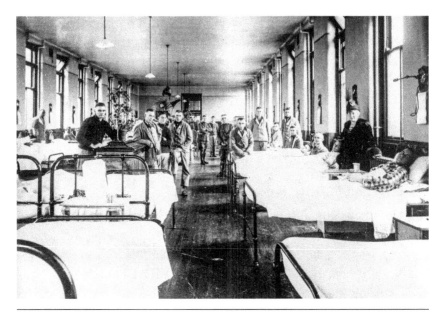

Figure 3.1 Influenza patients, 1918, American Ward, General Hospital, Glasgow, Scotland.

objected to wearing masks not only claim that they had the freedom to do so, but also take their cues from their political tribe, which can demand absolute adherence to its policies. Here, another Isaiah Berlin distinction might be useful. He argued that there are people who think like "hedgehogs" and see only one thing everywhere they look, and those who think like "foxes" and see many things and multiple ways to achieve a goal.[5] Berlin acknowledged that some people like to think of themselves as foxes, while actually behaving like hedgehogs, as we saw from those who think of themselves as free-market conservatives, open to a wide range of competitive activities, while also viewing politics in a singular way and demanding that their peers adhere to that view too.

This may help explain the paradoxical behavior of the "never-maskers." They may claim that wearing a mask constrains their freedom, but they also seem quick to deride anyone who wears a mask or asks them to wear one. They are hedgehogs, disguised as foxes. The opposite can happen as well. Public health officials may look like hedgehogs, focused on COVID-19 and telling us all to do the same few things – wear a mask, social distance, wash our hands, and avoid touching our faces – and yet they act more like foxes, as they responded to the unpredictable disease in sometimes improvisational ways.

The pandemic also showed how we should see freedom in temporal terms. Rather than being too much of a hedgehog when it comes to seeing freedom in only one way, we would do well to be more foxlike in our view of it. Negative freedom might serve us well in good times, when there is plenty to go around, but positive freedom has clear benefits in a pandemic, helping us get over our liberty-or-death mindset and put on masks for the good of the community as well as ourselves. If more people took a positive-freedom approach to the pandemic, as the Chinese did, the world would have conquered COVID-19 faster and gotten back more quickly to what so many Americans, at least, seem to yearn for: negative freedom.

Taking Exception to Exceptionalism

Another political paradox revealed by the pandemic is the idea of American exceptionalism. My father, a child and adolescent psychologist, used to advise me that, no matter how well I did in school or in other ventures, I should never think of myself as exceptional, since such thinking would make me anything but that. He taught me the paradox of exceptionalism: If you think you are exceptional, you are almost certainly not, since so many other people think of themselves as exceptional as well. In the U.S., that self-congratulatory frame of mind extends to how some people think about the country. As *New York Times* editor Jennifer Schuessler wrote during the pandemic, Americans tend to think that their country "stands apart from the forces shaping the rest of the world."[6]

The problem with such exceptionalist thinking is that it leads to overconfidence, something amply evident in America's bungled handling of the pandemic. By standing apart from the pandemic that had already begun to shape the rest of the world, the Trump administration did everything except prepare Americans for the disruption: denying it, mocking it, or calling it a hoax. Which raises another paradox of exceptionalism: Those who think they are exceptional may end up being the exception in all the wrong ways. As Schuessler put it, America is "a country that sees itself as the world's wealthiest, most powerful and scientifically advanced" that also "leads the world in both [COVID-19] cases and confirmed deaths."[7]

The complacency that comes from exceptionalist thinking makes the U.S. especially vulnerable in times like these. Schuessler quotes the Stanford historian, David Kennedy, who argues that the incompetence of the U.S. government in responding to the pandemic "laid bare the degree to which we've 'starved the public sector'."[8] After the Trump Administration closed the office charged with preparing for pandemics a year before the pandemic hit, as part of a larger effort to starve the public sector, the U.S. was, if anything, exceptionally lucky that it did not face more catastrophes, given its emaciated government.[9] Nearly four decades after President Reagan claimed that government is the problem, his observation came true: During the pandemic, the government proved to be the problem, after so many years of people on the political right working so hard to make it so.

The U.S. government's problem has also been its relative cluelessness about the real threats the country faces. For decades, right-wing leaders in Congress and in the White House built up the military, assuming that conventional warfare remained our biggest challenge, while denying the greater menaces, which are viral, digital, and climatological.[10] No amount of weaponry can protect us from pandemics, cyberattacks, and climate change, and if anything, they make those problems worse by diverting our money and attention. Indeed, we have military personnel armed and ready in a world that now largely stays at home. At the same time, too few soldiers have been allowed to help where they are really needed: in hospitals and testing facilities in our own country. Generals fiddle while Rome burns.

The pandemic taught the U.S. the lesson my father taught me. As Schuessler wrote, "the coronavirus, instead of affirming our distinctness, is revealing how much we have in common with the rest of the world."[11] The people of other countries are not our enemies; they are comrades in arms against our mutual enemy, an infection that ignored nationalities, ethnicities, or any allegiances. Novel viruses dissolve the illusion that we are exceptional and they dissipate the delusion that causes us to misunderstand each other – and ourselves. In that, they are truly exceptional.

But it takes a lot to break people of old habits. Growing up in the U.S. during the "cold war" years of the 1950s and 1960s, I heard a lot about a possible World War Three, a nuclear confrontation between America and Russia as a final showdown between capitalism and communism. Never once did I hear anyone talk about that war possibly being between us and a virus, but the pandemic turned out to be the real third world war, at least in terms of its casualties. The U.S. death toll as a result of COVID-19 went way past the total number of deaths from the Korean War (36,516), Vietnam War (58,209), World War I (116,516), and World War II (405,000), and as I write this, the deaths nearly equal the combined total of all of those wars.[12]

Yet unlike the unified way in which Americans fought in those contests, the war against COVID-19 divided the nation, with leaders who made it sound optional to do what it takes to defeat a viral foe: wearing of masks, social distancing, and self-quarantining. What leader of a country at war would act this way, pretending that it wasn't happening even as thousands died every day? The answer to that question eventually became clear. Two of the nations with the highest death rates – the U.S. and Brazil – both had presidents with authoritarian tendencies, who resisted acknowledging the pandemic and who refused to take precautions themselves, like wearing masks at public events.

Both countries also have strong cowboy cultures, and with that comes what the historian Carl Becker described as "an individualism of conformity," in which the self-reliant traits needed to survive on the frontier become a norm that everyone is expected to follow.[13] The popularity of Presidents Trump and Bolsonaro among residents in the rural and frontier sections of their countries reflected that mentality: real cowboys are not afraid of a virus, and if they are, they dare not show it.

Becker's individualism of conformity has another tragic aspect to it. Unlike soldiers in a war, who watch out for the well-being of their fellow soldiers, the individualism of America's and Brazil's cowboy culture made people especially prey to a killer like COVID-19. It's one thing to take a risk with one's own life, as a cowboy might out on the range, but another thing to risk the lives of others because of one's

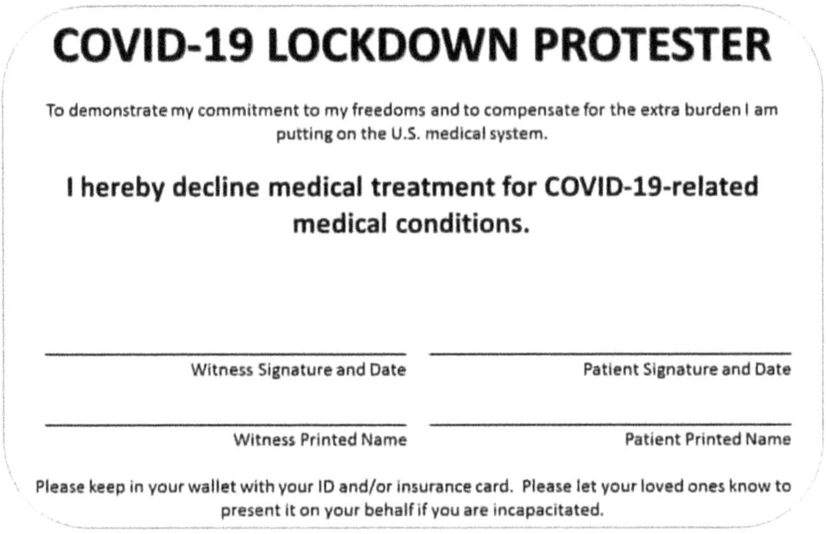

Figure 3.2 "COVID-19 protest" framed as personal freedom.

own carelessness, as was the case with the coronavirus. Not wearing a mask and not following the distancing and quarantining recommendations of the medical community threatened not only the people who ignored that advice, but also everyone with whom they came in contact. The conformist individualism that characterizes America's and Brazil's cowboy culture is really a contagious, irresponsible one.

Getting Our Analogies Right

Design offers one way of getting past the tension between individualism and conformism. Both Presidents Trump and Biden – as well as political leaders around the world – likened humanity's struggle with COVID-19 as a battle, an analogy that made all of us soldiers in the fight against the deadly virus. But war arises out of a win–lose view of the world, where one opponent seeks to prevail over another through force. An alternative analogy, though, might also apply to the pandemic, given the chances that COVID-19 or one or more of its variants may remain, like the common cold, within the human population for a very long time. In addition to warfare's win–lose view of the world, we might see the pandemic in terms of the win–win worldview of diplomacy, which accepts differences and seeks creative ways to resolve conflicts.

For example, we all might have avoided this war with COVID-19 by designing a better response to the initial outbreak of the disease, isolating those initially infected, preventing travel to or from its region of origin, and coordinating all of the nations of the world in a unified strategy to prevent its spread. War, in that sense, is a failure to imagine possible futures and act on the greatest threats before they get out of control. And those failures continued even as we did battle with our viral opponent, while failing to reframe the situation and seize unseen opportunities. The missed opportunity with the COVID-19 pandemic was not just that we let the coronavirus spread around the world, but also that we did not see this as an ideal opportunity to set aside petty political differences and unify globally against an enemy that threatened us all.

Most countries fought the war against COVID-19 as they would any other: as a nation, with leadership coming from the top elected officials and their public-health experts. The U.S., at least during the Trump administration, took another approach: letting every state fight the battle on their own, a strategy that, in a traditional war, would lead to certain defeat. And as a result, the U.S. had one of the highest death rates from the disease. For the richest and most powerful nation on the planet, that is a design failure of unprecedented proportion.

Indeed, it represented two types of design failures. One occurred as a result of a lack of clarity and consistency about the nature of the problem. Although some in the Trump administration recognized COVID-19 as a real threat, others saw it as an opportunity to gain and retain power by dividing states against each other as they vied for protective equipment and political points with their constituents.[14] If a nation cannot define a problem correctly, it cannot design an appropriate response, and the mixed messages and divergent responses to the problem of COVID-19 led to a sizable number of unnecessary deaths.

The other design failure resulted from how ordinary people responded to the problem. Wars typically get fought with well-trained soldiers who follow commands and who do what they need to do in order to protect themselves and to fight effectively. But the battle against COVID-19 was fought, at least in the U.S., more like guerilla warfare, with some people following public health commands and others refusing to do so, taking their orders from self-serving leaders or social-media conspirators. Countries cannot win wars if the troops refuse orders or claim that it is their right to decide what they do or not do, and the high number of U.S. casualties in this war against the coronavirus stemmed, in part, from the lack of discipline among its citizen soldiers.

As in any war, blame for that lay at the top. The responsibility for the behavior of undisciplined and unruly soldiers ultimately rested with their commanding officers, which in the case of the pandemic, were the elected officials rather than the military brass. But blame also lay with those in the ranks who were reprobate in their response to the pandemic, going about their normal lives as if nothing was happening, even as record numbers of fellow citizens fell ill and died from the enemy in their midst.

The design failure, in other words, was systemic. The U.S. may have the world's largest and strongest military, but the war against COVID-19 revealed the nation's underlying weakness when it comes to fighting the kind of wars we will increasingly face in the future, where we will all be enlisted, whether we want to or not. Redesigning our response to such scenarios is something the U.S. needs to start right now, since COVID-19 won't be the last or even the most threatening enemy we will face.

But is war the best analogy to use in such a situation? Does that analogy force us to think in certain ways that may be counterproductive? As the writer and theologian, Karen Hering, asked:

> Why are we so quick to label crises in terms of war and battle? Framing the Covid-19 contagion as "being attacked from abroad" … is not only inaccurate, but also unhelpful and dangerous … A better frame might be that we are experiencing a global natural disaster, and we must all work together and help one another with compassion and with courage.[15]

She has a point. When presidents declare a national emergency in times of war, it triggers a set of policies that allow the government to respond in more rapid and responsive ways. But as Ms. Hering observes, that analogy can also be unhelpful and dangerous. It can lead us to think of a novel virus as something we can defeat, when in fact, it is something we must live with, build immunity to, and be vaccinated against, probably on an annual basis, like the flu. In that sense, COVID-19 is more like an immigrant than an invader, more a part of us than an opponent of ours.

Hering offers the analogy of the COVID-19 pandemic as akin to a global natural disaster. Clearly the virus was a natural phenomenon and it had disastrous consequences across the globe, but that analogy might also distort the reality of the virus, since most natural disasters happen in relatively local areas: an earthquake or flood, a hurricane or tornado, a blizzard or drought, all have boundaries beyond which they have little effect and to which people and animals can flee when threatened. COVID-19 existed at a global scale. No person on the planet escaped its effect. Most of us isolated ourselves at various points and in various ways during the pandemic in order to slow its spread, but the virus eventually reached every corner of the planet, wherever we were, for better or worse.

Perhaps a better analogy might have been climate change, which is not an event, but a condition; not isolated, but global in its reach; and not avoidable, but modifiable depending upon our decisions and actions. Of course, in a political climate, at least in the U.S., where even mentioning the words "climate change" raises animosities, using it as an analogy for the pandemic might have been problematic. But getting the analogy wrong can also hamper our ability to fight the coronavirus, as we have seen in the inaction and delayed response of the Trump Administration.

Robert Grudin, in his book *The Grace of Great Things*, wrote about two different types of analogies: intra- and inter-disciplinary ones.[16] Intradisciplinary analogies occur within a field, as when we hear parallels between the COVID-19 virus and the 1918 flu epidemic. Such analogies have value in helping us put a phenomenon into perspective and to gage its impact in relation to similar occurrences.

But more creative responses come from interdisciplinary analogies, which make connections across different fields. The analogy of the pandemic to war or to a natural disaster are examples.

In such analogies, the measure of their value comes from what new insights they provide and what new meaning they give to the events of our lives. As I think about Ms. Hering's "global natural disaster" analogy and about how it felt to live through the COVID-19 pandemic, what comes to mind is more the asteroid impact over 65 million years ago, which killed all non-avian dinosaurs. The virus seems like an impact wave, making its way around the planet and eventually sweeping over us all.

While it was much less deadly to us than the asteroid was to the dinosaurs, the coronavirus did cause us to act as our distant, mammalian ancestors did millions of years ago. Mammals survived the asteroid's impact by burrowing in and waiting out the initial wave of devastation, and most of us did the same as we awaited the arrival of COVID-19: sheltering in place in hopes of avoiding the worst of the infection. If this were a war, such behavior would seem cowardly; but if this is like an asteroid strike, staying at home and keeping our heads down was exactly what we should have done in order to thrive once the threat has passed.

Designers deal with unknowns, having to make decisions that have consequences in the future without having much information about what those might be. The same is true for leaders during a pandemic. They need to act in the face of uncertainties and find a way, as designers do, to balance pessimism and optimism, skepticism and belief. President Trump skewed far in the direction of optimism and belief. He downplayed the seriousness of COVID-19, not wanting to panic the public, he claimed, but also reflecting his overly optimistic belief that the virus would, magically, just go away.[17]

Leaders do need to exude a degree of optimism during crises in order to give people hope and increase their confidence in their ability to overcome challenges. But when optimism goes too far, as it did with Trump, he became more a Pollyanna than a president, avoiding the unpleasant facts of the situation and misleading people as a result. That, in turn, led many of the president's supporters to become overly skeptical about the virus, the vaccine, and the advice of public health experts. Too much optimism in one direction can lead to too much pessimism in the other.

In situations like this, Pascal's wager might help.[18] A mathematician as well as a philosopher and physicist, Blaise Pascal made a logical argument for the existence of God. If we don't know if God exists or not, he argued, we would be better off believing in him than not, since believers have nothing to lose if he doesn't and everything to gain if he does. Meanwhile non-believers gain nothing if he doesn't and everything to lose if he does. Religious adherents have long embraced Pascal's optimistic argument as an upbeat way of explaining their belief in God. But when it came to COVID-19, many of those same believers, especially among the Christian evangelical community, became pessimists, skeptical about the existence of COVID-19, denying the seriousness of the illness, and hesitating to get vaccinated.[19]

Pascal's wager suggests that we should do the opposite during a pandemic like that of COVID-19. When confronted by a novel virus about which we knew little and for which we had no immunity, we should wager that it exists, listen to what the public health experts recommend and act accordingly. As Pascal would say, we had everything to gain by believing in COVID-19 and protecting ourselves from it, with nothing to lose if it didn't. Meanwhile, those who did not believe in the virus had everything to lose and nothing to gain by not doing so. Whether betting on the existence of God or the possibility of dying a horrible death at the hands of a virulent virus, better to wager on the side of caution than carelessness.

The analogy between the belief in God and in COVID-19 also highlights the importance of getting our analogies right when dealing with a life-or-death situation. Leaders deal in analogies, helping people understand a new situation or a potential threat by likening it to something we have experienced or do know. From that perspective, the analogies leaders choose to use make all the difference in terms of the stories they want to tell and the actions they want to encourage – or not. A different analogy, in other words, can make all the difference.

Generational Politics

The COVID-19 pandemic also shifted generational politics. For most of recorded history, older generations have dominated the younger, for obvious reasons. Older people have lived longer and have had time to accumulate money and experience and to ascend hierarchies to positions of power and influence, including the power to force youth to go to war. That, in particular, has constituted a kind of generational genocide in which one generation sends another to die, sometimes for irrational or self-serving reasons and often knowing that many young people won't make it back home.

Entrusting the lives of our youth to the decisions of their elders has been the norm for so long that few raise their voices against this generational inequity. But COVID-19 flipped that power dynamic. Those who were 65 or older or who had underlying health challenges died from COVID-19 at a much higher rate and in absolute numbers than younger people.[20] During the pandemic, younger generations threatened the longevity of older ones, not through military action, but through the inattention of many youth to the public health precautions that a mostly older generation of physicians recommended.

That differed from the 1918 flu pandemic, when soldiers lucky enough to return home unscathed after World War I had a to deal with a virus that killed young people at a far greater rate than the elderly.[21] From a generational point of view, the 1918 pandemic may have seemed more like a continuation of the war in just a different form and in a different place. The fact that the older generation in power at the time remained largely unaffected by the virus may have been one reason why that pandemic took so many lives. Not only was medical knowledge much less developed a century ago, but the pressure to find a vaccine may not have seemed as important as it did with COVID-19.

That had at least partly to do with the fact that COVID-19 most threatened those who have the most access to money and power. Of course, everyone, young and old, hoped that we would find a vaccine against the coronavirus so that everyone could return to some semblance of our former lives. But with youth surviving COVID-19 at a much higher rate than their elders, the latter's urge to spend whatever

Figure 3.3 "From turmoil to truce" during the pandemic lockdown.

it takes to find a cure became especially urgent. Presidents Trump and Biden, both in their seventies, rightly spent enormous amounts of money, first to develop vaccines and then to deliver them into people's arms. But let's also hope that older people in positions of power today learn what generational genocide feels like now that the tables have been turned. Maybe that will lead to a cure for the other great plague afflicting humanity: the power of elders to send youth off to war.

Political Inflammation

Not that youth were immune from the effects of COVID-19. The virus causes, especially in children, a condition called "multi-system inflammatory syndrome," in which many parts of the body – not just external organs like the skin and eyes, but also internal ones like the brain, heart, and kidneys – swell and become red and painful.[22] While children did not die nearly as often as adults from a COVID-19 infection, this syndrome can make them very ill and require hospitalization, where they are treated with anti-inflammatory drugs.

That condition suggests another possibly useful metaphor during the pandemic, the body politic of countries like the U.S. succumbed to their own multi-system inflammation. As happened with COVID-19, the political infection came quickly and spread rapidly through the population, not just through face-to-face interactions but also through Facebook and other social media. And yet, unlike COVID-19, the political virus traveled less through that air than through the Internet and, at least in the U.S., it took the form not of spiky viral balls, but instead that of 280-character Tweets containing their own RNA: Republican Nonstop Anger.

Just as the human body does not do well when inflamed, neither does a political body; it loses a sense of balance and an ability to function, to the point where the body's organs begin to attack each other: Senate against the House, States against the Federal Government. During the pandemic, that led to further political inflammation, as the body politic over-reacted with an excessive immune system attack from the media. This happened in different ways in different countries, but in several of them the pandemic made the nation as ill as many people within it.

What to do with a political infection like this? Perhaps we should do what the doctors do for children struck by multi-system inflammatory syndrome: focus on reducing the swelling through various therapies. For sickness of the body politic, that might include not responding to the inflammatory rhetoric, not over-reacting to its infective nature, and not losing a sense of balance and perspective – all of which is hard to do in the midst of political as well as personal illness.

And maybe we should see ourselves as the doctor rather than the ill patient. We might simply acknowledge the infection, monitor its course, and take the most prudent and least damaging steps in response to it. Leaders might insist, wrongly and recklessly, that illnesses like COVID-19 will someday just go away, but we should also remember that political infections will also someday go away if we refuse to let ourselves be inflamed by them. At that point we might begin to regain our mental health as well as our political one.

Part of regaining our mental health has to do with the question of control. During the pandemic, we saw repeated confrontations between elected officials who wanted to open up the economy and the schools prematurely, and public health professionals who advised against that for fear of unleashing a new wave of illness and death.[23] That confrontation revolved around the question of who had – or should have – more control. Legally, the elected officials had the emergency power to force both closures and re-openings during the pandemic, but their doing so against the recommendations of the public health community could be seen as irresponsible and possibly cause for their removal from office in the next election. In democratic politics, voters have the ultimate control.

But public health professionals exerted another type of control. Their command of population data, their insights into viral transmission, and their understanding of how epidemics have played out in the past gave the health community the upper hand when it came to determining the best course of action during the pandemic. And we saw that in the pronouncements of the directors of the Centers for Disease Control and Prevention and of the National Institute of Allergy and Infectious Disease in the U.S. They spoke from a position of authority not granted to them by the voters, but by virtue of their knowledge and experience in knowing that, despite our best efforts, we are never entirely in control when it comes to disease.

Which may be one of the most important lessons of the COVID-19 pandemic. We like to think of ourselves as having a degree of control over our lives and, through the deployment of modern science and technology, a degree of control over what happens to us. And yet, for all of our ability to control our world, the pandemic reminded us of how little control we actually have. Many people certainly demonstrated how little control they had over their own emotions as they refused to recognize the seriousness of the pandemic and acted as if it weren't happening, no doubt out of fear of losing their livelihoods if not their lives. Public health experts also admitted how little control they have over a novel virus about which we had little experience and for which we initially lacked a vaccine.

COVID-19, in other words, offered us a lesson in relinquishing control. That does not mean that we were helpless to protect ourselves and others or that we should not try to understand how the pandemic occurred and do what we can to prevent another one. But we would

Figure 3.4 COVID-19 mask requirement as a social compact.

be wise to recognize the extent to which we lacked control over it, and the degree to which we may never have full control over anything in the natural world. And with that wisdom comes an acknowledgement of the paradox at the heart of the human species: that the more control we try to exert over nature, the more nature reminds us of how little control we really have, whether that comes in the form of a novel coronavirus or extreme weather – or in the limitations of human nature itself.

Notes

1 Jia Tolentino, "What Mutual Aid Can Do During a Pandemic," *New Yorker*, May 18, 2020. www.newyorker.com/magazine/2020/05/18/what-mutual-aid-can-do-during-a-pandemic?utm_source=NYR_REG_GATE

2 Arthur M. Schlesinger, Jr., *The Cycles of American History* (New York: Clarion, 1999).

3 Justine Coleman, "Obama: The Republican Party 'Is the Minority Party in This Country,'" *The Hill*, December 16, 2020. https://thehill.com/homenews/media/530428-obama-republican-party-is-the-minority-party-in-this-country

4 Isaiah Berlin, "Two Concepts of Liberty," *Four Essays on Liberty* (Oxford: Oxford University Press, 1969) 118–172.

5 Isaiah Berlin, *The Hedgehog and the Fox: An Essay on Tolstoy's View of History* (New York: Simon & Schuster, 1957).

6 Jennifer Schuessler, "Will a Pandemic Shatter the Perception of American Exceptionalism?" *New York Times*, April 25, 2020. www.nytimes.com/2020/04/25/arts/virus-american-exceptionalism.html?ref=oembed

7 Schuessler, "American Exceptionalism?"
8 Schuessler, "American Exceptionalism?"
9 Beth Cameron, "I Ran the White Office Pandemic Office. Trump Closed It," *Washington Post*, March 13, 2020. www.washingtonpost.com/outlook/nsc-pandemic-office-trump-closed/2020/03/13/a70de09c-6491-11ea-acca-80c22bbee96f_story. html
10 World Economic Forum, *Global Risks Report, 2021*, 16th edition. www3. weforum.org/docs/WEF_The_Global_Risks_Report_2021.pdf
11 Schuessler, "American Exceptionalism?"
12 "Coronavirus in the U.S.: Latest Case Count," *New York Times*, August 5, 2021. www.nytimes.com/interactive/2021/us/covid-cases.html
13 Carl Becker, "Everyman His Own Historian," *The American Historical Review*, 37(2), January 1932, 221–236. https://academic.oup.com/ahr/article-abstract/37/ 2/221/19163?redirectedFrom=fulltext
14 Drew Altman, "Understanding the U.S. Failure on Coronavirus," *BMJ* 2020; 370:m3417. September 14, 2020. www.bmj.com/content/370/bmj. m3417
15 Karen Hering, "Coronavirus," *Star Tribune*, March 17, 2020. A6.
16 Robert Grudin, *The Grace of Great Things, Creativity and Innovation* (New York: Ticknor & Fields, 1990).
17 Juana Summers, "Timeline: How Trump Has Downplayed the Coronavirus Pandemic," *National Public Radio*, October 2, 2020. www.npr.org/sections/ latest-updates-trump-covid-19-results/2020/10/02/919432383/how-trump-has-downplayed-the-coronavirus-pandemic
18 "Pascal's Wager," *Stanford Encyclopedia of Philosophy*, September 1, 2017. https://plato.stanford.edu/entries/pascal-wager/
19 Elizabeth Dias, Ruth Graham, "White Evangelical Resistance Is Obstacle in Vaccination Effort," *New York Times*, April 12, 2021. www.nytimes.com/2021/04/05/ us/covid-vaccine-evangelicals.html
20 Kendra Cherry, "How Different Generations Are Responding to COVID-19," *Very Well Mind*, August 2, 2020. www.verywellmind.com/how-different-generations-are-responding-to-covid-19–4802517
21 John Berry, "Historian John Berry Compares COVID-19 to the 1918 Flu Pandemic," *University of Rochester Newscenter*, October 6, 2020. www.rochester. edu/newscenter/historian-john-barry-compares-covid-19-to-1918-flu-pandemic-454732/
22 "Multisystem Inflammatory Syndrome in Children (MIS-C) and COVID-19," Mayo Clinic. www.mayoclinic.org/diseases-conditions/mis-c-in-kids-covid-19/ symptoms-causes/syc-20502550
23 Christine Vestal, Michael Ollove, "Politicians Shunt Aside Public Health Officials," PEW, June 18, 2020. www.pewtrusts.org/en/research-and-analysis/blogs/stateline/ 2020/06/18/politicians-shunt-aside-public-health-officials

4
ECONOMICS

Pandemics have economic impacts as much as political and epide-miological ones. These global illnesses accomplish what not even a war can do: forcing countries to close themselves down and limit travel not only to other countries but also within their own territory as well. Shutting off the rest of the world, while it might make the most extreme nationalists happy, constitutes a type of economic self-harm, cutting off the very lifeblood of what sustains a country: the exchange of goods and services among its citizens and with other nations. Like a person deprived of food or water, a country cannot last long without the nourishment of people's interactions and the flow of materials across its borders.

We saw that happen in one country after another during the pandemic, and those remarkable measures seemed to work.[1] Most people obeyed the curfews and remained indoors, patiently waiting for release from their quarantine, but the closure of entire countries raised the question of what role countries may play in the future economy, especially in an era of pandemics and the global exchange of disease.

Jane Jacobs wrote over 50 years ago that the most important political and economic unit in the future will be city-based regions, competing with regions elsewhere around the world, while paying relatively little attention to national boundaries.[2] While sometimes

64 DOI: 10.4324/9781003198192-5

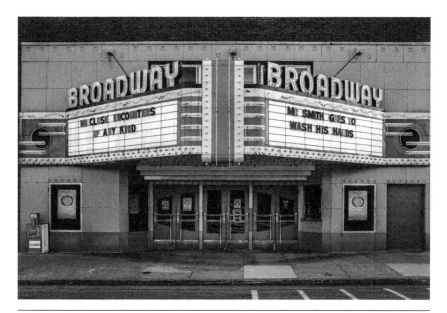

Figure 4.1 "Broadway Theater," closed during the pandemic.

dismissed by the economics community, Jane Jacobs got it right. We do increasingly live in regions competing with each other globally, and that has become especially apparent in recent years in the U.S. Some national policies, pushed by nationalistic and xenophobic leaders, have worked against the interests of various regions in the country, as local leaders – mayors, city council members, and county commissioners – have pursued their own economic futures.

The pandemic, though, offered a new twist on that plot. When trying to fight a virus that knew no borders, nations were the best entities to fight it. As in war, so in a pandemic, the enemy is too powerful and potentially pervasive to expect every local jurisdiction or regional economic unit to fight it on its own. One region cannot close while an adjacent one stays open; nor can one allow the transfer of people and goods while the other one prohibits it. If the best way to defeat a deadly virus, instead, involves shutting down an entire country, then that suggests a new and valuable role for national governments. They may not have as much economic value as they once had, but they may have more protective, public-health value than ever before.

The Economics of Import Replacement

Jacobs got something else right about economies as well. She recognized that regional economies thrive when they engage in what she called "import replacement," substituting imported goods and services with those made and provided locally. The pandemic highlighted the importance of that idea as global supply chains broke down and regions had to invent new ways of meeting their needs through more locally produced products. While the long-term effect of import replacement may take a while before it becomes clear, I suspect that we will see an abundance of new start-up businesses in regions around the world as a result of the economic opportunity that the pandemic created.

We already saw some of that start-up activity among restaurants during the pandemic. They were among the businesses most affected by the coronavirus, and so had some of the greatest incentive to innovate in order to stay open, with expanded take-out, drive-through, and home-delivery options.[3] Some restaurants also developed hybrid models in which they delivered the components of meals that peo-

Figure 4.2 "Barricade tape in a restaurant to keep people from sitting during the pandemic".

ple could then prepare at home, becoming a distributed network of kitchens in which the consumers of restaurant food also partly became its producers.

Such business hybrids point to another innovative aspect of the post-pandemic global economy: tapping the abundance of unleveraged talent and skill of people that exist within every community and that are rarely recognized or monetized. Prior to the pandemic, the global economy tended to separate producers and consumers, employees and customers, even though, obviously, most consumers needed to be producers – to have employment – in order to buy what they needed. Still, that division between producer and consumer led to the paradox of companies trying to reduce production costs, in part by laying off employees, while also trying to increase consumer spending, including by the very employees just laid off.

We saw with the pandemic how rapidly that whole system no longer works when consumption declines and production ends because of quarantines and forced closures. While companies and consumers lost a lot of money as a consequence, no one lost any of the talent, skill, and knowledge that they had before the pandemic arrived and that wealth remained, and in many cases grew, as people had more time to learn new skills and attain more knowledge. Which may be one of the greatest lessons of the pandemic: In a global economy that measures wealth in terms of the amount of money one has or controls, it overlooks other forms of wealth that hardly ever get measured, that rarely get monetized, and that have far greater value than anything money can buy.

The father of capitalism, Adam Smith, recognized this as the paradox of value.[4] He asked why we value diamonds, which we do not need, and do not value water, which we cannot live without. From a monetary point of view, the answer is obvious. Diamonds are rare so people who want them will pay more money for them than they will for water, which – at least in Smith's time and place – was widely available. But from a value point of view, his paradox is not obvious. Water is more valuable than diamonds and will always be so because of the essential role it plays in our remaining alive. And pandemics like the one we just endured, which highlighted our mortality and the fragility of life, should cause us all to question what is truly valuable and what is not.

That question is particularly pertinent now that the global economy has begun to recover. The epidemiologist Michael Osterholm once said, it may matter more that we know our neighbors than that we have a lot of money, since no amount of money can spare us from contracting a deadly illness, while some amount of neighborly aid might help us survive it.[5] We cannot buy neighborliness nor do we typically measure it, but it may be among the most valuable assets we have. And as we learned during the pandemic, the same is true of other, unmeasured forms of wealth, like personal resilience and family and friend relationships.

The Re-evaluation of Value

Post-pandemic economies, in other words, often lead to a re-evaluation of what we value. After the Black Death in medieval Europe, for example, people began to reject the feudal system, which oppressed them for so long, and to value worker protections and labor-saving technology that made their lives better and that helped give rise to the modern world.[6] Subsequent pandemics had similar effects. Research shows that unlike wars, which destroy cities, buildings, and infrastructure and often lead to increased interest rates as reconstruction occurs, pandemics tend to raise real wages as the competition for labor increases, while also lowering interest rates for a generation or two as the economy takes a while to recover.[7] After pandemics, people seem to matter more than just making money.

Evidence of that exists in the history of interest rates in the U.S.[8] Although conflicts like the Civil War and World War I led to spikes in interest rates, those rates also saw long periods of decline from around 1860 to 1900 after the cholera pandemics and from 1920 to 1945 after the flu pandemic. Economists caution that other factors may mitigate against this happening to such an extent after the COVID-19 pandemic, noting that it mostly affected the elderly no longer in the labor market and that it did not lead to nearly as many deaths as, say, the 1918 flu pandemic. Still, rising wages and lower interest rates may occur, to some extent, for several years to come.

That combination of factors might typically lead to a flurry of construction as people have more disposable income to spend and access to historically low interest rates on loans. But the COVID-19 pandemic coincided with – and accelerated – the rise of e-commerce, telecommuting, distance learning, and all the other forces moving us from a dependence on face-to-face, in-person interactions and toward remote, digitally enabled ones, all of which seems likely to reduce the need for built space rather than increase it. If anything, the current post-pandemic era has exacerbated the already over-built nature of especially commercial real estate in the U.S. and to varying degrees in other countries.

Other outcomes of higher wages and lower interest rates have also become apparent. For example, it has led to a tight residential real estate market as people take advantage of the low rates to move in search of more space in which to work remotely, sometimes in distant locations, not needing to commute to work as often.[9] At the same time, higher wages and the demand for workers have also led employers to focus on people's skills more than on their degrees, giving employees opportunities of upward mobility that they have not had before.[10] All of this represents a reassessment of the assets that already exist around us, be it under-valued houses or the under-appreciated abilities of people.

During the pandemic, for example, I watched school buses across the street from my house load boxes of food and then head out on their routes to deliver free breakfasts and lunches to the children and their families dependent on those meals and without access to them after the schools had closed. Rather than pick up children in the morning, the bus drivers handed out food to them. Many children needed such meals in order to focus on their studies in school, and they needed them just as much – of maybe even more – when trying to focus on their studies at home.

The pandemic, in other words, incentivized people to improvise, to appropriate something for a new use to meet a pressing need in a rapid and low-cost way. For all of its danger, COVID-19 enlarged our capacity to care for other people and to respond creatively to a crisis. The Roman poet, Horace, once wrote that "Adversity reveals genius;

Figure 4.3 "Getting Loaded": National Guard loading food onto school buses for students.

prosperity conceals it," and the pandemic proved his point.[11] Prosperity in countries like the U.S. have created myriad systems designed for specific purposes, like school buses, which typically sit unused much of the day and over most of the summer. But that prosperity also concealed their potential for other, useful purposes, like food delivery to people who need it. Adversity can open our eyes to the abundance all around us if we open our minds to it.

After a pandemic, adversity often continues for some time, as prosperity takes a while to return. The economist Paul Romer estimated that the pandemic cost the U.S. economy 500 billion dollars per month, while the Congressional Budget Office predicted that the U.S. economy would not get back to where it was before the pandemic until 2028.[12] Romer also noted that the people "most disadvantaged will be the ones who suffer the most, and their kids." His comments brought to mind the argument of the philosopher, Matthew Stewart, that "The meritocratic class has mastered the old trick of consolidating wealth and passing privilege along at the expense of other people's children."[13] Inequality in America, Stewart notes, has not been this high since the 1920s, just prior to the last Great Depression.

The toxic wave of wealth concentration that arose in the Gilded Age and crested in the 1920s finally crashed on the shoals of depression and war … As long as inequality rules, reason will be absent from our politics; without reason, none of our other issues can be solved …. Unreasonable people also tend to be ungovernable.[14]

To deal with inequality without crashing again on the shoals of depression and war, countries like the U.S. need programs that provide employment to all who seek it. And the opportunities to do so – to tap the unleveraged wealth of people and put it to work – are abundantly available. Take the global effort by several non-profits to end deforestation and replenish the tree cover lost to large-scale agriculture and land development.[15] Such an effort makes a lot of sense not just environmentally, but also economically as large-scale reforestation could employ millions of people in relatively low-skilled and highly rewarding work in their communities. It could help create a greener and more equitable economy, one tree at a time.

An Economics of Living

That is something that America's most under-appreciated economic thinker, Henry David Thoreau, would have liked.[16] Thoreau moved to the woods by Walden Pond to "live deliberately, to front only the essential facts of life," and in some ways, the pandemic made Thoreau's of us all, whether we wanted to or not. It forced us to simplify our lives, to focus on essentials, and to give up many of the distractions of pre-pandemic existence, even as we discovered – as Thoreau did – how busy a self-quarantined life can be. Thoreau lived alone and busied himself with building his cabin, growing his food, and writing about the natural world around him and what he might learn from it. For many of us, during the pandemic, the busyness came instead from juggling work and family life, much of it happening in the same location, at the same time.

In 2020, some people followed Thoreau's example and moved to the woods – to family cabins or vacation spots – to socially distance themselves during the pandemic. Most, however, self-quarantined in place, which made the global furlough all the more challenging, as we lived in the spaces and with the possessions of our former lives, while knowing that our lives had forever changed. As Thoreau wrote, "Our life is frittered away by detail," and we were all forced, during our quarantines, to consider what details really mattered to us and which ones did not.

Thoreau, however, also went to Walden Pond to imagine a new kind of economy in which "the cost of a thing is the amount of ... life which is required to be exchanged for it, immediately or in the long run."[17] He wrote that we focus too often on "political economy" – on the cash-based economy that drives our daily lives – and that we pay little or no attention to "the economy of living," which is time based: the amount of life's experiences we have to exchange in order to purchase something.

During the pandemic, with many people having less money because of layoffs, furloughs, or pay cuts, the cash economy sometimes seemed like our enemy, a threat to our homes and families. At the same time, we had to learn to be economical in how we lived: reducing our expenditures, eliminating inessentials, and stewarding what we had. While the political economy that drives our legislatures and stock markets seemed increasingly disconnected from our lives, the economy of living, as Thoreau called it, defined the deposits and withdrawals of our day-to-day struggles.

What possibilities does Thoreau's economy of living offer us in this post-pandemic era? What if we put a price on what every moment in our life meant to us and evaluated the cost of everything in terms of the time it would require us to give up in order to have it? Would we really assess our time in terms of some wage that someone else has decided to offer us or would we, instead, demand a wage commensurate with the real value that our life has for each of us? And would we allow others to use up or abuse the time we have and to chip away at it until there is nothing left, or would we care for it, protect it, and make sure it lasted as long as possible?

The contemplation of one's own death that occurs during a pandemic can make such questions more urgent. Money comes and goes, but time is all we have and Thoreau's economy of living provides a measure of what, in the end, is the scarcest asset of all: our own individual lives. Some people may be fine with wasting that asset, frittering their lives away in details, as Thoreau said, or letting others waste our time for us in meaningless work. But with a novel virus reminding us that we are mere mortals, weighing the cost of things according to the time we have to give up in return for them may be the basis for a post-pandemic economy worthy of what we all just went through.

Ledger Economics

With an economy of living might come a new kind of currency, one that measures what we value rather than what we have or own. We have long thought of money in terms of the exchange of physical tokens – coins and bills – in order to purchase goods and services, although cash accounts for only 26% of all transactions in the U.S., with digital transactions – via debit and credit cards – accounting for more than 50% of them.[18] That trend was well under way prior to 2020, but the pandemic greatly accelerated the shift away from the physical exchange of cash toward the digital exchange of payments among ledgers. And that trend will likely continue as e-commerce continues to grow.[19]

Pandemics have long triggered important transitions in the history of money. Europeans, for example, moved from a feudal and mostly barter economy toward a market-based, cash economy in the wake of the Black Death.[20] In the U.S., the government established the national banking system and a national currency in the mid-19th century during the Civil War and just after the third cholera pandemic.[21] And in the wake of the social distancing trend after the influenza pandemic of 1918, banks established the loan policies in the 1920s and the Federal government, the Home Owners Loan Act of 1933, which transformed the ability of ordinary people to buy their own single-family houses.[22]

The COVID-19 pandemic seems to have affected a transformation of a different sort. With the decline in use of physical cash and the increasing use of digital debit and credit cards has come a recognition of the difference between money and wealth. As my colleague, Joel Hodroff, and I have argued, many of us tend to confuse money, a unit of exchange, with wealth, a measure of excess capacity.[23] We often call people with a lot of money, wealthy, and those with little money, poor. And yet most of us also recognize that there are many forms of wealth – a wealth of human knowledge, lived experiences, social connections, personal wisdom, community cohesiveness, environmental benefits – that exist in abundance all around us.

Think of the difference between money and wealth like the difference between a photograph of a place and the place itself. As in a photograph, money is a useful abstraction of reality and a valuable tool that we can exchange when we need to, but also like a photograph, money cannot capture nor substitute for all the unseen wealth of a place. A place and its people may lack money, but they may not feel poor if its people have a lot of family and friend relationships, social and cultural traditions, and personal and practical knowledge and skill. Nor does any wealth disappear during the economic downturns of pandemics. People may lose jobs or money, but they lose none of their knowledge and capability, which can continue to grow if they so choose.

The distinction between money and wealth is particularly relevant, given the inequities that the COVID-19 pandemic revealed. While many people struggled to make ends meet during the pandemic, and while communities of color suffered higher rates of infection and death than most whites, we also saw the emergence of the Black Lives Matters movement and the global protests against police brutality on the part of many people, black and white, in many communities, urban, suburban, and rural. While economic inequality increased in many countries during the pandemic, so too did collective action and the community wealth that represents.[24] Many people lost paychecks during the pandemic, but also gained purpose and pursued passions.

The pandemic also showed how much a focus on money rather than wealth has created an enormous amount of excess capacity, wasted resources, and under-used assets of all kinds. It took the closure of most stores and offices during the pandemic and the shift on the part of many people to e-commerce and telecommuting to show how much competitive duplication of goods and services existed in the old economy, how much time we wasted going from one place to another, and how much under-used space existed all around us.

That duplicate effort, wasted time, and excess space did not just represent the normal cost of doing business. They are the result of our confusing money and wealth, as we chased money while decreasing our wealth by over-producing and over-consuming what we did not need. Chasing money in this way also puts downward pressure on profits, wages, and people's purchasing power, and misses the fact that there is a tremendous amount of untapped wealth in the world, side-by-side with a lot of excess capacity and unmet need.

Once we make the distinction between money and wealth, we can see that the amount of wealth in the world greatly exceeds the amount of money in circulation. And yet we continue to compete for money without monetizing or measuring our wealth, a paradox that the pandemic revealed. The events of 2020 forced us all to depend upon those with whom we quarantined and to seek help from and to help out others, drawing upon familial and social connections as well as the aid of communities and the relief of nature in relational rather than transactional ways. The pandemic, in other words, accelerated a shift not only from a cash-based to a debit- and credit-card-based economy, but also from competition over money to an appreciation of the multiple forms of wealth in our communities and among ourselves.

That does not mean that money is unimportant. During and after the pandemic, many people lost their jobs and livelihoods, faced bankruptcy or eviction, and exhausted checking and savings accounts.[25] And in response, many governments came to people's aid with various forms of modern monetary theory.[26] That theory holds that because nations have a monopoly over the printing of their currency, governments – especially in the wake of a dramatic downturn like the one that followed the COVID-19 pandemic – need to print more money and put it into circulation in order to aid citizens and restart economies. If inflation starts to rise as a result, they can control it by taking money out of the system through taxation.

Critics of this theory point to the debt problems this can create for governments and to the out-of-control inflation that this can cause, with taxes unable to rise fast enough or far enough to rein it in.

At some level, though, modern monetary theory also tries to solve our economic problems with the same tool that caused these problems to begin with: money. We already have enormous excess capacity – empty tables at restaurants, empty seats in theaters, empty aisles in stores – and pumping more money into the economy may only increase that which we already have in excess.

Instead, we need what we might call a "modern ledger theory" of economics. A ledger-based, digital economy would help people and communities leverage their untapped wealth and let businesses absorb their excess capacity in ways that fully utilize the talents, skills, and knowledge of people as well as the assets that they already have at their disposal. Ledgers may seem boring: Who wants to talk about accounting protocols and financial transactions? And ledgers may appear an unlikely basis upon which to build a new economic model. But they highlight the difficulties that occur in an economy based upon money. As Hodroff puts it,

> ledgers do not crash or inflate in value, do not experience scarcity or hoarding, and do not lend themselves to speculation or theft. Moreover, ledgers allow us to measure not just the exchange of cash, but other currencies as well, accounting not only for money, but also for other forms of capital that we have not tallied before.[27]

Post-Pandemic Healthcare

Modern ledger theory views wealth as an abundant resource as opposed to the scarcity mentality that surrounds money: There is never enough money to do all the things that need doing, but we exist within almost inexhaustible amounts of wealth. A ledger-based system would also address some of the perverse aspects of the modern economy. The U.S. healthcare system, for example, profits off illness and receives relatively little financial gain by promoting wellness. A heart attack produces a major economic benefit for the system, while people quitting smoking lowers the gross domestic product. Meanwhile, as the pandemic showed, health disparities continue among those who lack sufficient purchasing power to lead healthier lives.

Many employers now track and reward their employees for wellness activities, programs that have proven to reduce healthcare costs, absenteeism, workers compensation, and disability claims.[28] But those savings mostly occur at the edges of the system and mainly benefit those who are already employed, while the most health disparities occur along ethnic and racial lines, regardless of employment status.[29] Nor do these wellness programs address the systemic cause of so much ill health in a country like the U.S., with a food system awash in sugar, salt, and fat, in a physical environment that leads many people to engage in a lot of sedentary behavior.[30]

Changing such a situation will require change in the underlying economics that drive it. That might have seemed impossible prior to the pandemic, but we saw how quickly and profoundly so many things changed in 2020. Why can't we also change the economy, which is just another designed system and one with perverse outcomes, as the health system shows? What if, for example, the ledgers with which we track wellness activities went one step further and paid people to lead healthier lives in a currency that could extend people's purchasing power with merchants who have excess capacity in their establishments?

That idea could extend beyond the health system and wellness programs. Most non-profits need volunteers to help do the work these organizations want to do in the world, without the funding to pay for that help. At the same time, most businesses could use more customers, who have choices as to where they spend their limited funds, and most people could use more goods and services that they do not have enough money to purchase. These three entities often occupy the same communities, with money – cash – as the only missing ingredient. Meanwhile, the enormous amount of wealth that exists in every community goes unleveraged and unmonetized.

Continuous Economic Improvement

That misalignment of money and wealth suggests the need for what Hodroff calls: continuous economic improvement. We continue to improve our personal and collective wealth: our technology and skills, our knowledge and understanding, and our personal and social networks; and we continue to have access to the abundant ecosystem services that nature provides us: solar and wind energy, forests and row crops, carbon sinks, and oxygen supply. So why do we continue to accept the boom-and-bust cycles that come from win–lose competition over money in our economy? Instead, we should expect an economy to provide an ever-improving standard of living and quality of life, with shorter working hours for everyone.

Instead of holding down production to the level of available purchasing power, continuous economic improvement would raise the purchasing power for individuals, families, and communities by capturing their ever-increasing productive capacity. It would not raise employer labor costs, increase taxes, or deepen debt, but would instead leverage untapped wealth without requiring government subsidy, based on the idea that business innovation and the profit motive are more effective than politics at solving social, economic, and environmental challenges.

An early embrace of this idea came in the summer of 1945, when the psychologist B.F. Skinner wrote a book a couple of blocks from where I write these words, published in 1948 as *Walden Two*.[31] That book is among a long line of utopian novels seeking to imagine a better world. But Skinner presented a version of a ledger-based economy in chapter 8 of the book, when he wrote about people receiving labor credits for the work they do, with more credits for doing unpleasant jobs and fewer credits for pleasant ones, with everyone working on average four hours a day. There would be no cash exchanged and no accumulation of money on the part of some at the expense of others; instead, everyone's contribution would be accounted for and credited in a ledger, with people using those credits to meet their needs.

While *Walden Two* depicted a community apart from the world around it, its labor-credit idea can exist within – and complement – mainstream economies. Rather than replace money, a labor-credit system – a ledger economy – could extend people's purchasing power to address the paradox of people having excess wealth and insufficient cash. But how might such an economy work in the real world, as opposed to a novel?

Ledger Dollars

Employers would continue to pay their employees in cash, but their workers might also receive payment in a second currency, let's call them "ledger dollars," for their wellness achievements or their volunteer activities. Alternatively, an employer with an excess amount of goods or services might offer, as an employee benefit, ledger dollars with which to buy down the business's excess capacity. People would redeem their ledger dollars, which would then be taken off the books.

Businesses could redeem the ledger dollars of non-employees in the same way. Let's say a person earned ledger dollars for doing valuable work in a community – mentoring children in the local school, helping a community group clean up a vacant lot, or taking care of elderly parents. Merchants with excess capacity – unfilled seats, unused equipment, unsold goods – could offer those at discounted prices by accepting purchases partly in cash and partly in ledger dollars, which would move their merchandise or utilize their services while also reducing the costs to their customers and benefiting the communities within which they exist. Businesses would, in other words, accept both cash and ledger dollars, monetizing the wealth of the people they serve.

Monetizing wealth through a second ledger-dollar currency would extend the capacity of the public and non-profit sectors as well. A city, for example, could credit its residents for contributions of time or insights they provide to planning processes or committee assignments. Or a non-profit could credit volunteers for their contributions to the mission of the organization or the aid they provide. These sectors would not only expand their impact, but also engage more people in their work by recognizing and compensating that effort. It would literally return us to the origin of the word "economy" with roots in the Greek words for "household management," and to the original connotation of the word, involving ideas of thrift and frugality. Instead of wasting the talent and good intentions of the people in a place, a ledger economy would fully utilize the physical, social, and natural assets of a community.

All of what we need to make such a system work already exists. There are digital ledgers aplenty on the Internet, most of them downloadable for free. Nor would such a system need cash in order to operate: It only needs agreement among the public, private, and non-profit sectors, each looking to either attract more customers, aid more citizens, or expand purchasing power. And once available, a second currency would require little coaxing of people to participate: Who would not want recognition and compensation for the voluntary, unpaid work they already do to further a mission they believe in or to take care of those for whom they feel responsible? While many people might say that they do not do this work for the money, most would welcome being rewarded in another way that would also extend their ability to purchase what they need.

All it takes is an openness to the idea that the economy is a designed system and money a human creation, both of which are not working well for most people. Faced with such a dysfunctional system, we cannot just do more of what makes the system not work in the first place: looking for more money to do what money does not do well. We have a responsibility, instead, to re-imagine how to make our economy work for more people, in more equitable ways. Indeed, equity lies at the heart of why we need to redesign the economy.

As the pandemic helped reveal, too many women, youth, and people of color face too many disparities as a result of the current, cash economy, as ever fewer people amass ever greater fortunes at the expense of everyone else. Governments and foundations have historically sought to address those inequities through fiscal means – taxation and subsidies – or philanthropic ones – gifts and grants. But those monetary methods miss the mark by assuming that we can eliminate inequities with more cash, perpetuating the idea that people without money need charity.

Instead, the less cash a community has, the more it has had to rely on non-monetary forms of wealth, be they familial, social, cultural, or spiritual, just waiting to be tapped. Wealth, in this sense, is relational rather than transactional, as the exchange of money often becomes. Ledger dollars would honor that relation-based wealth and enable people to exchange it for what they need as much as they do with cash. A dual-currency system would also allow those with more cash to help those with less in a very simple and direct way.

Let's say that a restaurant needs a certain amount of cash to cover its costs and to make a reasonable profit, but it also needs more customers in order to do so. The restaurant could establish a system where those customers with greater financial means could pay a larger percentage of their bill in cash, which would allow those with less money to pay more of their bill in ledger dollars. Some might argue that everyone would try to pay as little in cash as they can, whatever their financial wherewithal, but pay-what-you-can restaurants have shown that the model works, that most people willingly pay more if it allows those with less to benefit from that largess.[32]

That also suggests an economy that operates at a different scale than the traditional one, based on national currencies that are, by nature, scarce. Ledger dollars would work less like cash, and more like loyalty rewards programs, which are a kind of business-issued currency backed by its products and services. But unlike loyalty rewards, which encourage more consumption and consumer spending, ledger dollars would be entries in a ledger, matching the production of goods and services with business, employee, customer, family, and community wants and needs.

National currencies are a blunt instrument to address economic inequity, as traditional money chases the highest rate of return, while interest and dividends bring ever more money to those who already have plenty. Ledger dollars, instead, would encourage a more level economic playing field through smarter production and distribution of real wealth. Finally, national currencies encourage consumerism to promote traditional economic growth, which has negative social and environmental consequences. In contrast, ledger dollars would promote a higher quality of life by engaging everyone in greater economic efficiency and voluntary sharing of currently idle resources, advancing better living, with less consumption. In a post-pandemic world, weary of the physical idleness and social isolation that COVID-19 caused, a new, more equitable and less wasteful economy might be just the cure we need.

Figure 4.4 "Loyalty cards" show the potential of rewarding community work.

Notes

1 Phillip Connor, "More than Nine-in-Ten People Worldwide Live in Countries with Restrictions amid COVID-19," Pew Research Center, April 1, 2020. www.pewresearch.org/fact-tank/2020/04/01/more-than-nine-in-ten-people-worldwide-live-in-countries-with-travel-restrictions-amid-covid-19/
2 Jane Jacobs, *Cities and the Wealth of Nations, Principles of Economic Life* (New York: Vintage Books, 1984).
3 Eve Turow-Paul, "How Restaurants Are Innovating During the COVID-19 Pandemic," *Forbes*, March 23, 2020. www.forbes.com/sites/eveturowpaul/2020/03/22/how-restaurants-innovating-during-the-covid-19-pandemic/?sh=6de9da4a2c2b
4 Adam Smith, *An Inquiry into the Nature and Causes of the Wealth of Nations* (Amsterdam: MetaLibri, 2007) 26. www.ibiblio.org/ml/libri/s/SmithA_Wealth-Nations_p.pdf
5 "Michael Osterholm," Center for Infectious Disease Research and Policy. www.cidrap.umn.edu/about-us/cidrap-staff/michael-t-osterholm-phd-mph

6 Adam McBride, "The Black Death Led to the Demise of Feudalism. Could This Pandemic Have a Similar Effect?" *Salon*, April 26, 2020. www.salon.com/2020/04/26/the-black-death-led-to-the-demise-of-feudalism-could-this-pandemic-have-a-similar-effect/

7 Oscar Jorda, Sanjay J. Singh, Alan M. Taylor, "The Long Economic Hangover of Pandemics," *Finance and Development, International Monetary Fund*, 57(2), June 2020. www.imf.org/external/pubs/ft/fandd/2020/06/long-term-economic-impact-of-pandemics-jorda.htm

8 Dorothy Neufeld, "Visualizing the 200-year History of U.S. Interest Rates," *Markets in a Minute*, October 1, 2020. https://advisor.visualcapitalist.com/us-interest-rates/

9 Ben Winck, "5 Trends Fueling on the Hottest Housing Markets in U.S. History," *Business Insider*, May 26, 2021. www.businessinsider.com/trends-fueling-hot-housing-market-structural-shifts-bubble-inflation-shortages-2021-5

10 Steve Lohr, "Up to 30 Million in U.S. Have the Skills to Earn 70% More, Researchers Say," *New York Times*, December 3, 2020. www.nytimes.com/2020/12/03/technology/work-skills-upward-mobility.html

11 Eduard Fraenkel, *Horace* (Oxford: Oxford University Press, 1957).

12 Paul Romer, "To Save American Jobs, We Must Bring Virus to 'Screeching Halt'" *PBS News Hour*, July 2, 2020. www.pbs.org/newshour/show/economist-paul-romer-to-save-american-jobs-we-must-bring-virus-to-screeching-halt

13 Matthew Stewart, "The 9.9 Percent Is the New American Aristocracy," *Atlantic*, June 2018. www.theatlantic.com/magazine/archive/2018/06/the-birth-of-a-new-american-aristocracy/559130/

14 Ibid.

15 "Impact Report, 2016–2020," *Trillion Trees*. https://trilliontrees.org/sites/default/files/2021–04/Trillion_Trees_Impact_Report_2016–2020b.pdf

16 Henry David Thoreau, *Walden or Life in the Woods* (Boston: Ticknor & Fields, 1854), chapter 1.

17 Ibid.

18 Raynil Kumar, Shaun O'Brien, "2019 Findings from the Diary of Consumer Payment Choice," Federal Reserve Bank of San Francisco, June 2019. www.frbsf.org/cash/publications/fed-notes/2019/june/2019-findings-from-the-diary-of-consumer-payment-choice/

19 Carolyn Said, "The Pandemic Pushed Us Toward a Cashless Economy. It Could Be the New Normal," *San Francisco Chronicle*, July 1, 2021. www.sfchronicle.com/bayarea/article/The-pandemic-pushed-us-toward-a-cashless-economy-16288252.php

20 Remi Jedwab, Noel D. Johnson, Mark Koyama, "The Economic Impact of the Black Death," Institute for International Economic Policy, The George Washington University, August 2020. www2.gwu.edu/~iiep/assets/docs/papers/2020WP/JedwabIIEP2020-14.pdf

21 "Lincoln and the Founding of the National Banking System," Office of the Comptroller of the Currency. www.occ.gov/about/who-we-are/history/founding-occ-national-bank-system/lincoln-and-the-founding-of-the-national-banking-system.html

22 "The Home Owners Loan Act, 1933," *Living New Deal*. https://livingnewdeal.org/glossary/home-owners-loan-act-1933/

23 Thomas Fisher, Joel Hodroff, "From Money-Centered to People- and Planet-Centered Ledger Economics: Leveraging the Hidden Wealth of Underutilized Productive Capacity," *Investment Strategies in Emerging New Trends in Finance* (London: IntechOpen, February 1, 2021). www.intechopen.com/chapters/75019

24 Zia Qureshi, "Tackling the Inequality Pandemic: Is There a Cure?" Brookings, November 17, 2020. www.brookings.edu/research/tackling-the-inequality-pandemic-is-there-a-cure/
25 Felix Richter, "COVID-19 Caused a Huge Amount of Lost Working Hours," World Economic Forum, February 4, 2021. www.weforum.org/agenda/2021/02/covid-employment-global-job-loss/
26 Steven Globerman, "A Primer on Modern Monetary Theory," Fraser Institute, May 18, 2021. www.fraserinstitute.org/studies/primer-on-modern-monetary-theory
27 Fisher, Hodroff, "From Money-Centered to People- and Planet-Centered Ledger Economics."
28 "Control Health Care Costs," Centers for Disease Control and Prevention. www.cdc.gov/workplacehealthpromotion/model/control-costs/index.html
29 "The State of Health Disparities in the United States," National Academy of Sciences, 2017. www.ncbi.nlm.nih.gov/books/NBK425844/
30 Michael Moss, *Salt Sugar Fat, How the Food Giants Hooked Us* (New York: Random House, 2014).
31 B.F. Skinner, *Walden Two* (Indianapolis: Hackett, 1948).
32 Grant Trahant, "The Pay What You Can Café Model May Revolutionize the Restaurant Industry in America," *Causeartist*. https://causeartist.com/pay-what-you-can-cafe-place-at-the-table-future-restaurant-industry/

5
EMPLOYMENT

The pandemic created a paradox when it came to employment.[1] On one hand, many people wanted and needed to get back to work after the pandemic waned, whether in person, remotely, or some combination of both. On the other hand, the context around work had changed for many people, presenting barriers to their returning to jobs. Many childcare centers went out of business during the pandemic and so many parents had no one to watch their children, which prevented many women, especially, from re-entering the job market. At the same time, the pandemic gave many people an opportunity to reassess what they wanted to do with their lives and careers, perhaps because we were all reminded of the brevity of life in the midst of so many COVID-19 deaths. As a result, many employers had difficulty finding enough workers and many workers took their time seeking the right employer or the right job.

Adding to those short-term challenges in labor markets was a longer-term trend toward the automation of much of the work that people have done in the past. The pandemic did not cause that trend, which had been under way for many years, but as in so many other areas of human activity, the pandemic accelerated the transformation in work in ways that will likely have long-term impacts and profound effects.[2] This automation of work aligns with the rebalancing

DOI: 10.4324/9781003198192-6

Figure 5.1 "Might." The essential work of women became evident during the pandemic.

of the digital and physical worlds triggered by the pandemic. Just as many workers now have a choice whether to do something remotely or in person, so too do many employers have a choice in whether a task needs to be done by an employee or if it might be better done digitally, through computer automation, artificial intelligence, and robotics, in partnership with or in place of a person.

One reason for the accelerated shift to automation stems from the struggles companies had during the pandemic to maintain their supply chains with workers required to quarantine. "The pandemic," wrote business journalist Anjani Trivedi, "made 'humans the risk to continued operations' in supply chains," according to analysts from

Sanford C. Bernstein and Company, as people fell ill and forced the closure of key points along those chains. Unlike people, robots don't get sick and computers don't quarantine.[3]

Trivedi goes on to note that "60% of production work globally is in areas that can easily be automated. In China, almost 40% of jobs are machine-replaceable," and that while many companies have reduced the number of employees, "only 15% are planning to cut investments for automation, artificial intelligence, and industrial internet-of-things."[4] The pandemic, in other words, propelled a move toward automating a substantial percentage of the work that people have traditionally done, especially in activities that computers can be programmed to do more quickly, efficiently, safely, and accurately.

Automation-Resistant Work

What, then, is the future of work in the post-pandemic world? In a ground-breaking paper, Oxford University researchers Carl Benedikt Frey and Michael A. Osborne looked at 702 different occupations in terms of their susceptibility to replacement or at least major disruption by computers.[5] They concluded that 47% of those occupations – a percentage similar to those that Trivedi mentions – are at high risk of being automated, mostly jobs that involve work that is dangerous for people to do or repetitive and predictable enough that a machine can be programmed to do it more efficiently and correctly than what even the most skilled person can do. As a McKinsey study shows, relatively few jobs – less than 5% – lend themselves to complete automation, but at least half of all jobs will see at least 40% of their activities automated, indicating the extent to which most work in the post-pandemic era will continue to evolve in terms of what gets done digitally or physically, and how much of that work needs a human being's involvement at all.[6]

Automation, though, does not affect all jobs equally. Research by the economists Andy Feng and Georg Graetz has suggested that many high-skilled and also many low-skilled jobs resist automation, for different reasons.[7] Jobs like hotel maid, restaurant waiter, or residential roofer require relatively little training and few specialized skills, but the variety of the tasks these workers need to do and the necessity of their responding to a wide range of different situations make their jobs difficult to automate. Meanwhile, highly skilled jobs – attorneys, physicians, psychologists, architects – involve lengthy training, specialized knowledge, and deep expertise, as well as an ability to respond to a lot of different situations, making those jobs also hard to automate. Even so, many professional fields have seen computers take on the more repetitive or predictable aspects of their jobs in order to do their work more quickly and efficiently.

The jobs most threatened by automation are "middle-skill workers (who) compete directly with machines."[8] This has led to a hollowing out of labor markets, with more wage inequality between high-skilled workers and everyone else, and with a growing percentage of jobs occurring at the low-skilled end of the market. In many ways, workers benefit from the automation of boring, repetitive, or dangerous work, which few people want to do or are good at doing, but that trend also clearly threatens a lot of jobs. Which raises a key question in the post-pandemic era: What are the jobs left for people to do, after we have automated the rest, and how should we prepare people for a very different work world than what existed in the past?

Frey and Osborne identify three categories of work that are "bottlenecks" to computerization, resisting automation:

- work that involves perception and manipulation, manual dexterity and working in cramped spaces or awkward positions,
- work that demands creative intelligence, original problem-solving and artistic production,
- work that requires social intelligence, negotiation, persuasion and caring for others.

They conclude that "generalist occupations requiring knowledge of human heuristics, and specialist occupations involving the development of novel ideas and artifacts, are the least susceptible to computerisation."[9] They further note that "as technology races ahead, low-skill workers will reallocate to tasks that are non-susceptible to computerization – i.e., tasks requiring creative and social intelligence.

For workers to win the race, however, they will have to acquire crea-tive and social skills."[10]

The pandemic made that race even more competitive. As much of the world quarantined, we all became aware of how dependent we were on essential workers, both low-skilled workers such as dis-tribution and delivery personnel as well as high-skilled workers like epidemiologists and ICU doctors and nurses. The pandemic also highlighted the importance of "bottleneck" workers able to work re-motely and to keep the wheels of the economy turning as they taught classes, managed projects, made decisions, and provided services of all sorts remotely, via digital platforms and the Internet. Meanwhile, those hardest hit by the pandemic's economic downturn – restaurant and hospitality staff, travel and transportation personnel – found the race to acquire new skills or move into new lines of work especially urgent.

Frey and Osborne's list of the jobs most vulnerable to automation, however, goes well beyond the travel and hospitality industries. Their list also includes jobs that software has already begun to replace, from tax preparation to telemarketing to insurance underwriting to medical diagnosis.[11] Of note in this list is how much automation now threatens white-collar jobs as much as blue-collar ones. The automation of in-dustrial production has gone on for a long time and many factory jobs have already disappeared, but that process was also well under way before the pandemic in administrative and professional offices, where secretarial and clerk jobs had largely vanished and where repetitive tasks had begun to succumb to algorithms. The pandemic forced us to ask not only who needs to return to the office, but also who is needed to do the work of the office, as many employees discovered how much can be done remotely and independently of support staff.

The jobs at the other end of Frey and Osborne's list – the jobs most resistant to automation – tell another story. They generally fall into seven categories, in what I will call the seven "Cs": Computer, Caring, Communication, Community, Construction, Craft, and Creative jobs. Technology may eventually replace some of these jobs; their resistance to automation does not make them permanently im-mune to computerization. But these seven types of jobs will probably remain areas where human capabilities will surpass those of computers, however sophisticated the latter become. Those seven "Cs" also indicate where we might want to focus our educational and workforce-training efforts in the post-pandemic era.

Computer Jobs

It may seem obvious that one category of jobs resistant to computerization are those that involve the programming and applications of computers, but that isn't necessarily so. Frey and Osborne place jobs like computer-systems analysts and engineers high on their list, although computers can already program themselves to some extent and artificial intelligence and machine learning promise to make it possible for non-coders to define what they want a computer to do and it will create what is needed itself.[12] Computer jobs may change accordingly. While the growth of the digital economy makes computer-related work highly likely to continue, those jobs may entail less coding and more of the kind of work that the other six "C"s involve, such as the development of computer interfaces that enhance communication, facilitate creativity, and promote a sense of craft.

That, in turn, suggests that post-pandemic education may demand not just some knowledge of coding, but also a much greater understanding of what computers can – and cannot – do. Some might think that, with so many people having worked remotely during the pandemic, most work can now be done digitally and remotely, without the need for a physical workplace or even for co-workers. While that might be true for a limited number of jobs, shifting the balance between the digital and the physical worlds so far toward the former makes the same mistake as those who might want to dismiss the experience gained during the pandemic and to go back to in-person work as if nothing happened. The most important jobs related to computers may ultimately involve knowing what work will benefit from computerization and what will not and may never.

Caring Jobs

Many of the job categories most resistant to automation involve caring for ourselves and other people. The work highest on Frey and

Figure 5.2 "Operation COVID-19," temporary emergency beds for COVID patients.

Osborne's list includes recreational and occupational therapists, social workers, surgeons, and nutritionists: all jobs that entail attending to the physical or mental health of people. As the global population grows and as aging societies become more common with improvements to public health, these caring jobs will almost certainly remain in high demand, requiring human interactions that computers or robots may never fully replace.

Nor does the demand only involve caring for people. Farmers and foresters, microbiologists and hydrologists are all jobs high on the automation-resistant list, aimed at understanding and caring for the natural world and for other species. Farming and forestry, in particular, remain among of the oldest jobs in human societies, which raises another aspect of the future of work: It may look a lot like the work that happened prior to the industrial revolution of the 18th and 19th centuries, when machines first began to take over from human labor. Many people had caring jobs in that pre-industrial era – caring for families and farms, communities and congregations, livestock and landscapes – and we might see a widespread return to that in the post-pandemic economy.

In terms of preparing for that future, educators may need to see caring in new ways. Right now, we face an enormous pay divide between low-skilled caring jobs, like home health aides, and high-skilled ones, like surgeons, even though we need far more of the former than the latter as both an aging population and non-invasive medical procedures continue to grow. For example, the median pay of surgeons, at least in the U.S., is over 7.5 times that of home health aides.[13] Reducing that gap and paying lower-skilled but essential workers more will need to happen if we hope to attract people to the caregiving that more and more of our population needs. At the same time, we need to educate more of our population to care about caring, to see this as one of the greatest areas of demand for work in the future and to frame it not just as a technical skill, but also as a deeply interpersonal one. We need not only more caregivers, but also a more caring society grounded in the Old English root word of care – carian – which means to feel concern for or interest in another. What better outcome of an education is there than that?

Communication Jobs

Caring for others demands communication skills, an area of work that also does not lend itself to automation. Most people prefer to talk to another person rather than a machine, and however much we might try to replicate human speech or to simulate human empathy in a computer, it misses the point that communication remains a relational activity among people rather than a transactional one with machines. The Frey and Osborne list has a wide range of automation-resistant jobs involving communication, including teachers, administrators, managers, curators, clergy, and counselors – whose work involves judgment, self-reflection, and the ability to respond appropriately and constructively to unanticipated situations.

Communicators have benefited enormously from computers in order to gain access to information and to connect to people remotely, as so many did during the pandemic. However, the primary work of communication – listening and observing, knowing what to say when and when not to say anything – demands a mix of intuition and experience among people and requires strong interpersonal, intrapersonal, and verbal intelligence that, again, are difficult, if not impossible, to replicate with a computer.[14]

This, too, suggests a very different kind of education that most students currently receive. As some have observed, we have an educational system based on an older, industrial model in which students move through a curriculum like products on an assembly line, with teachers performing similar tasks over and over again like assembly line workers.[15] This worked well when the economy needed educators to produce future industrial-era employees who could follow instructions and perform repetitive tasks without complaint. In a post-pandemic, post-industrial world, though, when students have access to far more information via their digital devices than a teacher could possibly give them and when the economy needs people able to generate paradigm-shifting ideas and produce innovative goods and services, our industrial-era educational system interferes with students' ability to thrive once they graduate.

What employers say about what they want in their employees – an ability to communicate and collaborate, a capacity for continuous learning and critical thinking, and a willingness to be adaptable, curious, and flexible – all have little to do with the content-related coursework offered in most schools.[16] These so-called "soft skills" may be hard to teach or measure, but their demand among employers shows how much work has changed in our time. What matters is not what people know but how they apply and communicate what they know and how they go about getting the information and ideas they need. Even if students do not pursue specific communications jobs, the ability to communicate has become an essential part of every job as well as a way that workers can ensure that they do not get replaced by a computer.

Community Jobs

Another reason for teaching communication skills comes from the recognition that many jobs in the future will involve engaging and working with communities of people and coordinating their efforts, be they in a local geographical area or among people physically dispersed. Examples of such community jobs in Frey and Osborne's list

Figure 5.3 "Memorial for U.S. COVID-19 Victims," Washington D.C.

include: emergency management directors, firefighters, instructional coordinators, and human resource managers. While diverse in what they involve, these jobs all entail serving community members, whatever the reasons for it. Whether facing a crisis or having a concern, most people will seek the advice or aid of other human beings, however much technology – like fire trucks or emergency vehicles – assist in that response.

There is also overlap in these job categories. The clergy, for example, engage in community work as much as they do communication work, serving the spiritual needs of people whether through word or action. Other jobs, like coaching, also rank high on the automation-resistant list in part because it involves caring for athletes' health and wellbeing, communicating performance improvements, and building a sense of community among team members. The more "Cs" a job covers, the more likely it will resist automation for a very long time. The range of what constitutes a community also varies widely, from a clergy member's congregation to a coach's sports team to a fundraising manager's donor pool to a chief executive's customers, stockholders, and employees. The clearer a community's identity, the more likely that members of that community will rely on the person or people leading them.

Here, too, education needs to change. The focus on individual grades and test-taking during a student's education works against the importance of community skills in the post-pandemic economy. Employers look for people who work well in teams and have the ability to lead teams, which rarely get explicitly conveyed in schools. As a result, the educational system often depends upon a student's inherent interpersonal intelligence, which downplays the fact that community building skills can – and should – be taught. Some curricula have increasingly had students work and learn in teams, but all the way through the modern educational system, up through college and graduate school to hiring and promotion, the focus remains on grading or assessing individual achievement, even though almost nothing happens in the modern world that involves just one person.

Construction Jobs

The above jobs all involve the interactions of people with each other, be it in a community setting or in one-on-one caring or communication activities. But another group of jobs resistant to automation involve the interactions of people with things, with the creating, crafting, and constructing of the physical world at various scales, for a variety of purposes.

Among these, construction jobs may seem the most unexpected. Construction differs from other automation-resistant fields in that it often gets classified as "blue-collar" work, which has suffered greatly from the automation of many factory jobs. The construction trades have also seen many tasks replaced or at least aided by technology, from robotic brick laying to 3D-printed building components to virtual reality construction training.[17] Nevertheless, construction jobs resist replacement by computers not only because of the relative fragmentation of the construction industry, with a lot of small businesses rather than a few multinational players able to automate, but also because of the physically awkward positions and manually dexterous tasks that most builders face. While robots are good at repetitive construction tasks, work that demands a high degree of bodily balance and kinesthetic skill may never get replicated robotically.

Unless, of course, we start constructing buildings in new ways. A 3D-printed house in the Netherlands shows how far the automation of construction has come.[18] While the 3D printer needed an operator to maintain or change the nozzle heads, the shell of the house went up in six days without the help of any contractors. Interior equipment and finishing still required human handiwork, so even the most automated forms of construction need hand labor, but the printing of buildings marks a milestone in the industry, where physical dexterity and manual skill no longer shield contractors from the machine.

The nature of construction jobs will likely change as a result. For some, it might mean becoming the operators of machines that do much of the construction, following a path that many former assembly line workers have taken in the past. For others, the 3D printing of new structures may lead many contractors to do what cannot be easily printed, like interior renovation and repair of existing buildings as well as the interior fit out of new ones. But as Marshall McLuhan wrote, "Each new technology .... turns its predecessor into an art form," and that may very well happen with construction jobs: technologies like 3D printing may turn the handiwork of contractors into an art form – or at least an artistic form of craft.[19]

Craft Jobs

The pandemic made craft work even more in demand than it was prior to that event, and even more unlikely to succumb to automation. Many people in quarantine during the pandemic took up a craft to pass the time or possibly to move their career in a new direction.[20] Meanwhile, the sale of hand-craft goods saw a 200% increase over pre-pandemic numbers.[21] And craft work will likely continue to grow in popularity and demand in the post-pandemic era since it, too, is hard to computerize. Craft work like fabric and apparel patternmakers, makeup artists, and music directors, are all high on Frey and Osborne's list of automation-resistant jobs.

In some sense, resistance to automation lies in the very word "craft," which means the exercise of human skill. While even now we have machines that can make things look handcrafted, the lack of a person's involvement means, by definition, that it does not involve craft. Indeed, a lot of the value of craft work lies in the fact that what it produces is not machine made or mass produced; a big part of its value lies in the fact that a person rather than an algorithm imagined and made it.[22]

Crafts, however, have also embraced technology when it facilitates what a person can do by hand. The brewing of craft beer, for example, involves the use of sophisticated technology, as do myriad other crafts, from glass blowing to jewelry making to prosthetic fabrication. The distinction lies in how we use technology: as a tool or implement that enables or enhances a person's craft or as a machine that replaces it. This suggests that, in the post-pandemic era of work, we might keep in mind Marx's caution that

> As soon as man, instead of working with an implement ... becomes merely the motive power of a ... machine, it is a mere accident that [it requires] human muscle; and it may equally well take the form of wind, water, or steam.[23]

Here, too, the educational system needs adjustment. Although craft schools have emerged over the years to teach people handiwork, the education system still has a mind–body split, with most coursework focused on mental skills and with the teaching of crafts in decline in schools in many countries.[24] The irony here is that we can more easily automate many of the mental skills taught in schools, like memorizing information or solving equations, than we can craft skills, like carpentry, sewing, or cooking, which schools increasingly do not offer. If we want an educational system that prepares students for the economy in which they can thrive, as opposed to being in jobs threatened by automation, we should rethink the role of the crafts in schools for children of all ages.

Creative Jobs

A similar irony occurs with the final "C": Creative jobs. Many schools have cut arts classes, mainly for budgetary reasons, that prepare students for jobs like choreographer, set designer, artist, or archi-tect.[25] Those fields rank high on Frey and Osborne's list because of the unpredictability and paradigm-shifting aspects of creative work, which makes it almost impossible for a computer to replicate. Just as craft work requires the hand and mind of a person in order to call it a craft, so too does creative work demand not just the human hand and mind, but also the human ability to imagine what does not yet exist and to play with what we know in order to create something new and unexpected from it.

In many ways, all of the "C" jobs relate to each other in various ways. Creative jobs, for example, all involve a level of craft, most of them involve the construction or fabrication of something, many of them depend upon computers to varying degrees, and some of them also involve caring, communication, and community work. Likewise, all of the other "C" jobs demand creativity in the sense of understanding a

Figure 5.4　"The COVID Chronicles." Creativity and humor can reframe a pandemic.

situation, imagining possible responses or outcomes, and judging how best to achieve that goal. If social commentators like Richard Florida are correct, they are all part of the rise of a creative class and a creative economy, which the educational system has yet to embrace fully.[26]

That is evident in recent research which has shown that, while IQ scores have risen since 1990, creative thinking scores among students have dropped dramatically, the result of educational systems that often prioritize students being correct in their answers rather than creative in their responses.[27] The World Economic Forum has taken on this problem, arguing that schools across all ages should teach creativity along with a host of other "soft" skills, like complex problem solving and critical thinking, which many schools often address only in passing as they continue to focus on content, which students can acquire in other ways.[28]

Post-Pandemic, Pre-Industrial Work

The growing importance of the seven "Cs" suggests that we may be coming out the back end of the industrial revolution, which arose over two centuries ago. While that revolution began with the mechanization of onerous physical labor, it has ended with the replacement of predictable and easily quantifiable intellectual work, resulting in a post-industrial economy much like the pre-industrial one, based on computing, caring, communicating, coordinating, constructing, crafting, and creating. The pandemic provided a pause in that evolution and an opportunity for each of us to ask: What do I want to do, what do I like to do, and what can I do better than a machine?

The pandemic also showed how we need to do better when it comes to caring, communicating, and coordinating. Failure to do so, especially on the part of several national governments, helped COVID-19's spread and hampered our ability to fight it. A lack of creativity on the part of many leaders also resulted in a failure to anticipate the pandemic before it occurred. In the U.S., for example, the slow reaction to the COVID-19 pandemic will cost the U.S. economy almost $8 trillion over the next decade, largely a result of the government's inability to imagine such a black-swan event and to anticipate its effects beforehand.[29]

If we invested a substantial portion of what we now spend on reacting to problems, instead, on their prevention, we would not only save a lot of money, but also see how essential the seven "C" skills are to our future. It would mean having people in positions of authority who are creative and caring enough to imagine possible futures before we suffer negative consequences, attuned to community needs and to communicating with a diversity of people, and able to compute, craft, and construct more effective responses to a crisis. These are no longer "soft" skills; they are survival skills.

Many people, of course, profit greatly from the reactive economy, from what Naomi Klein has called "disaster capitalism."[30] Doctors make a lot of money healing people who are ill, and private prisons make handsome profits incarcerating people for committing crimes. And there are undoubtedly many in positions of power who would resist changing this expensive, reactive mode of problem-solving because of the money they receive from well-healed donors whose profits depend upon maintaining the status quo.

But the pandemics that came to a head in 2020 – not just of COVID-19, but also of institutionalize racism and climate change – may have marked a turning point in this equation. As communities took over some of the public-safety work of the police during the pandemic, it showed how many jobs can be created in places where people currently live and care about. While often comprised entirely of unpaid volunteers, those efforts showed the effectiveness of community policing and the potential of that creative, caring work becoming regularized and paid.

The same is true with healthcare. The more that we focus on public health and getting ahead of both physical and mental health issues among the members of a community, the more "C" jobs like caring and communicating become important, and the more likely we can address the causes of illness and injury before they become acute. Not everything a community needs, of course, exists within its borders and so there will remain a demand for specialized expertise, whether it be police responding to an active shooter or emergency medical personnel responding to an injured person. But spending much more on an ounce of prevention will more than pay for itself in what we save from the extraordinary amount we spend on a pound of cure.

Notes

1 Nick Bunker, "Indeed Job Search Survey June 2021: COVID Concerns and Financial Cushions Make Job Search Less Urgent," Indeed Hiring Lab, June 29, 2021. www.hiringlab.org/2021/06/29/indeed-job-seeker-survey-june-2021/
2 "The Future of Work After COVID-19," McKinsey Global Institute, February 18, 2021. www.mckinsey.com/featured-insights/future-of-work/the-future-of-work-after-covid-19
3 Anjani Trivedi, "The Robots-Are-Taking-Our-Jobs Threat Gets Real," *Bloomberg*, May 20, 2020. www.bloomberg.com/opinion/articles/2020–05–20/robot-makers-like-japan-s-fanuc-will-get-a-post-coronavirus-boom
4 Ibid.
5 Carl Benedikt Frey, Michael A. Osborne, "The Future of Employment: How Susceptible are Jobs to Computerisation?" Oxford Martin School, September 17, 2013. www.oxfordmartin.ox.ac.uk/downloads/academic/The_Future_of_Employment.pdf
6 "A Future That Works: Automation, Employments, and Productivity," McKinsey Global Institute, January 2017. www.mckinsey.com/~/media/mckinsey/featured%20insights/digital%20disruption/harnessing%20automation%20for%20a%20future%20that%20works/a-future-that-works-executive-summary-mgi-january-2017.ashx
7 Andy Feng, Georg Graetz, "Rise of the Machines: The Effects of Labor-Saving Innovations on Jobs and Wages," London School of Economics, April 17, 2013. https://conference.iza.org/conference_files/ESSLE2013/graetz_g9265.pdf
8 Feng, Graetz, "Rise of the Machines," 2.
9 Frey, Osborne, "The Future of Employment," 40.
10 Ibid., 45.
11 Ibid., 57–72.
12 Dom Galeon, "Computers Are Learning How to Code Themselves, Human Coders Beware," *Futurism*, February 24, 2017. https://futurism.com/4-our-computers-are-learning-how-to-code-themselves
13 "Healthcare Occupations," U.S. Bureau of Labor Statistics. https://www.bls.gov/ooh/healthcare/home.htm
14 Howard Gardner, *Multiple Intelligences, New Horizons* (New York: Basic Books, 2006) 3–24.
15 Allison Schrager, "The Modern Education System Was Designed to Teach Future Factory Workers to Be 'Punctual, Docile, and Sober'," *Quartz*, June 29, 2018. https://qz.com/1314814/universal-education-was-first-promoted-by-industrialists-who-wanted-docile-factory-workers/
16 Forbes Human Resources Council, "The Top 10 Skills Recruiters Are Looking for in 2021," *Forbes*, November 9, 2020. www.forbes.com/sites/forbeshuman-resourcescouncil/2020/11/09/the-top-10-skills-recruiters-are-looking-for-in-2021/?sh=720d99be7e38
17 Michael Chui, Jan Mischke, "The Impact and Opportunities of Automation in Construction," McKinsey, December 1, 2019. www.mckinsey.com/business-functions/operations/our-insights/the-impact-and-opportunities-of-automation-in-construction
18 Daniel Boffey, "Dutch Couple Become Europe's First Inhabitants of a 3D-Printed House," *Guardian*, April 30, 2021. www.theguardian.com/technology/2021/apr/30/dutch-couple-move-into-europe-first-fully-3d-printed-house-eindhoven
19 Andrew McLuhan, "Understanding Understanding Media," *Medium*, February 1, 2019. https://medium.com/@andrewmcluhan/understanding-understanding-media-8cdd40d46908

20 Maile McCann, "Retailers are Betting on the Crafting Boom to Continue into 2021," *Modern Retail*, May 10, 2021. www.modernretail.co/retailers/retailers-are-betting-on-the-crafting-boom-to-continue-into-2021/
21 Miles Brignall, "Hobbycraft Reports 200% Boom in Online Sales since Start of Pandemic," *Guardian*, August 2, 2020. www.theguardian.com/business/2020/aug/03/hobbycraft-reports-boom-in-online-sales-since-start-of-pandemic-crafts-coronavirus
22 Teleri Lloyd-Jones, "What Is the Role and Value of Crafts Today?" British Museum, August 17, 2011. https://blog.britishmuseum.org/what-is-the-role-and-value-of-crafts-today/
23 Karl Marx, *Capital* (Chicago: University of Chicago Press, 1952), vol. 50, 183.
24 Rachel Williams, "End of the Creation Story? Design and Crafts Decline in Schools," *Guardian*, February 11, 2014. www.theguardian.com/artanddesign/2014/feb/11/design-craft-subjects-decline-in-schools
25 "Why We Should Care about The Decline of Arts Education in Our Public Schools," *Teach & Kids Learn*, February 13, 2020. www.teachnkidslearn.com/why-we-should-care-about-the-decline-of-arts-education-in-our-public-schools/
26 Richard Florida, *The Rise of the Creative Class* (New York: Basic Books, 2002).
27 Kyung Hee Kim, "The Creativity Crisis: The Decrease in Creative Thinking Scores on the Torrance Tests of Creative Thinking," *Creativity Research Journal*, 23(4), 2011, 285–295. www.nesacenter.org/uploaded/conferences/SEC/2013/handouts/Kim_Creativity-Crisis_CRJ2011.pdf
28 Rebecca Weicht, "Education Systems Can Stifle Creative Thought. Here's How to Do Things Differently," World Economic Forum, April 4, 2018. www.weforum.org/agenda/2018/04/education-systems-can-stifle-creative-thought-here-s-how-to-do-things-differently/
29 Jeff Cox, "The Coronavirus Will Cost the Economy Nearly $8 Trillion, Congressional Budget Office Says," CNBC, June 1, 2020. www.cnbc.com/2020/06/01/the-coronavirus-will-cost-the-economy-nearly-8-trillion-congressional-budget-office-says.html
30 Naomi Klein, *The Shock Doctrine: The Rise of Disaster Capitalism* (New York: Metropolitan Books, 2007).

PART 2
POST-PANDEMIC FUNCTIONS AND FACILITIES

6
WORKING

As pandemics accelerate us into the future, they also disrupt a lot of what we once took for granted. One such assumption, disrupted by the COVID-19 pandemic, held that living and working need to occur in different places, in houses and apartments on one hand and in offices and factories, stores and restaurants, schools and colleges on the other. But as many people who quarantined at home during the pandemic know, the spatial separation of living and working largely collapsed for all but the most essential workers. Prior to the pandemic, 20% of the U.S. workforce worked from home, but that grew to 71% once the coronavirus came. And there is no going back to the old normal: 54% of the respondents to one survey reported that they wanted to continue to work from home, at least part of the week, once the pandemic ended.[1] That has major implications for the built environment, for both homes and workplaces.

The world's largest architecture firm, Gensler, tracks global workplace trends, with indicators of how the home and office may change going forward.[2] In a survey of over 2,300 U.S. workers, the Gensler data showed that 29% want to return full-time to an office because they see it as a place where they are more productive, with better access to technology and needed workspace, while 71% of those who want to telecommute at least part of every week see the home as the

DOI: 10.4324/9781003198192-8

place where they can be more productive and more comfortable, while saving money, reducing commuting time, and avoiding distractions.

This, of course, depends upon one's situation at home. A survey by one consulting firm highlighted both the good and bad aspects of working at home.[3] Among those who like telecommuting, 67% say that they feel more connected to their family, while among those who do not, 74% say that it blurs work and family life and 58% say that they feel disconnected from co-workers. There are also generational and personal differences among those responding. Older workers, as well as childless couples, report wanting to work from home more than younger, single workers or those who have children. Whether because of cramped quarters or a desire to remain connected to colleagues socially, this latter group expresses a stronger desire to go to an office most or all of the time, although younger workers also seem more comfortable than older colleagues using technology and working remotely when they do.

Regardless of personal or generational differences, though, these data suggest that telecommuting from a home is here to stay, and that distraction-free workspace, high-bandwidth Internet access, and perhaps even some meeting and maker space may become the norm in single-family houses and multi-unit residential buildings. Residential districts will likely change too: many home-based workers may need facilities like co-working spaces, affordable childcare, and technology hubs within a reasonable distance to their work space. Even as the home and office have merged for many employees, there remains a natural human desire to get out of the house every so often, if only to walk to a corner coffee shop or travel a short distance to a co-working space.

The Home-like Office

These surveys of employers and employees also indicate a need for offices to become more home-like. The trend toward more home-like offices existed prior to the COVID-19 pandemic, in part to appeal to younger employees who often prefer more casual apparel and informal settings when they work.[4] But in the post-pandemic era, with so many people able to telecommute, the office will have to compete

Figure 6.1 The post-pandemic office will need to be more home-like to attract workers back.

in order to remain relevant, including the provision of some of the features that many people like about working from home: comfortable furniture, softer lighting, and access to food and beverages. The Gensler research captures those changing attitudes. While 69% of those surveyed worked in open offices prior to the pandemic and only 21% had enclosed offices, now almost half – 47% – would prefer a more private work environment, like many people have at home.[5]

One company, Prime Therapeutics, exemplifies this trend. It shifted the traditional strategy of an office headquarters with branch offices to what it calls its hub-and-home arrangement, in which its 2,200 employees rotate through the main office during agreed-upon days of the week, with everyone working half the week or more at home.[6] At the same time, the company remodeled its main office, getting rid of the old, open-office cubicles and replacing them with easily moved furniture, acoustical partitions that can shift to accommodate different-size meetings, collaborative work spaces, brighter lighting, and storage lockers for rotating rounds of employees. At the same time, the company gave up a large office in another location, consolidating into the headquarters building.

Anecdotally, smaller professional firms are doing the same. One large law firm, now on four floors of a downtown office building in my city, plans to consolidate onto one floor, with office hoteling, in which lawyers share their offices with each other, with a schedule to show what offices are free at any given moment. Design firms have moved in a similar although somewhat different direction. Several firms that I have visited both before and after the pandemic have their staff working at long tables or clustered workstations in large, open spaces, with only a few enclosed meeting rooms for acoustical privacy. In many cases, those workstations are plug-and-play, available to anyone in the office to use and rarely assigned to a particular employee. Freedom and flexibility abound.

Tech companies have long been a model for this. Well before the pandemic, many of these companies had more informal office interiors, with stress-reducing games, comfortable seating, and good food as a way to attract and keep employees, but also as a way to one-up what staff might find at home.[7] The 2020 pandemic simply turned that evolution of the office into a necessity for employers who want to appeal not only to younger staff, but also to their more experienced workers, who now have a choice of whether to go to the office or not.

The idea of the home-like office has advantages beyond that of employee morale. One company in a nearby suburb began offering flexible work schedules several years ago, and converted its headquarters' interiors to appeal to employees able to work from home by getting rid of its office cubicles and assigned desks and instead, installing a wide range of work areas, from an in-office coffee house to living room and family room setups. At the same time, the company vacated six of the seven office buildings it had formerly occupied, even as employees reported higher levels of satisfaction and a greater degree of productivity.

My own center offers another example of this. We dramatically downsized our square footage in the middle of the pandemic, with office space half as large as what we previously had in a nearby building. While my staff and I worried, before COVID-19 arrived, about how everyone in my center would fit in the smaller space, after we worked successfully and productively for well over a year at home because of the pandemic, we wondered just the opposite: How much space do we really need and will we even need offices, as traditionally defined, now that the pandemic had ended? Any employer who has not asked that question in the past, will undoubtedly need to do so in the future.

The technology needed to make these changes in the workplace has long existed. In the early 1980s, I purchased my first laptop computer and after seeing how productive I became, I convinced my boss to buy laptops for all of the staff. At the same time, we reduced to a couple of days a week the mandatory time for everyone to be in the office when we held all of our joint meetings. What had been a company suffering from a revolving door of staff members became just the opposite after we moved to flex time and laptops. We had a staff that remained with us much longer, reported being much happier and, from the evidence of their work, showed how much more productive they became. I learned from this that, when given the freedom to determine where and how they do their work, employees will do far more than maybe even they thought possible, perhaps in part to maintain their freedom.

While we have had the means to achieve more flexible work since the 1980s, it has taken much longer to change our minds about work. After the pandemic closed the campus in which I work, I taught my students and met with my colleagues remotely, with most of us sitting in our living, dining, or bedrooms and working at desks or tables that were probably never intended to serve as our offices. I have no doubt that the home office will evolve in ways that none of us can predict, just as the office has continually changed since it first appeared.

The Home–Office Community

The downsizing of office space and allowing staff to work at home has affected not just homes and office buildings, but main streets and the traditional office cores of cities as well. In my city, a major corporate employer announced that it would no longer need almost 1 million square feet in one of the downtown's office buildings, representing two-thirds of the space in the 51-story tower.[8] Some 3,500 of its 8,500 employees in the downtown would work primarily from home from now on, using the two million square feet of space in one of the company's other towers as a home base when staff needed to come in for meetings or other joint activities. The company emphasized that it was not laying off any of the 3,500 people; indeed its business did well during the pandemic. But what it called its "Flex for a Day" program would become standard practice, a practice that will no doubt become common among many employers as they compete for talented staff.

The remote-work statistics show why.[9] In one study, 80% of the employers surveyed said that they plan to allow employees to work from home at least part-time from now on and in another study, 78% of employers see remote working as a permanent part of their operations. For companies, this translates not only into less real estate to own or lease, but also into more talent attraction and employee retention. Yet another survey showed that 27% of workers would accept 10% to 20% less in pay if they could work from home, while 81% said they would feel more loyalty to a company that allowed them to work remotely. And other research indicated that remote work, overall, makes people 33% to 40% more productive than those working full-time in the office, where businesses lose an estimated $600 billion annually in workplace distractions.

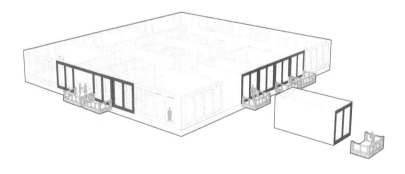

Figure 6.2 Office floors will likely accommodate a wider range of uses to fill empty space.

The rise of telecommuting as a dominant practice presents social and environmental opportunities as well as personal ones. It raises the question, for example, of how much office space, parking space, and commuter lanes we will need going forward. Over 11 billion square feet of office space currently exists in the U.S.[10] If the post-pandemic demand for that space decreases by, say, half of what it was prior to COVID-19, that would free up 5.5 billion square feet of office space for other uses, such as affordable housing, business incubators, or even indoor agriculture. We may well see a lot of mixed-use office buildings in the future, where people might not just work, but also live and produce goods as well, in a kind of vertical city in which the elevators and stairs substitute for the roads and highways that now connect these activities in the city.

That would have substantial environmental benefits. Electrically powered, widely shared, and highly efficient elevators in buildings require much less energy – and produce much less pollution – than the fossil-fueled, personal vehicles so many people need in order to live. The mixed-use of office buildings would also save a lot of embodied energy. With buildings equaling anywhere from 24 metric tons of embodied CO_2 for wood construction to 45 metric tons of embodied CO_2 for concrete construction per 1,000 square feet, repurposing that 5.5 billion square feet of space rather than tearing it down would sequester between 132 and 247 million metric tons of CO_2.[11] That equals the amount of CO_2 sequestered by between 2.1 and 4 billion trees growing over a 10-year period.[12]

Reducing the total square footage needed for offices can have both good and bad effects. It clearly benefits employers, who have lower costs and increased flexibility, and it also benefits employees, who now have options for where they work and with whom. But it remains to be seen what impact this will have on office cultures and interpersonal relations among coworkers and how that plays out on organizations' bottom lines. There is no question, though, that in the post-pandemic era, employees and their employers will need to re-imagine work and how it gets done.

Some businesses may also need to re-imagine the services they offer. Coffee shops, for example, had become popular meeting- and workspaces prior to the pandemic, but in the wake of COVID-19 that trend will almost certainly increase. As more people work from home and may look for places near their homes to gather with colleagues or to simply to get out of the house, coffee shops will become de facto workplaces or what some have called "neighborhood clubhouses," in which you pay a monthly fee and the food and beverages are free.[13] Other business hybrids will also likely become more common: health clinics in grocery stores, childcare centers in exercise facilities, and maker spaces in libraries. Combining such activities not only provides convenient outlets for home workers, but also suggests how the physical world will successfully compete with the digital one in the post-pandemic era, by mixing services in ways not possible online.

The Re-Imagined Home

These trends will also shape the nature of built space going forward. The shift to home-based work recalls a time when agriculture constituted a majority of the economy and when most work occurred in the homestead and farmstead. The post-pandemic economy, in other words, may represent a high-tech version of a pre-industrial economy,

Figure 6.3 Office buildings might also have housing units as well as production facilities.

moving us rapidly into the future while also taking us back to a past most have forgotten. Prior to the industrial revolution, offices mainly existed in people's houses, as people worked in rooms that doubled as living, dining, or sleeping spaces at night or weekends.

The growing interest in convertible furniture, allowing a space to serve as an office by day and a bedroom by night, shows how much that pre-industrial idea has returned. In one survey 91% of architects and interior designers reported that their clients wanted more flexible spaces that could multi-task along with the needs of their occupants.[14] The adaptability of residential interiors and furnishing also lets owners do much more in less space, saving money in rent or mortgage payments in the process. For many people, of course, the home–office never disappeared, remaining a feature of farmsteads and small, home-based businesses to this day. The COVID-19 pandemic simply expanded that phenomenon to a wider swath of the workforce, among people who long considered themselves office workers rather than home workers.

History offers some clues of what working at home can involve. I once served as the historical architect for Connecticut's State Historic Preservation Office, and in that capacity, I visited myriad old houses and saw how dramatically their uses had changed over time. In most of the houses that predated the Civil War, a relatively small number of rooms accommodated the diverse activities that still occur in most households today: the preparing and consuming of food, receiving visitors and conversing with family members, the washing of clothes and bathing of children, and of course the sleeping and grooming of the house's inhabitants.

But many rooms in those early houses also doubled as work spaces. In an 1848 house we owned near the center of New Haven, Connecticut, the main-floor rooms as well as the upstairs sun porch had hooks that held the drying lines of a laundry that its former owners ran out of the house. The business specialized in the washing, drying, and pressing of linens and the main living rooms also served as the place where the household made its living, among the drying lines, hanging fabrics, and ironing boards that once filled those spaces. In another, much older house I worked on in Guilford, Connecticut, the 1639

Henry Whitfield House, the structure served not only as a residence for Reverend Whitfield and his family, but also as a church, a meeting house, and even a fort, with thick stone walls to protect people in case of attack. The home, in this case, was literally a castle.

These homes were places of production as well as consumption, although those two areas of activity began to diverge in the 19th century. In another house we owned in Connecticut, dating from the late 19th century, it had former servants quarters in a series of rooms on the third floor, with a back stair that gave access to the kitchen at the back of the house and the laundry in the basement. That house embodied the division of labor between household owners and servants, although that split between production and consumption did not last long. After the Great Depression and World War II, servants became rare in all but the wealthiest households, as domestic work fell increasingly on the occupants and owners. And residential design shifted accordingly. Gone were servants' quarters and in their place came open spaces, island kitchens, easily cleaned surfaces, and a legion of labor-saving devices and appliances.

Those older houses, however, foretold what may increasingly happen in post-pandemic households. At least in the U.S., roughly 50% of all small businesses, even before the COVID-19 pandemic, existed in people's homes.[15] That percentage jumped to 60% if the business had no employees and almost 70% if in a start-up phase. The pandemic broadened that to include not just small business owners, but also employees of large organizations and professional service firms as well as independent consultants, all of whom can now work wherever there exists a good Internet connection. We have entered a high-tech version of an earlier era when there were fewer employer/employee relationships and more autonomous workers and self-sufficient families who made their living wherever they were.

Sharing Space

The post-pandemic era will also likely change our expectations of housing. On one hand, the rising cost of living, especially in economically thriving cities, has led to a downsizing in the amount of people's living space, with micro-unit and studio apartments increasingly common in such places.[16] On the other hand, many realtors have seen a growing demand for larger houses that can accommodate working as well as living spaces. That shows the greater choice – and different choices – of people when it comes to housing, leading to seemingly contradictory data that are really part of the same, larger trend.

We can see those same apparent contradictions play out in short-term rental housing, like Airbnb. On one hand, such short-term rentals endured a dramatic drop in the demand during the pandemic as tourism largely ended because of travel restrictions.[17] Community opposition to short-term rentals because of the impact it can have on the cost and availability of housing also continued during the pandemic.[18] On the other hand, short-term rentals and the sharing economy more generally align with the new post-pandemic reality, as people seek flexibility in a rapidly changing economy as they access and pay for what they need rather than own it. In some situations, it can cost less to live out of Airbnbs as longer-term rentals than to rent a traditional apartment.[19]

However the sharing economy evolves, the pandemic highlighted the flaw in how we have typically conceived of the built environment, especially over the last century or more: as a set of structures designed to accommodate particular purposes at particular points in time. The labels we give these structures – office, house, store, garage – further limit our ability to think about them in new ways, as if their original purpose prevents them from becoming something else – something more – than what we imagined them to be.

The post-pandemic period will see the functions of some building types change rather dramatically, given the declining demand for some functions and the growing demand for others. The dynamics of space will also likely change. The sharing economy has provided digital platforms that enable us to trust and transact with strangers over who uses a space, how and when, which can change from day to day, even hour to hour. Finally, the demand for space will also undoubtedly change. It will take years to understand the lasting impact of the pandemic, but there seems to be no question that we need less traditional office space and far more affordable housing, far fewer parking ramps and far more recreation space. That shifting demand may change over time and from place-to-place, depending upon the marketplace and the stock of structures that already exist, but it will likely happen everywhere to some extent.

Those changes suggest that we value built space according to how well it functions, not just for what it was initially intended to do, but also for the range of other activities it can accommodate. In that light, we might stop calling buildings by their original function – office, home, store, etc. – and instead call them by their potential futures – work-homes, maker schools, distribution stores. And as workplaces become more home-like and homes more work-like, we will also likely see other, similar transformations: former office buildings that become co-housing, former malls that become business incubators, former parking ramps that become urban farms, and so on.

The Barriers to Innovation

That trend may encounter resistance in some quarters. Building codes, for example, have different loading criteria and egress requirements for different functions, making it difficult to adopt some buildings for other purposes. But those code requirements also reflect older ideas of what these different buildings involve, and as we move to a more digitally driven economy, the idea of an office containing a lot of

Figure 6.4 Empty parking structures might become extremely affordable housing.

paper-based files or homes containing a lot of heavy bookcases may need revisiting.

The same may apply to egress requirements. Will entertainment in the future always involve large crowds or might some such venues in the future be more virtual and digital, more a matter of personal rather than collective experiences? We might not know the answers to such questions for a while, but we should remain open to rethinking what constitutes life safety as people increasingly live more lightly on the land and in buildings.

Another barrier to the reuse of buildings involves their dimensions and services. Most office buildings, for example, have floor widths wider than the typical depth of an apartment, making it hard to insert housing into an empty office floor. Such buildings also typically have their restrooms located in or near the elevator and stair core, making the insertion of kitchens and bathrooms in housing units especially challenging.[20] Such obstacles can be overcome with design strategies like raised floors or hung ceilings that can accommodate additional plumbing and service runs.

The adaptive reuse of buildings also suggests new opportunities for how we live and work. An office floor, for example, can lend itself to the shared kitchens and bathrooms found in co-housing and dormitory-like accommodations, not only reducing the cost of housing, but also increasing the sense of shared responsibility and community among those who live there. While many people experienced living in dormitories with shared bathrooms and communal dining when in college, we often view that type of housing as fit only for teenagers or young adults. In fact, in an era in which the cost of housing and the isolation of especially older people have become major issues, such co-housing may turn out to be a solution for people of all ages.[21]

Overcoming the Housing Monopoly

A further barrier has to do with monopolies that limit our ability to think about housing in new ways. James Schmitz of the Federal Reserve Bank has written about the harm that monopolies in the home-building industry inflict, especially upon low- and middle-income Americans.[22] Schmitz argues that we tend to think of monopolies in terms of large corporations driving out their competitors, but he observes that the failure of home builders to adopt technologies that would increase their productivity and reduce the cost of housing and to expand factory-built modular housing also constitutes a form of monopoly.

Continuing to hand-build houses in an era of mass-production and mass-customization seems outdated, but it remains largely the case, at least in the U.S. Such practices also make it more difficult to construct housing in unconventional settings, where homebuilding, for example, intersects with office interiors, and it makes Schmitz's argument all the more pressing. Monopolistic power, though, can also fall of its own accord as disruptions make that power irrelevant. Homebuilders depend upon us continuing to build homes as we have known them, but the rebalancing of the digital and physical in the post-pandemic era suggests that home-seeking, home-sharing, and home-adapting may become more common, where people re-imagine the space already built rather than wait for someone to build new space.

Zoning has also played a monopolistic role in housing. Highly prescriptive policies related to the size, setbacks, and single-family occupancy of housing has effectively excluded lower-income residents and people of color. Yet, here too, a changing economy has begun to make many zoning policies self-defeating for the communities that often enforce them. Many prescriptive land-use policies – like single-family residential districts that are now full of workplaces and small businesses – may become barriers to a municipality's economic competitiveness in the post-pandemic world. The monopoly of power on the part of existing residents in a community needs to empower – and learn from – those who might want to reside in that community in new and more flexible ways, if that community hopes to thrive in the wake of COVID-19.

The pandemic came upon us unexpectedly, and we need to prepare ourselves for all of its unexpected long-term effects by letting go of the unquestioned assumptions, rigid categorization, and outdated thinking of the sort that helped spread the pandemic in the first place. Flexibility, adaptability, equity, and sustainability: Those qualities served us well in fighting COVID-19 and they will serve us as well as we adjust to post-pandemic realities, not just in our homes and offices, but in myriad other building types as well.

Notes

1 Kim Parker, Juliana Menasce Horowitz, Rachel Minkin, "How the Coronavirus Outbreak Has – and Hasn't – Changed the Way Americans Work," Pew Research Center, December 9, 2020. www.pewresearch.org/social-trends/2020/12/09/how-the-coronavirus-outbreak-has-and-hasnt-changed-the-way-americans-work/

2 Gensler Research Institute, "U.S. Workplace Survey 2020, Summer/Fall," Gensler. www.gensler.com/gri/us-workplace-survey-2020-summer-fall

3 "The Future of Work, How the Pandemic Has Altered Expectations of Remote Work," *Morning Consult*. https://go.morningconsult.com/rs/850-TAA-511/images/Remote%20Work%20Report%20-%20Morning%20Consult%20-%20Final.pdf

4 Steve Hemsley, "How Businesses Are Looking to Replicate Home-Like Atmosphere in Future Office Layouts," *Digiday*, February 4, 2021. https://digiday.com/media/businesses-replicate-home-like-atmosphere-in-future-office-layouts/

5 Gensler, "U.S. Workplace Survey."

6 Jackie Crosby, "For Business Leaders, Office Space Issues Loom as Return-to-Work Time Gets Closer," *Star Tribune*, March 15, 2021. www.startribune.com/for-business-leaders-office-space-issues-loom-as-return-to-work-time-gets-closer/600034348/

7 Daisuke Wakabayashi, "Google's Plan for the Future of Work: Privacy Robots and Balloon Walls," *New York Times*, July 29, 2021. www.nytimes.com/2021/04/30/technology/google-back-to-office-workers.html

8 Burl Gilyard, "Target Ending Operations at City Center," *Twin Cities Business*, March 11, 2021. https://tcbmag.com/target-ending-operations-at-city-center/

9 Emily Courtney, "Remote Work Statistics: Navigating the New Normal," *FlexJobs*, www.flexjobs.com/blog/post/remote-work-statistics/

10 Kimberly Amadeo, "Commercial Real Estate and the Economy," *The Balance*, July 5, 2021. www.thebalance.com/what-is-commercial-real-estate-3305914

11 "Construction Carbon Calculator," Buildcarbonneutral.org. www.buildcarbonneutral.org/

12 "Greenhouse Gas Equivalencies Calculator," *United States Environmental Protection Agency*, March 2021. www.epa.gov/energy/greenhouse-gas-equivalencies-calculator

13 Connor Sen, "Workplace of Future Is More Clubhouse than Cubicle," *Bloomberg*, July 29, 2021. www.bloomberg.com/opinion/articles/2021–07–29/workplace-of-future-is-more-clubhouse-than-cubicle

14 Haley Chouinard, "How the Pandemic Has Put Flexible Furniture on the Map," *Business of Home*, December 11, 2020. https://businessofhome.com/articles/how-the-pandemic-has-put-flexible-furniture-on-the-map.html

15 Nina Godlewski, "9 Home-Based Business Statistics You Need to Know (2021)," Fundera, December 16, 2020. www.fundera.com/resources/home-based-business-statistics

16 Anna Dorothea Ker, "Can Co-Living Survive in a Socially Distanced Future?" Dwell, November 18, 2020. www.dwell.com/article/future-of-coliving-covid-19-pandemic-1937333b

17 Lea Lane, "How Bad Are Covid-19 Pandemic Effects On Airbnb Guests, Hosts?" *Forbes*, June 9, 2020. www.forbes.com/sites/lealane/2020/06/09/how-bad-are-covid-19-pandemic-effects-on-airbnb-guests-hosts/?sh=3cef8c274328

18 Mokter Hossain, "The Effect of the COVID-19 on Sharing Economy Activities," *Journal of Cleaner Production*, 280(1), 20 January 2021, 124782. www.sciencedirect.com/science/article/pii/S0959652620348265

19 Benji Stawski, "The Case for Living out of Airbnbs Full Time," The Points Guy, November 4, 2020. https://thepointsguy.com/guide/airbnb-monthly-stays/

20 Henry Grabar, "Could Your Empty Office Turn into Apartments?" *Slate*, April 20, 2020. https://slate.com/business/2021/04/residential-conversions-housing-offices-manhattan-boston.html

21 Nancy P. Kropf, Sherry Cummings, "From Cohabitation to Cohousing: Older Baby Boomers Create Living Arrangements to Suit New Needs," *The Conversation*, September 5, 2019. https://theconversation.com/from-cohabitation-to-cohousing-older-baby-boomers-create-living-arrangements-to-suit-new-needs-121592

22 James A Schmitz, Jr. "Solving the Housing Crisis will Require Fighting Monopolies in Construction," Federal Reserve Bank of Minneapolis, Working Paper, No. 773.

7
Shopping

Pandemics often lead to a transformation in how we access goods. After the 19th-century cholera pandemic, with the emergence of large cities, department stores and downtown specialty shops emerged to meet the needs of growing urban populations, offering access to a wide range of goods that customers once had to travel far and wide to find or, more often, to do without.[1] Along with the rise of large cities in the 19th century, post-cholera era, retailing became more spatially concentrated and retailers, more expansive and more specialized in what they offered.

The 20th-century flu pandemic had the opposite effect spatially, at least in the U.S. Along with the rise of single-family housing and private automobiles, which allowed people to socially distance, retailing became equally spread out, with suburban shopping centers and malls emerging far from the former concentration of retailing in downtowns.[2] With this came a geographical spread in the ownership of stores, with regional and national chains pushing out a lot of locally owned businesses, as well as in the origin of goods, as products from around the world became more readily available. This, of course, also forced people to drive much greater distances in search of the stores with the goods they wanted, and so the inconvenience

DOI: 10.4324/9781003198192-9

Figure 7.1 Auto-oriented retailing consumed people's time and valuable land for parking.

of traffic congestion worked against the supposed convenience of suburban shopping centers.

(E)Commerce

The seemingly contradictory trend of greater concentration and then greater dispersal of retailing after the previous pandemics became even more extreme during and after the COVID-19 pandemic. Online retailers like Amazon became an ever-larger presence during the pandemic as they offered people quarantined at home access to almost any type of product made almost anywhere in the world, with a distribution network that could readily deliver it to our doors.[3] Part of Amazon's success lay in the fact that it offered the benefits of both of the trends that emerged after the previous pandemics: extreme concentration, as one company became the source of almost every type of product, and extreme dispersal, as it made those products available to almost everyone.

Not that in-person shopping ended with the COVID-19 pandemic; people continued to go to stores for various reasons, including simply wanting to get out of the house or to have the experience of being in a physical space with other people. But the pandemic accelerated e-commerce especially among those who rarely if ever engaged in it before COVID-19 arrived. During the pandemic, the online purchase of many goods soared: medical supplies went up 500%, baby products up 400%, groceries up 150%.[4]

Meanwhile, many bricks-and-mortar stores struggled. One study indicated that the retail sector may lose 11% to 17% of stores by 2025, with 100,000 to 150,000 stores closing in the next five years in the U.S., as the pandemic accelerated a trend already underway.[5] The pandemic also revealed inefficiencies as well as inequities in the retail world.[6] The U.S., for example, has 8.5 billion square feet of retail space or roughly 24.5 square feet per person, which is five times that of Europe. Were retail space in the U.S. to equal the average amount in Europe, the U.S. would need only 1.5 billion square feet or 7 billion square feet less than what it has now – creating an abundance of excess space that could be used for other priorities, be it incubator facilities for people wanting to start businesses or housing for the over 553,000 people experiencing homelessness, on average, in the US.[7]

While the amount of retail space in the U.S. may not decline to that extent, at least anytime soon, it seems inevitable that the online world will permanently alter the way in which many people access goods and services. One study showed, for example, that 81% of those who shopped online for groceries during the pandemic intended to do so afterward, indicating that the recent pandemic, like those before it, bring long-term transformations in how we conduct our daily lives.[8]

Access Inequities

Pandemics also alter who benefits – and who does not – from the transformations they trigger. The COVID-19 pandemic revealed the inequities that have long existed in underserved urban and rural communities, which had been retail and food deserts for quite some time. While online shopping and the home delivery of goods did increase the access to goods among some in underserved communities, it also highlighted the inequality that comes from a lack of digital devices or Internet access. For those without those assets, e-commerce can isolate them even more, as both bricks-and-mortar stores and online shopping remain unavailable to them. Previous pandemics brought investments in infrastructure, and the COVID-19 pandemic showed the need for high-bandwidth access to the Internet for everyone.

That will require major government investment at a time when the public sector has also been facing economic challenges. Most municipalities depend on taxes from commercial property for a sizable part of their budgets and large numbers of employees receive their primary income from serving customers and stocking goods in stores. Because of that impact, many cities subsidize commercial property, whether directly through tax incentives or indirectly by upgrading infrastructure to serve retail developments, and that clearly cannot continue.[9] Instead, cities will need to adopt more flexible zoning policies, to relax single-use designations and expensive parking requirements, and to welcome mixed-use developments that can accommodate whatever combination of activities the market needs, in whatever ways people need to live and work in response to an increasingly digital economy.

Hybrid Retailing

The architecture and design community will play an important role in this. At the neighborhood scale, mixed-use walkable communities had already begun to take a market share, prior to 2020, from car-oriented commercial development.[10] The pandemic propelled that trend, not only because of the flexibility that a combination of uses allows, but also because such communities typically have higher densities and more people able to secure goods faster by walking rather than waiting for on-demand delivery.

Meanwhile, at the scale of individual stores, retailers will need to offer what people cannot get online: human interaction, serendipitous encounters, and immersive experiences. Some experts point to models like IKEA and Barnes & Noble as pre-pandemic models of experiential retail, offering gathering spaces, food and beverages, and even children's play areas that encourage people to make the store itself a destination.[11] Physical stores also began to mimic digital sites. For example, Amazon re-imagined bookstores as the physical parallel of its online experience, focusing not on stocking a large number of books, but instead displaying related books based on a reader's interest, as they do on their website, which leads to more in-store purchases as well as more online ones.[12]

Such hybrid retailing continued to grow in the post-pandemic era. Giant retailers, like Target, did well during the pandemic because it turned its bricks-and-mortar stores partly into distribution centers, with same-day pickup locations "within 10 miles of most Americans," as Target's CEO Brian Cornell observed.[13] At the Minnesota Design Center, we have explored what hybrid retailing might look like in the post-pandemic future, with stores that offer not just in-store shopping, but also drive-through pickup and delivery options, along with mobile, pop-up stores and the equivalent of food trucks for other types of goods that bring experiences as well as products to where people live. We have also examined how empty retail space and their adjoining parking lots might offer other services ranging from maker spaces, co-working destinations, recreational activities, child-care facilities, hydroponic agriculture, to a wide range of other uses.

In-person shopping in bricks-and-mortar stores will not disappear. Although e-commerce in the U.S. grew by 44% during the pandemic, such commerce still accounted for only 21.3% of all retail sales.[14] But the greater choice we have in the post-pandemic world in terms of how we access goods and services forced every retailer to have a digital

Figure 7.2 Stores and even alleys might become places for the pick-up and delivery of goods.

presence and to reassess what it will take to attract shoppers back to their stores. Retail has long been at the forefront of the experience economy, and many retailers will figure this out, but the pandemic certainly raised the temperature on this issue – as pandemics do.[15]

The Pall over Malls

A renewed focus on the experience of in-person shopping is particularly important to imperiled parts of retailing, including shopping malls and department stores. In 2020, five times the number of major department stores in the U.S. declared bankruptcy than the year before, with foot traffic half of what it was the prior year.[16] And a quarter of the shopping malls, about 1,000 facilities, face closure over the next five years in the U.S.[17] The two forms of retailing that the last two global pandemics triggered – department stores and shopping centers – are among the most threatened by the most recent pandemic.

That does not mean that these facilities will simply disappear. One major mall owner has explored converting empty department stores in its malls into Amazon fulfillment centers, joining the competition rather than fighting it.[18] And one study of repurposed shopping malls showed that almost 70% had been converted to uses ranging from housing, offices, and warehouses to churches, medical clinics, and entertainment centers.[19] A contagion can, at least indirectly, prompt creativity.

The malls themselves have a history that might be creatively revisited. The first enclosed, climate-controlled shopping mall, Southdale, stands less than 10 miles from where I live, and it has gone through many of the same disruptions and transformations that other malls have faced. It lost department stores and converted one into a fitness center and considered converting another into a regional library. Meanwhile, apartment buildings and stand-alone stores arose in the mall's parking lots as the number of parking spaces needed has dwindled.

That mix of uses at Southdale recalls the original vision of its owners, the Dayton family, and their architect, Victor Gruen.[20] Born in Vienna, Gruen came to the U.S. in 1938 and soon began designing stores in New York City. After the war, he designed open-air shopping malls in Michigan and Indiana prior to the design of Southdale, completed in 1956. Gruen originally conceived of Southdale having housing, schools, medical facilities, and community assets such as parks and play areas for children in or immediately adjacent to the mall, but with the exception of a nearby medical facility, the facility initially consisted of just stores, restaurants, and two department stores at either end of an indoor concourse, surrounded by parking lots.

That model of anchor department stores at the ends of an enclosed mall became the formula for the thousands of shopping malls that followed Southdale, so much so that Gruen became known as the "Father of the Shopping Mall," a label he later came to detest.[21] He designed the central concourse at Southdale to be the width of the commercial streets in his native Vienna, and he wanted shopping malls to bring an urban, pedestrian-oriented experience to the suburb, which they did to some extent on the interior, however much their vast parking lots destroyed any sense of urbanity outside.

That history, though, has become newly relevant in the post-pandemic era. Even as e-commerce continues to grow as a competitor to shopping malls and department stores, the latter offer some things the digital environment cannot, and therein lies the future of those facilities. As Gruen knew, most people like pedestrian-oriented places and in the original Southdale, he – and his clients, the forward-thinking Dayton family of retailers – had an outdoor café (complete with umbrellas over the tables), a pool stocked with fish, an aviary, and a children's play space in the mall itself, replicating the experience that people might have in a dense, diverse city, where one could people-watch and encounter others different from oneself.

The digital environment cannot match such experiences. If anything, it divides us into groups of people like ourselves and distances us from those who differ from us. Malls and department stores may compete most successfully, not by trying to offer more goods than e-commerce, but instead by providing experiences other than what the digital environment can. What if malls and department stores, for example, became participatory runways, where customers could try on and try out products they are interested in buying. Southdale, in its early years, hosted fashion shows in its main concourse, and ideas like that might once again draw people out of their homes and away from their digital devices to malls.

Malls and retail stores might also provide essential services rather than try to compete with the online world for the provision of goods. The original Southdale had a grocery store, a hardware store, and a tailor shop, all of them locally owned and offering services that their suburban customers might need as part of their daily lives. And more tellingly for a pandemic-plagued future, the mall also had a major medical center built immediately adjacent to it, providing healthcare for what Gruen envisioned as a sizable urban center in the suburbs. While the medical center remains at Southdale, most of the local businesses long ago disappeared as regional and national chains took over most of the retail space, as happened in myriad shopping malls around the U.S. and other parts of the world.

Southdale finally began to attain the mixed-use diversity that Gruen envisioned for it, when multi-family housing began to rise in its parking lots. The more that malls become diverse districts, with people living and working as well as shopping there, the more they will thrive. And the more they attend to the daily needs of people – as the successor to the Dayton's department stores, Target, has done in the U.S. – the more they will prevail in the competition with the digital environment for people's time and attention.

A Physically Disjointed Future

Still, the physical world can only go so far in that competition. Dennis Snower, a Senior Fellow at the Brookings Institution, has argued that the economic crash triggered by the COVID-19 pandemic was different from previous pandemic-related downturns.[22] Now, he writes, "all the economic activities that involve physical interactions – for both production and consumption – are imploding, whereas the physically disjointed activities are exploding," leading to what he calls "the Great Economic Mismatch." He urges governments not to subsidize everyone equally, since not everyone needs it, but to spend substantial amounts of money on "hiring and retraining subsidies, relocation benefits, and investment credits for transforming production processes from physically integrated to physically disjointed activities."[23]

What does a "physically disjointed" economy look like? Snower uses Amazon as an example, replacing what once happened in the interactions of people in physical space with a "disjointed" process of people shopping online for the home delivery of goods. But there are other ways to think about the "physically disjointed" consumption of goods, suggesting a new way forward for bricks-and-mortar retailing. Amazon and other online retailers have developed a highly efficient form of production and consumption by eliminating most physical interactions, but they have also altered the experience not just of consuming goods, but of producing them as well.

Prior to the 19th century, many goods were made locally, often by people that customers knew – if not made at home by the customers themselves. The retailing that followed in the wakes of the previous pandemics – the department stores that arose in large, industrial cities, and the shopping centers that spread through post-war suburbs – represented a separation of production and consumption, with the former happening often in far-away places, physically separated from the consumers purchasing a product. The boost to e-commerce in the wake of the recent pandemic, has simply perpetuated that separation between making and buying a product. It has given us efficiency at the expense of experience.

Vulnerable Supply Chains

But the pandemic showed that with efficiency also comes vulnerability. As people cleared the shelves of essential goods in grocery stores and big-box retailers when COVID-19 arrived, it revealed how dependent many people had become to global supply chains that help keep those shelves stocked. That global supply chain provides plentiful goods at low prices in locations convenient to most people, but it relies upon one assumption: that all the parts of the supply chain function as intended. Any break in the chain can lead to the shortages – and the panic buying and product hoarding – that we saw during the pandemic.

Retailers are as vulnerable to this as their customers. When the COVID-19 pandemic took off, factories closed, ships stayed in port, and the flow of goods among countries greatly slowed, causing shortages around the world. And even products made within the country in which they will sell relied upon a functioning transportation system, which in turn depended upon restaurants and filling stations, many of which closed as the virus spread. As the supply chain started to crumble, e-commerce as well as bricks-and-mortar retail suffered equally.

Being part of a global economy, in other words, means that what goes on around the world affects us in some way, wherever we might be. An epidemic almost anywhere can mean empty shelves almost everywhere else, depending upon the type of product and its distribution network. The COVID-19 pandemic not only revealed the vulnerability of the global supply chain, but the need to develop a far more resilient system that can withstand unpredictable stoppages and closures and maintain the flow of especially essential goods.[24]

The pandemic also exposed the delusion that one country can insulate itself from the woes of another simply by closing its borders or stopping international travel. Borders cannot stop the spread of the virus, nor can they prevent shortages of goods. And we can guard against both by attending to the health of our global supply chain and workforce, whose well-being is directly connected to our own, not just medically, but also economically.

Restoring Restaurants

Supply chain breakdowns affect perishable goods like food even more than non-perishable ones, and restaurants felt the stoppage in the flow of goods as much or more than many other industries. By the end of July 2020, restaurants, globally, had seen a 54.4% decline in the number of customers that they had seated.[25] While many restaurants responded quickly and creatively by offering take-out meals, the impact of COVID-19 on the industry was extraordinary, with declines in year-over-year restaurant sales from mid-2019 to mid-2020 anywhere from 50% to 70% in major American cities.[26] And while the industry saw jumps in sales in the wake of the pandemic, a lot of that came from "off premises" dining, as people continued to order food for pick-up or delivery to their homes because of the convenience it offered.[27]

As many restaurants closed and those that remained rebalanced on- and off-premise service, that shift revealed the inequalities that have long plagued this industry. As Madalyn Nones of the Restaurant Opportunities Center of Minnesota put it,

> We cannot go back to the "normal" that allowed restaurant workers to be so vulnerable to systemic shocks. We need to correct the imbalance of power in the restaurant industry that makes its workers functionally expendable labor ... we need to make all restaurant jobs secure, dignified and professionally compensated.[28]

Such challenges offer restaurants an opportunity to re-imagine their industry and possibly return to their roots as a social institution. While dining out dates back as far as 11th-century China, restaurants as we know them today began in 18th-century France, when people went to restaurants for medicinal reasons, to be restored by drinking healthy broths.[29] Closed during the French Revolution and viewed by the French king as places where revolutionaries would meet to plot their next moves, restaurants reopened after the fall of the monarchy, becoming symbols of people's new-found freedom to gather and to speak their minds.

The medicinal and political roles of restaurants have long been forgotten by most restaurant goers, but in that past may lie a key to the industry's future. As take-out dining became much more common during the pandemic, it raised the question: Why go to a restaurant at all, even after it is safe to do so? While the experience of dining will certainly draw some people back to restaurants, these establishments might also reconsider their original purpose as places where people can go to engage in good conversation as well as good food. Rather than be transactional places, restaurants might return to being relational ones, in which the workers are not anonymous laborers in the kitchen, but part of the exchange of information and ideas in the dining room.

To restaurants struggling to get as many customers back as possible just to stay in business, such a proposal might not seem promising. Focusing on food that "restores" our health and well-being and on dialogue that "restores" our sense of community and camaraderie might appear to limit the potential customers of restaurants. But that idea might be just the thing that "restores" an industry that has become dominated by take-out dining. In a digitally dominated future, diners may go to restaurants to get what we cannot find any other way: conversations among diverse people about issues of common interest. In a post-pandemic world, restaurants might again become the places they once were: a space unlike any other, where one could get food and food-for-thought.

The Integration of Production and Consumption

This is part of a larger trend in the post-pandemic world: the integration of production and consumption. In the retail industry, for example, additive technologies enable the consumers of products to be producers of them as well, 3D-printing goods whenever needed. The U.S. military has done this as an economical way of supplying troops, using 3D printers to make parts and equipment in the field rather than having the military ship materials from distant locations.[30] As often happens, innovations in the military find their way into the commercial world.

Commercial applications of 3D printed products have, indeed, begun to happen. Companies like Kor Ecologic have produced 3D-printed automobiles, which suggest that products that once

Figure 7.3 Restaurants might become places of interaction as well as dining.

required big capital expenditures in large, hierarchical companies can now be produced at a relatively low cost, by small companies, with a mass-customization appeal.[31] While most consumers might not have the skills to produce a functioning vehicle like this, the ability to manufacture such a product wherever the 3D printing capacity exists shows how the customers of such products might be able to witness their fabrication and interact with the fabricators. The experience of a car might include the making as well as the driving of it.

For other types of goods, the integration of production and consumption could create a digital version of cottage industries, in which small groups of people create customizable goods for local as well as global markets, with the interaction of the consumer and producer at the center of the experience. The making of goods becomes relational as much as transactional, involving in-person as well as digital communication. This democratization of manufacturing and democratization of skills can both boost local economies and employ the people who have been displaced by the economic mismatch that Snower describes.

This could transform bricks-and-mortar retailing as well. Malls and department stores might become places where people can go not only to purchase goods, but also to experience the production process, interact with those making the desired goods, and maybe even learn how to produce goods themselves. The store could become a place in which to seek education as well as experiences. And the blurring of the distinction between the consumer and producer could turn retail spaces into maker spaces as well, as the retail experience becomes a creative experience at the same time.

Retailers, of course, need to be open to such ideas. When a major retailer announced their intention to close their flagship department store in my city, I suggested that they turn the upper levels of their multi-story, block-long building, instead, into a production place for apparel and other small-scale goods, enabling their customers to interact with designers and fabricators and to have some say in how they might customize or personalize the products they are making and buying. The idea did not get any traction, which is not surprising given the company's need to cut costs quickly. But the

Figure 7.4 Stores and restaurants might become places of production and consumption.

subsequent purchase and renovation of the former department store into a mixed-use building, containing offices, food venues, and spaces for leisure activities, shows how much the post-pandemic economy seeks to blur once distinct or, to use Snower's term, "disjointed" efforts.

Restaurants have also recognized the value of integrating production and consumption. Many have visually linked the food preparation area with the dining space, and some even let customers eat in the kitchen, giving whole new meaning to family style dining. A further enhancement of that idea are the cook-it-yourself restaurants, in which diners partly or completely prepare the meal at their tables.[32] Are "make-it-yourself" stores next? While the COVID-19 pandemic forced us to re-balance the digital and physical worlds – something felt perhaps most acutely in the retail and restaurant industries – the pandemic also enabled us to rethink those industries and relearn from their past where they might go in the future. With e-commerce has come what we might call "re-commerce" – a chance to re-imagine what it means to produce and consume what we need.

Notes

1 Nikolaus Pevsner, *A History of Building Types* (Princeton: Princeton University Press, 1976), pp. 267–272.
2 Ibid., 272.
3 Jeffrey Dastin, Akanksha Rana, "Amazon's Sales and Profits Rise as Retailer Rides Wave of Pandemic Shopping," Reuters, April 30, 2021. www.reuters.com/technology/amazon-first-quarter-sales-beat-expectations-2021-04-29/
4 Susan Meyer, "Understanding the COVID-19 Effect on Online Shopping Behavior," *Big Commerce.* www.bigcommerce.com/blog/covid-19-ecommerce/#product-categories-shifting-during-covid-19
5 Clare Kennedy, "UBS Estimates 100,000 More Retail Stores Will Close by 2025," *LoopNet*, April 27, 2020. www.loopnet.com/learn/ubs-estimates-100000-more-retail-stores-will-close-by-2025/174318906/
6 Gregory Scruggs, "The Unmalling of America," Lincoln Institute, December 16, 2019. www.lincolninst.edu/publications/articles/2019-12-unmalling-america-municipalities-navigating-changing-retail-landscape
7 "The State of Homelessness in America," National Alliance to End Homelessness. https://endhomelessness.org/homelessness-in-america/homelessness-statistics/state-of-homelessness-report-legacy/
8 James Melton, "68% of Shoppers Buy Groceries Online for Home Delivery During the Pandemic," *Digital Commerce 360*, October 1, 2020. www.digitalcommerce360.com/2020/10/01/68-of-shoppers-buy-groceries-online-for-home-delivery-during-the-pandemic/
9 Kate Meis, "The Decline of Retail: What Governments Can Do," Local Government Commission, June 26, 2017. www.lgc.org/newsletter/decline-of-retail/
10 Tracy Hadden Loh, Christopher B. Leinberger, Jordan Chafetz, "Foot Traffic Ahead," *Center for Real Estate and Urban Analysis, Smart Growth America*, 2019. https://smartgrowthamerica.org/wp-content/uploads/2019/06/Foot_Traffic_Ahead_FINAL-compressed.pdf
11 Emmy Hawker, "Has Coronavirus Brought Brick-and-Mortar Retail to an End?" *Business Because*, July 27, 2020. www.businessbecause.com/news/insights/7119/the-end-of-brick-and-mortar-retail?page=2
12 Anna Schaverien, "Five Reasons Why Amazon Is Moving into Bricks-and-Mortar Retail," *Forbes*, December 29, 2018. www.forbes.com/sites/annaschaverien/2018/12/29/amazon-online-offline-store-retail/?sh=7212ad205128
13 Steven Bertoni, "Why Target, Walmart and Best Buy are Booming Amid the Pandemic – and Being Hailed as Heroes," *Forbes*, October 14, 2020. www.forbes.com/sites/stevenbertoni/2020/10/14/why-these-retail-giants-are-booming-amid-the-pandemic-and-being-hailed-as-heroes/?sh=715d49f43858
14 "U.S. Ecommerce Grows 44% in 2020," Digital Commerce 360, January 29, 2021. www.digitalcommerce360.com/article/us-ecommerce-sales/
15 B. Joseph Pine III, James H. Gilmore, "Welcome to the Experience Economy," *Harvard Business Review*, July–August 1998. https://hbr.org/1998/07/welcome-to-the-experience-economy
16 Rani Molla, "The Death and Rebirth of America's Department Stores, in Charts," *Vox*, December 2, 2020. www.vox.com/recode/21561046/death-rebirth-department-stores-retail-charts
17 Lauren Thomas, "25% of U.S. Malls Are Expected to Shut in Five Years. Giving Them a New Life Won't Be Easy," CNBC, August 27, 2020. www.cnbc.com/2020/08/27/25percent-of-us-malls-are-set-to-shut-within-5-years-what-comes-next.html

18 Lauren Thomas, "Simon Shares Jump on Reported Talks with Amazon. But Converting Stores to Warehouses May Face Hurdles," CNBC, August 10, 2020. www.cnbc.com/2020/08/10/mall-owner-simon-shares-jump-on-reported-real-estate-talks-with-amazon.html

19 "Case Studies on Repurposing Vacant Retail Malls," National Association of Realtors, Research Group, 2020. www.nar.realtor/sites/default/files/documents/2020-case-studies-on-repurposing-vacant-retail-malls-05–08–2020.pdf

20 Victor Gruen, Anette Baldauf, editor, *Shopping Town, Designing the City in Suburban America* (Minneapolis: University of Minnesota Press, 2017).

21 Southdale Center," *10 Buildings that Shaped America*, WTTW. https://interactive.wttw.com/tenbuildings/southdale-center

22 Dennis J. Snower, "Waking Up in the Post-Pandemic World," *Brookings*, March 27, 2020. www.brookings.edu/blog/future-development/2020/03/27/awakening-in-the-post-pandemic-world/

23 Ibid.

24 Willy C. Shih, "Global Supply Chains in a Post-Pandemic World," *Harvard Business Review*, September–October, 2020. https://hbr.org/2020/09/global-supply-chains-in-a-post-pandemic-world

25 S. Lock, "Daily year-on-year impact of COVID-19 on global restaurant dining 2020–2021," *Statista*, June 28, 2021. www.statista.com/statistics/1103928/coronavirus-restaurant-visitation-impact/

26 "National Restaurant Association Releases 2020 State of the Industry Report," National Restaurant Association, February 27, 2020. https://restaurant.org/2020-soi-release

27 Peter Romeo, "Restaurant Sales to Jump 10.2% in 2021, National Restaurant Association Says," *Restaurant Business*, January 26, 2021. www.restaurantbusinessonline.com/financing/restaurant-sales-jump-102–2021-national-restaurant-association-says

28 Madalyn Nones, "We Need a Reformed Economy, Not Just a Reopened One," *Minneapolis Star Tribune*, May 21, 2020. www.startribune.com/we-need-a-reformed-economy-not-just-a-reopened-one/570675362/

29 Katie Rawson, Elliot Shore, *Dining Out: A Global History of Restaurants* (Chicago: University of Chicago Press, 2019), Chapter 2.

30 Kyle Rempfer, "Army Announces New Push to Get 3D Printing, Advanced Manufacturing to the Troops in the Field," *Army Times*, October 4, 2019. www.armytimes.com/news/your-army/2019/10/04/army-announces-new-push-to-get-3d-printing-advanced-manufacturing-to-troops-in-the-field/

31 Bridget O'Neal, "Three Wheels & Two Seats: Will the 3D Printed Urbee 2 Be Your Car of the Future?" *3D Print*, March 14, 2016. https://3dprint.com/124086/3d-printed-urbee-2-car/

32 Allison Levine, "Breaking Down a Trend: Cook it Yourself Restaurants," *Foodable Network*, March 3, 2016. www.foodabletv.com/blog/2016/3/1/breaking-down-a-trend-cook-it-yourself-restaurants

8
LEARNING

Among the many effects that the COVID-19 pandemic had on societies globally, the one felt perhaps most acutely by families with children was the closure of schools in most places around the world, and the switch on the part of most students to learning at home. That switch relied on the availability of technology, which put many lower-income or remotely located students at a disadvantage and revealed often-overlooked educational inequities within countries as well as among them. At the same time, the pandemic previewed a future of hybrid digital-and-physical education, even as it revived aspects of education from the past.

As children of different ages learned at home, often in the same space, it recalled the education encountered in one-room schoolhouses, where older youth modeled learning behaviors and even served as mentors or tutors for younger ones. That had its challenges, of course. A one-room schoolhouse near my home once served the farm families in what was then a small, country community, and many students no doubt had household chores and farmstead responsibilities that they juggled with their schooling, something that has re-emerged as an issue during the COVID-19 pandemic, as students balanced demands at home with their school work.

DOI: 10.4324/9781003198192-10

Figure 8.1 Hybrid learning at home and at school may continue, integrating learning and life.

Learning in viral bubbles throughout the pandemic also expanded who we think of as teachers: not just those professionally trained to educate our youth, but also parents, grandparents, older siblings, and even neighbors and friends. In my family's compound, where my two daughters and their families live on either side of us, my grandson, Gus, learned from home during the pandemic, with various adults in our compound serving as his teachers. His extended family, in other words, played a more active role in his education than ever before, in a mix of professionals (my one daughter is a primary school teacher) and amateurs, with the latter done – as the root word of amateur implies – out of love.

Many students, though, did not have that same parental involvement nor the same opportunities as Gus did. At the height of the pandemic, somewhere between 1.2 and 1.5 billion school children went home to learn, constituting over 90% of global enrollments.[1] In the U.S. over 56 million school children faced that situation, as did about 18 million U.S. college students.[2] While many did fine during their immersion into home-schooling, many did not, and almost everyone – students, teachers, and parents – welcomed the return to the classroom and the resumption of in-person learning. Still, post-pandemic education will invariably differ from what came before.

The use of educational technology – or Ed Tech – was already well under way prior to COVID-19's arrival. The percentage of college students taking at least one online course saw steady growth before the pandemic, increasing from over 33% in 2017 to well over 37% in 2018.[3] During the 2020 pandemic, however, that percentage jumped to over 90%, a rate of growth that will inevitably affect the demand for remote learning in the future.[4] COVID-19 may have pushed the accelerator, but the engine of digital-communications platforms and high-bandwidth Internet access had already started, fueled by students and educators seeking more flexible and convenient ways of teaching and learning.

Ed Tech

Prior to the pandemic, Ed Tech market had grown to become an almost $19 billion industry, projected at that time to reach $350 billion by 2025.[5] But now, those projections look low, as schools and colleges invested even more heavily in educational platforms, digital devices, and server space in order to function and to support their faculty and students during the COVID-19 shutdown. In one study, 87% of the educators surveyed said that they had become better at using Ed Tech in their courses, with similar numbers of teachers planning to continue to use online-learning tools in their classrooms, even after they return to teaching in person.[6]

Access to Ed Tech, however, remains very uneven, depending upon the budgets of schools and the income, race, or location of a student's family. In one study, 67% of the educators in schools with a high percentage of low-income children reported that their students had challenges accessing coursework remotely, compared to just 21% in schools with few low-income students.[7] Another study showed that 40% of black students and 30% of Latinx students could not access online coursework during the pandemic, compared to just 10% of white students.[8] And in yet another study in California, only about a third of rural households have Internet access, compared to 78% in urban areas.[9]

Communities tried interim solutions to this problem during the pandemic. Some created mobile Internet hotspots that students could go to in order to gain access to schoolwork, while others advocated deploying Citizens Broadband Radio Service networks, once used only by the Department of Defense, but now open for public use, to provide shared wireless broadband access.[10] And students and parents also improvised in creative ways, sitting or parking next to stores or restaurants to access their wireless connection in order to study or do other work. Still, with about 25% of American students lacking remote access to their classrooms and coursework, and with over 30 million Americans having little or no Internet connection, according to the Biden Administration, the only lasting solution is a major Federal investment in high-speed connectivity for every U.S. household.[11]

Still, the educational community remains divided on the benefits of distance learning. Some research has shown that e-learning can help students retain course content from three to six times more than when learning in person, and absorb five times more content in the same amount of time.[12] At the same time, other studies highlight the value of social interaction and face-to-face communication, representing a type of learning that can get lost in online courses.[13] While most teachers and students have returned to their bricks-and-mortar classrooms after the pandemic, it seems inevitable, given the experience gained during the shutdown, that various hybrids of online and in-person learning will remain a part of the educational system, given their complementary strengths and weaknesses.[14]

The Future Classroom

That hybridization needs to have the support not just of teachers, but of students and their parents as well. The "just ask us movement" has begun to listen to the diverse voices of both students and parents, who have the most at stake in attaining a quality education and who often have some of the most creative ideas about it.[15] Implementing those ideas, though, will require a more innovative mindset than what often exists in the educational system. That includes becoming more open to the kinds of experiments students, parents, and teachers want to explore, while accepting, as a recent Brookings Institution report says, an iterative approach: evaluating, course correcting, and scaling up what works best.[16]

Hybrid digital and physical education will affect school facilities as well. Many older school buildings represent an industrial model of education, in which students sit in fixed-walled, standard-sized classrooms aligned down double-loaded corridors, with only a few spaces – often just the cafeteria, library, and gym – allowing for gathering or interaction among classmates. In that form, many 20th-century school buildings reflected, in microcosm, the modern city, with its single-use districts and standardized zoning requirements, producing a lot of repetitive structures, with only a few places – mainly parks, libraries, and other public buildings – available for community gatherings.

The repetitive physical structure of school buildings also matched the curricular structure of the modern educational system. Students took required courses in particular sequences, determined by the faculty and administrators, that culminated in grades at the end of the term and a degree at graduation, like cars coming off an assembly line. Yet, students now graduate into a world that increasingly needs a different kind of product: a person more creative and critical than what the current educational system typically provides.

Standardized Education

The one-size-fits-all model of K-12 education had its origins in the thinking of one, Ivy League man. Most of the systems and assumptions about education in the U.S. – grades, bell curves, standardized tests, multiple-choice exams – arose in the late 19th and early 20th century, inspired by the work of the mid-19th-century president of Harvard, Charles Eliot.[17] Eliot's ideas affected the design of school buildings as well.[18] Although often draped in historical styles, evoking an earlier pre-industrial era in education, school buildings became, by the early 20th century, as standardized as the education Eliot thought they should offer. And while the architecture of school buildings changed, especially after World War II, to become more modern and utilitarian in appearance, the curricula of many schools became even narrower, reducing the number of classes related to creative activities like art and music for budgetary reasons.

Despite the investments in technology in recent decades, many school buildings continue the standardized classroom arrangement, even though research shows how most students thrive in more flexible, adaptable, and natural settings.[19] Human beings did not evolve, for example, to learn in environments closed off from the natural world, nor did we evolve to sit in regimented rows of desks within fluorescently lit spaces. As informational processing beings, seeking a balance between order and improvisation in the natural environment, students instead need educational environments that offer variety, while accommodating their creativity and encouraging their agency.

The post-pandemic era offers an opportunity, in the design of schools as well as in their curricula, to focus on the performance outcomes for students, staff, and teachers, rather than on the prescriptive goals found in standardized curricula and in the school buildings themselves. The industrial model of 20th-century education does not produce the kind of educational outcomes we will need in the 21st century. And there is mounting evidence that a more varied and stimulating approach to education and a more adaptable and nature-based approach to school design might better prepare students for work environments in which those same characteristics have also become more common.

Learning Communities

The pandemic brought that point literally home. While it revealed the inequities students and their families face in accessing online learn-

Figure 8.2 Schools may become more open and diverse, responding to different pedagogies.

ing resources, the pandemic also gave us a taste of what education might be like in less institutional and more residential settings, where synchronous and asynchronous instruction can happen across the day and week, depending upon how different students like to learn. And school design seems poised to respond. In an article on post-pandemic school design, architect Prakash Nair talks about schools becoming learning communities, replacing classrooms and corridors with learning studios, teacher collaboration spaces, areas for wet or messy work, and a media bar where students can access information when needed.[20]

And he is not alone in thinking this way, evident in the design awards given out in recent years by the American Institute of Architects Committee on Architecture for Education.[21] Flexible learning spaces, ample areas for collaborative work, extensive amounts of daylight and access to the outdoors, varied places for students to work, ready access to technology and equipment, and sensitivity to environmental sustainability and social equity – all characterize the best school buildings. Many of these schools dispense with the standardized, assembly-line quality of older facilities, but many also have concrete floors, durable surfaces, and exposed structures that convey a sense of education being about not just thinking, but also making, about not just knowledge acquisition, but also creative experimentation.

The flexibility of these facilities will serve students well in the post-pandemic era. As we move toward more hybrid forms of learning – at home as well as in school – those two environments will likely have qualities of both. The home may become more of a learning environment, with technology that allows students to connect to their schools remotely and to do their schoolwork at various times of the day or week. At the same time, the school may become more of a living environment, in which students, staff, and faculty have more comfortable furniture, daylighting, and adaptable spaces to complement – and to some extent, compete with – what people often have at home.

Nomadic Learning

I learned this from my own students. Prior to the pandemic, I taught a class nomadically, letting my students choose where they wanted to meet, and not once did they select a classroom or lecture hall.[22] Instead, they preferred places like coffee shops, hotel lobbies, and campus lounges, all of which had more relaxed furniture arrangements, more daylight and views outdoors, and more activity going on around us as we held the class. In the cold, winter months, students even found places on or just off campus with working fireplaces and warm beverages.

Some of my colleagues thought that I was crazy to allow my students to select our meeting place every week, although I had pedagogical reasons for doing so: the course addressed the role that the built environment had on the behavior of those who occupy it. Accordingly, the students had to explain why they selected the spaces they did and the entire class evaluated the effect of those spaces on their own behavior, applying what they learned in the course and assessing its value in real time. While the digital environment enabled the class to meet remotely, as we had access to the Internet everywhere we went, the course also showed how much in-person learning in physical space can offer something no online class ever could. When allowed to vote with their feet, my students did not want the standardized learning environments we had created for them. Instead, they chose visual variety over uniformity, active spaces rather than quiet ones. And more importantly, that environmental diversity seemed to help students better remember the content of the course. They would often attach a concept or conversation to where they heard it, using the physical environment as a kind of mnemonic device, jogging their memory through the association of a particular space with a specific idea.

From that perspective, the uniform user interface of most online educational platforms, like the repetitive classrooms and lecture halls that pervade schools and colleges, inhibit students' retention of information and ideas. It may be easier and cheaper to build such uniform environments and to pack in the students to maximize the efficiency of a teacher lecturing, but it does not maximize student learning or utilize the associative power of diverse places in helping us remember ideas and information. Which may be another reason to hybridize post-pandemic education: the more varied the places in which students can learn, the more valuable place becomes in their learning.

As I taught that nomadic course prior to the pandemic, I watched my university continue to build structures full of classrooms and lecture halls, based on standard space-use and classroom-utilization formulas, and I wondered if anyone responsible for those buildings ever asked students if they actually wanted to learn in those settings. Given the lessons of my class, most do not. And given what we saw during the pandemic, many students now have a choice in how and where they learn – and they, too, may vote with their feet.

Facilities Lessons

That is not to dismiss the value of face-to-face education in school buildings. But the value of that, especially after the pandemic's lockdown of schools, may lie less in the conveyance of information and acquisition of knowledge – increasingly available online – and more about conversations with teachers, collaborations with classmates, and interactions with peers. That in turn suggests that we will need far fewer fixed-seat, sloped-floor lecture halls and classrooms full of individual chairs with tablet arms, and far more spaces like the libraries, lounges, and cafés where students often gather after class. We need to look at where students go when given a chance, and do more of that.

Figure 8.3 We can learn a lot from students about how – and where – they want to learn.

This isn't about dumbing down our facilities, as one tradition-minded colleague put it to me, but about saving them: giving them a new purpose at a time when they have begun to lose their old one. Prior to the pandemic, most of us still held on to the idea that to teach and to learn, we had to be in a classroom or lecture hall, speaking or listening, showing slides or taking notes about the content of the course. We had plenty of technology in the room – laptop computers, digital screens, smart phones, and tablets – but we continued to behave in ways unchanged from over a century ago. And, as I learned in a lecture class that I used to teach, when students could look up the information I was conveying as fast as I could say it and correct me if I got something wrong, education has almost nothing to do with the amount of "seat time" students spend in class.

As many of my colleagues had done in their courses, I flipped that lecture class, posting videos of my talks and slides online, so that students could view them at their leisure and listen to them more than once if they wanted. But the old system continued to operate and my students and I kept coming to a space at the appointed times each week and improvising as best we could with fixed seats and sloped floors, which made it almost impossible to have smaller, group conversations or to do collaborative teamwork. Too many educational facilities get in the way of education, and I fully understood why the students in my nomadic class never chose to learn there.

But in the post-pandemic era, even bigger disruptions lie ahead. Digital platforms, which became the dominant way of delivering education during the global shutdown of schools, raise fundamental questions about the nature of education itself. Who are our students when a digital platform like Zoom allows up to 300 participants, of any age or location, to audit a class or hear a lecture? Who are our faculty when experts from around the world can log on to a class to teach and interact with students? And why have a campus when professors and students can teach and learn from almost anywhere in the world?

Such questions do not mean to devalue in-person learning, but they do suggest that schools, colleges, and universities have largely unexplored opportunities to make education more accessible, affordable, and equitable than ever before.[23] In the case of high-price higher education, fully utilizing a digital platform like Zoom could offer adults lower-cost, life-long learning from wherever they live, without adding appreciably to the work of those teaching a course. Students in such a scenario could include everyone from traditional, degree-seeking pupils to workers seeking new skills in order to remain competitive in the marketplace to retirees looking for new ideas and information to enhance the quality of their lives. In the wake of the pandemic, learning has the potential to become pervasive, in what Arizona State University's President Michael Crow has called the "fifth wave" in higher education, where equity and excellence complement each other.[24]

Platforming Higher Education

This platforming of education is part of a larger "platform revolution," as authors Geoffrey G. Parker, Marshall W. Van Alstyne, and Sangeet Paul Choudhary call it in their book by that name.[25] They write about how, across the economy, platforms are replacing what they describe as "pipeline" organizations, which act as gatekeepers to knowledge that is in high demand and packaged in one-size-fits-all bundles. Education – and especially higher education – fits the pipeline-organization model perfectly. Colleges often tout their selectivity and guard their gates in terms of who they let in, while promoting the success of their graduates and touting their one-size-fits-all degree programs.

Higher education, in other words, seems poised for a serious disruption by platforms, as already began to happen during the pandemic. At a time when people increasingly expect knowledge to be widely available, with greater choices in how and when they access it, at little or no cost, higher education will have to change or find itself forced to do so by the very thing it embraced during the pandemic: the digital platforms on which most classes were taught and most research conducted. The pandemic brought the platform revolution to education and higher education, especially, needs to pivot … or perish.

What might that pivot look like? As Parker, Van Alstyne, and Choudary write, "Platforms beat pipelines because platforms scale more efficiently by eliminating gatekeepers ... unlock new sources of value creation and supply ... (and use) data-based tools to create community feedback loops."[26] That offers an outline for how pipeline education organizations can avoid the disruption of platforms and instead become platform-like themselves. Rather than be gatekeepers and make it hard for people to access knowledge, every educational institution should focus on making it as easy as possible for prospective students to do so, whether remotely or in-person or both. Rather than let their facilities sit empty evenings, weekends, and summers, every institution should look at filling them with other value-creating activities, since almost everything involves education of some sort. And rather than see education as a one-way stream of information from faculty to students, every school and college should engage their communities in feedback loops, looking at what their members have to teach as well as learn.

Such ideas may seem antithetical to the way in which we have seen education in the past and it may seem unlikely that any except the most desperate schools will embrace them. But that complacency is precisely where the danger lies. The Platform Revolution authors end their analysis of education with this prediction: "It wouldn't be surprising if many of the 3,000 colleges and universities that currently dominate the U.S. higher education market were to fail, their economic rationale fatally undercut by the vastly better economics of platforms."[27] Schools turned to digital platforms in a matter of weeks at the start of the pandemic, and now that the contagion has subsided, they need to see that as their first step into a very different post-pandemic future – or if they return to the old way of doing things, their last step before platforms flatten them.

Alternative Universities

The steps educational institutions take in response may differ quite a lot. In the book *Alternative Universities*, the historian David Staley lays out a number of possible paths colleges and universities might consider, facing the disruption of their centuries-old model.[28] Staley argues that higher education institutions have innovated in the past, and that

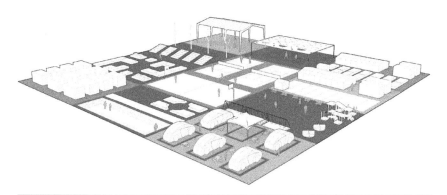

Figure 8.4 Universities might become more open, flexible, and life-long-learning oriented.

> the problem is not that universities are lacking in innovation,
> but rather that they suffer from a poverty of imagination of
> what that innovation might be … the main existential crisis
> facing the university is a poverty of ideas about what univer-
> sities can become.[29]

He goes on to imagine all sorts of institutional designs, from platform universities and micro-colleges to the nomad university, the interface university, and the polymath university among many others.

Staley's point is profound and in the post-pandemic world, a pressing one as well. Pandemics expand the choices people have and the recent pandemic was no exception: It has shown how rapidly we can change when forced to do so, how inefficient and inequitable our old ways of doing things have been, and how digital tools have freed us from the old habit of thinking we had to do everything in person in order to do it at all. Educational institutions that go back to their inefficient, inequitable, and in-person-only ways will be forced to change or left to die, rapidly or slowly depending upon the lag time that their legacy allows them.

And while legacy institutions may be buffered somewhat by their endowments and their sense of entitlements, that in no way protects them from the fate that faces those unwilling to change. As we saw with Ponzi Schemes, those who think they will have a guaranteed return on their investment, as those who attend the most prestigious schools sometimes think, also have the farthest to fall and the most to lose when the scheme collapses. Higher education likes to think of itself as an engine of opportunity for those who have lacked it, and for some number of students, that is true. But others have argued that colleges and universities also widen the inequality gap through their competition for higher-income students in order to meet ever increasing institutional budgets.[30] When Ponzi Schemes run out of those willing to play, they fall, and as students and their prospective employers have started to accept online degrees as equivalent to those of much higher-priced degree-granting institutions, the latter may face a swift decline.

Higher Education's Public Health

Averting such a decline will require that we start to see higher education in a new way. Many people think of going to college like going to a doctor: a sometimes scary and somewhat painful process in which students pay a fee (tuition) in order to receive expert knowledge (from faculty) and to get an outcome (a degree) that will help them have a (financially) healthy future. That medical model of higher education works for those who can pay those fees and devote that time, but it leaves out far too many other people, who have just as much need for – and have just as much right to – an education.

Medicine helped solve the problem of inequitable access to healthcare by giving birth to public health, a field that sees the entire global population as its purview. Fee-based higher education might need to do the same – develop a public-health version of itself – if it hopes to thrive in a post-pandemic world, threatening to flatten – or platform – its current financial model. Just as public health coexists with medicine, so too should a public-health version of higher education coexist with the current tuition-based model, with the former attending to the knowledge needs of the entire global population in the same way that public health attends to humanity's health needs.

Massive open online courses or MOOCs, often free or available at a very low cost to anyone with access to the Internet, provide one path toward that goal. Like the vaccines that eliminated global diseases such as polio and smallpox, such courses might help eliminate the inequitable access to knowledge across the globe and improve the educational attainment of under-served populations. A colleague of mine, Brad Hokanson, teaches a MOOC on creative problem-solving that engages thousands of students.[31] He has them do ordinary activities in some unusual way, to help them see how creativity involves making the familiar seem strange, and he also has them interact with other people in their immediate environment in a way that disrupts their expectations and causes them to think about why they have those expectations to begin with.

Few of Brad's students have ever come to campus; instead, he brings to his geographically dispersed class the kinds of experiences that relatively few students can have on campus. This is nothing new for higher education: community colleges, extension services, and continuing education programs have long embraced aspects of this idea, delivering knowledge to a non-traditional group of students. Such efforts, though, often remain attached to an expert-based model of education, in which the exchange of information largely goes one way, from the professor to the public. MOOCs like Brad's show how learning needs to go both ways, from teachers to students and back again, with everyone generating creative insights in a global teaching and learning community.

The Redesign of Education

That dynamic and immersive approach to higher education has taken root in a few universities around the world. I saw that when serving as a reviewer for an innovation in education prize competition, sponsored by the International Union of Architects.[32] Some higher education institutions did not just explore innovative pedagogies, but also did so in ways that dramatically reduced the cost of instruction and increased the relevance of students' education. In several of the most imaginative curricula, colleges embedded students in the communities with whom they worked, gaining knowledge from both their professors and community members and applying that knowledge in actual situations in order to evaluate and learn from the results.

In doing so, these schools adjusted their coursework to fit the situations that their students encountered, using the design methods of empathetic listening, problem reframing, creative ideation, rapid prototyping, and critical evaluation. While not every discipline can connect to communities in exactly this way, those curricula showed how universities can re-imagine themselves and deliver knowledge more efficiently and effectively by seeing not just their campuses and buildings, but entire communities and the planet itself as their classroom. For the design community, that has meant seeing its role beyond the creation of educational facilities to include the facilitation of a process – in partnership with faculty, staff, students, and the communities they serve – to redesign education itself. Our future depends on it.

Notes

1 Cathy Li, Farah Lalani, "The COVID-19 Pandemic Has Changed Education Forever. This Is How," World Economic Forum, April 29, 2020. www.weforum.org/agenda/2020/04/coronavirus-education-global-covid19-online-di2gital-learning/
2 "Back to School Statistics," National Center for Education Statistics. https://nces.ed.gov/fastfacts/display.asp?id=372
3 Doug Lederman, "Online Enrollments Grow, but Pace Slows," Inside Higher Education, December 11, 2019. www.insidehighered.com/digital-learning/article/2019/12/11/more-students-study-online-rate-growth-slowed-2018
4 "The Evolution of Distance Education in 2020," The University of Kansas, School of Education & Human Sciences, September 17, 2020. https://education-online.ku.edu/community/distance-education-evolution-in-2020
5 Research and Markets, "Online Education Market Study 2019/ World Market Projected to Reach $350 Billion by 2025, Dominated by the United States and China," Intrado. www.globenewswire.com/news-release/2019/12/17/1961785/0/en/Online-Education-Market-Study-2019-World-Market-Projected-to-Reach-350-Billion-by-2025-Dominated-by-the-United-States-and-China.html
6 Kevin Bushweller, "How COVID-19 Is Shaping Tech Use. What That Means When Schools Reopen," *Education Week*, June 2, 2020. www.edweek.org/echnology/how-covid-19-is-shaping-tech-use-what-that-means-when-schools-reopen/2020/06
7 Benjamin Herold, "The Disparities in Remote Learning Under Coronavirus (in Charts)," *Education Week*, April 10, 2020. www.edweek.org/technology/the-disparities-in-remote-learning-under-coronavirus-in-charts/2020/04
8 Emma Dorn, Bryan Hancock, Jimmy Sarakatsannis, Ellen Viruleg, "COVID-19 and Student Learning in the United States. The Hurt Could Last a Lifetime,"

McKinsey & Co., June 1, 2020. www.mckinsey.com/industries/public-and-social-sector/our-insights/covid-19-and-student-learning-in-the-united-states-the-hurt-could-last-a-lifetime

9 Sydney Johnson, "Disconnected: Internet Stops Once School Ends for Many Rural California Students," Ed Source, December 6, 2019. https://edsource.org/2019/disconnected-internet-stops-once-school-ends-for-many-rural-california-students/620825

10 Adam Stone, "6 Ways to Close the Broadband Gap Between Rural and Urban Students," Ed Tech, March 6, 2021. https://edtechmagazine.com/higher/article/2021/03/6-ways-close-broadband-gap-between-rural-and-urban-students

11 "The American Jobs Plan," The White House, March 21, 2021. www.whitehouse.gov/briefing-room/statements-releases/2021/03/31/fact-sheet-the-american-jobs-plan/

12 Karla Gutierrez, "Facts and Stats That Reveal the Power of eLearning," Shift Learning. www.shiftelearning.com/blog/bid/301248/15-facts-and-stats-that-reveal-the-power-of-elearning

13 Adam Driscoll, Karl Jicha, Andrea N. Hunt, Lisa Tichavsky, Gretchen Thompson, "Can Online Courses Deliver In-Class-Results?: A Comparison of Student Performance and Satisfaction in an Online versus a Face-to-face Introductory Sociology Course," *Teaching Sociology*, May 16, 2012. https://journals.sagepub.com/doi/full/10.1177/0092055X12446624

14 "Weighing the Pros and Cons of Online vs. In-Person Learning," National University. www.nu.edu/resources/weighing-the-pros-and-cons-of-online-vs-in-person-learning/

15 Just Ask Us. www.justaskusmovement.org/

16 Emiliana Vegas, Rebecca Winthrop, "Beyond Reopening Schools: How Education Can Emerge Stronger Than Before COVID-19," Brookings, September. 8, 2020. www.brookings.edu/research/beyond-reopening-schools-how-education-can-emerge-stronger-than-before-covid-19/

17 Russlynn Ali, "The New 'New Education'," *Atlantic*, February 18, 2019. www.theatlantic.com/ideas/archive/2019/02/charles-eliot-saw-promise-public-high-schools/582967/

18 Bryn Nelson, "School Design Through the Decades," *Mosaic*, November 4, 2014. https://mosaicscience.com/story/school-design-through-decades/

19 Thomas Fisher, "The More Buildings Run Counter to the Environments in Which We Evolved, the More Problematic They Become," *Dialogues*, 3, Fall, 2019. https://pubs.royle.com/publication/?m=31173&i=621535&p=4&ver=html5

20 Gideon Fink Shapiro, "Post-Vaccine K-12 Education and School Design," *Architect*, February 24, 2021. www.architectmagazine.com/design/post-vaccine-k-12-education-and-school-design_o

21 Maggie Brown, "About the Award Program," American Institute of Architects, Committee on Architecture for Education, April 14, 2020. https://network.aia.org/viewdocument/education-facility-design-awards-bo?CommunityKey=-1b63a201-a510–41b7-b801-bca8083b5727&tab=librarydocuments&LibraryFolderKey=011bbfa7-e0f7–440a-bae7-adb65cffad4e&DefaultView=folder

22 Thomas Fisher, "My Nomadic Class," *Chronicle of Higher Education*, April 15, 2015. www.chronicle.com/blogs/conversation/my-nomadic-class

23 Victor J. Garcia-Morales, Aurora Garrido-Moreno, Rodrigo Martin-Rojas, "The Transformation of Higher Education after the COVID disruption: Emerging Challenges in an Online Learning Scenario," *Frontiers in Psychology*, February 11, 2021. www.frontiersin.org/articles/10.3389/fpsyg.2021.616059/full

24 Michael M. Crow, William B. Dabars, "The Emergence of the Fifth Wave in American Higher Education," *Issues in Science and Technology*, 36(3), Spring 2020. https://issues.org/american-higher-education-accessibility-fifth-wave/

25 Geoffrey G. Parker, Marshall W. Van Alstyne, Sangeet Paul Choudhary, *Platform Revolution: How Networked Markets Are Transforming the Economy and How to Make Them Work for You* (New York: Norton, 2016).

26 Ibid., 8–10.

27 Ibid., 268.

28 David J. Staley, *Alternative Universities, Speculative Design for Innovation in Higher Education* (Baltimore: Johns Hopkins University Press, 2019).

29 Ibid., 279.

30 Josh Freedman, "Why American Colleges Are Becoming a Force for Inequality," *Atlantic*, May 16, 2013. www.theatlantic.com/business/archive/2013/05/why-american-colleges-are-becoming-a-force-for-inequality/275923/

31 Brad Hokanson, "Creative Problem Solving," *Coursera*. www.coursera.org/learn/creative-problem-solving

32 UIA Endorsed Awards, *International Union of Architects*. https://competitions-awards.uia-architectes.org/en/uia-endorsed-awards/

9
STUDYING

The COVID-19 pandemic proved especially problematic for museums, whose purpose of gathering people together, indoors, to engage with art or other media also made them ideal places for the coronavirus to spread. Most museums have survived the pandemic's shutdown, although as many as 15% of them faced "significant risk of closure" because of revenue declines and budget cuts, leading some to cut staff or consider selling art work to pay the bills.[1] As the restaurant and hospitality industries discovered, museums have also had to deal with the hesitancy on the part of many people, even after the pandemic, to return to crowded interior spaces. Like so many other public, private, and non-profit organizations, museums emerged from the pandemic permanently changed; however, much their buildings and interiors may appear as they did before.

Museums were established to expose people to the products of human imagination and understanding and to inspire those who might make their own creative contributions to societies and culture. While that overall institutional role has not changed, the pandemic accelerated an on-going change in how we interact with and think about the contents of museums, as well as in how museums see their responsibilities to under-represented voices and to the artifacts of colonization. The pandemic also made access to museums harder, with their

DOI: 10.4324/9781003198192-11

Figure 9.1 Digital access has allowed collections to become pervasive and part of daily life.

buildings closed, and also easier as people viewed exhibitions, lectures, and performances online, often for free, on their digital devices.

Many museums had moved in these directions prior to 2020: Many had begun to diversify their holdings and repatriate misappropriated works, and many had also begun to digitize their collections and post videos of lectures and gallery talks. The pandemic simply made that activity, happening behind the scenes or at the margins of the museum experience, much more central to it. Most museums made their commitment to diversity more explicit and extensive, while also expanding their digital presence in order to remain relevant to the publics they serve, including everything from online chats with curators to entire exhibitions delivered digitally. *New York Times* critic Jason Farago wrote about this change to museum culture: "With cheaper and rougher digital tools ... every exhibition should become a Zoom classroom, a podcast lecture, a Twitter thread."[2]

The Museum as an Art Form

The previously mentioned observation of Marshall McLuhan about old technology becoming an art form has relevance to museums in a post-pandemic era, with digital technology playing an ever-more central role in delivering their mission.[3] Museums might become not just the holders of art, but also, as McLuhan might say, an art form in and of themselves. Well before COVID-19 arrived, many museums had begun to commission and complete new and often iconic buildings or additions to lure visitors and donors to their doors and to make a statement about the important, creative role they play in their communities. As much as their collections, museum buildings became destinations in their own right.

In the post-pandemic world, those iconic buildings offer a way in which the physical museum can compete with its digital twin by providing experiences almost impossible to replicate online. They have become their own art form as technology has replaced their former role as the only place in which to view art. The question remains, though: How much new museum building will occur going forward? Or rather, how might the physical museum change in the post-pandemic world, given the greater, more convenient, and less costly access that the digital environment offers? What can only be done in person and what kind of space does that require? Those questions, too, had begun to be asked prior to the pandemic. In a 2014 article entitled, "Is the Era of Big Museums Over?" the architecture critic Aaron Betsky wrote that

> the making of stand-alone, expensive, and iconic object [buildings] rarely benefit their communities and their arts. Investments that make use of existing facilities—working with, rather than building on top of existing conditions—and energize, rather than merely temporarily creating audiences make more sense.[4]

The pandemic, in other words, accelerated a process already under way in museums, as they increasingly moved away from a singular focus on objects – be they art or architectural in nature – and toward a much greater appreciation of community connections, public education, and under-represented artists and audiences. What changed as a result of the pandemic was the assumption that, to engage in an activity like viewing art, we needed to go to a purpose-built space in order to do that. We realized that we could enjoy museum experiences from many different locations, letting the museum come to us rather than our always having to go to the museum. We also recognized that we could access multiple museums at the same time, from the same place, and that, to borrow from the Beatles song, the museum existed not just "here," in one physical location, but also "there," in many other locations, and "everywhere," in digital space.

The Museum without Walls

To understand the implications of such experiences, we might revisit the ideas of André Malraux, who served as France's Minister of Cultural Affairs after World War II.[5] Malraux famously argued for the idea of the "museum without walls," which seems to capture the impact that the digitization of collections has had on museums. But, as the critic Derek Allan has observed, Malraux had a broader – and more radical – notion in mind than simply making images of art accessible to people wherever they were.[6] He wanted us to re-imagine the idea of the museum itself and to see it not just as an institution that collects, conserves, and displays art and artifacts, but also as an on-going activity of identifying, locating, and preserving culturally important art and artifacts, wherever they exist, far beyond the walls of museums. Malraux believed that what the art establishment considered to be significant works of art in no way limited what others may find meaningful and what constitutes their own "museum," wherever that may lie.

In many ways, Malraux's idea recalled the origin of the word "museum" – mouseion – meaning "seat of the muses."[7] For the ancient Greeks, it meant a place in which to muse, which could happen almost anywhere that enabled such contemplation, in nature as much as in a building, in a temple or school as much as in a space created to house works of art. The museum, in that sense, has many walls as well as no walls, since different people may find many different places in which to muse, as well as many different artifacts that prompt reflection.

Many museums have pursued Malraux's path. In addition to the art collected, conserved, and displayed in their galleries, numerous museums also have historic structures and archeological sites that they curate and care for, and many offer walking tours and trips to distant locations to expose visitors to significant works that remain in place. But in the post-pandemic era, museums might go even further: to preserve not only work important to the canon, but also work that diverse groups of people find meaningful. Museums might use digital technology not only to push out images and information to various publics, but also to listen to diverse perspectives of people in order to understand what leads them to "muse."

In doing so, museums could enrich their collections with a much greater diversity of work, in a much wider range of places. And museums might curate exhibitions that involve digital maps and street-view images as well as museum guides, showing where visitors can find the work that others find meaningful to them as well as explaining the history and context of that work. In Malraux's sense of the term, such geographically dispersed exhibitions would not just create a "museum without walls," but would also get the museum outside of its walls to engage communities of people in co-creating what the museum shows, what it represents, and who it is for.

Figure 9.2 Museums may return to their roots as diverse places that prompt us to muse.

The Decolonized Museum

That intellectual defenestration of museums might also advance their decolonization.[8] Long before the pandemic arrived, curators and critics had begun questioning the right of a museum to collect and store materials stolen from other people and cultures and to present those materials in ways that do not reflect the values of those who made them.[9] With the closure of museums during the pandemic, many had a chance to assess their collections and their responsibilities with this in mind, and to hear calls to accelerate the process of returning artifacts to their rightful owners or communities.[10] This recalled another side of Malraux's argument. As museums return objects to those who had no voice in their appropriation, museums have increasingly listened to the "voices of silence," as Malraux put it, in order to determine what objects they should or should not collect or exhibit in the future.

The decolonization of museums also constitutes a recontextualization of work in their collections. Appropriated artifacts should be returned not only to the people to whom they belong, but also to the places where they are from. This, of course, does not apply to all art since much of it from more recent centuries was intended for purchase and display in other places. But as museums must now compete with the digital environment for the time and attention of people, the return of place-based work to the people and locations for which they were intended also highlights the role of the museum in the preservation and curation of culture in addition to individual works of art. Enabling visitors to see works in their original settings offers yet another way to think about Malraux's museum without walls: Museums might have as many different kinds of walls as there are works in their collections, all displayed in a manner as true to the original context of the work as possible.

Those experiences will be aided by advances in digital communication tools, like virtual reality and artificial intelligence. In part fueled by the pandemic, such tools allow museum goers to visit locations remotely, without disturbing those places or damaging the work or its context. And as a result, museums might have a diversity of spaces around the world in their "collection," connecting a visitor to them virtually or physically, depending upon a person's ability and the environment's accessibility. Here the value lies not just in the technology that can immerse us in diverse places, but also in the interpretive reading of the places and the depth of contextual knowledge that can help bring a site alive.

The Serendipitous Museum

That points to another way in which museums can compete for our attention in the post-pandemic era: by creating unexpected connections and serendipitous experiences. A weakness of social media lies in its continually trying to assess what we like and to connect us to more of the same, which might work when trying to sell something, but which fails to offer people what they did not know they needed until they have experienced it. As some museums have begun to do, this might mean moving away from chronological, geographical, or thematically related exhibitions according to some canon, and toward the juxtaposition of apparently unrelated works within a collection. In this way, museums can not only inform us about the work on display, but can also help us find unexpected connections or unseen commonalities among diverse work.[11] While that may sound irrational or even an abrogation of curatorial responsibility, it can accomplish what few digital environments do: to provoke us into musing upon what we had not thought about before and to let us co-curate the experience we have in a museum.

That may also recall the way in which museums displayed work in the 19th century, with work of widely varying quality stacked up the walls or in cases with little information or explanation. But in many ways, the 21st-century museum faces the opposite problem: We now have almost too much information about – and images of – most works readily available on our digital devices. The role of the museum then becomes one of making meaningful connections among things and helping us do the same.[12] In this way, museums serve not only to inform us about art or culture, but also to prepare us for a post-pandemic world in which co-creativity and openness to innovation are key. This, in turn, implies a new social role for museums: as instructional and inspirational places that help instill in us a habit of mind able to adjust to the rapid economic, environmental, and demographic changes occurring all around us. By inviting the public not just to view the work on display, but to re-imagine and reconnect it in new ways, museums can prepare us for a post-pandemic world in which we are all both the producers and consumers of work.

Re-imagining Libraries

Libraries have a related, but somewhat different role to play in the post-pandemic era. During the pandemic, most libraries faced the same challenges as museums: building closures, budget cuts, and staff furloughs, and as the pandemic waned, they both had hesitant patrons, unsure whether they want to return to large, indoor spaces even if vaccinated against the virus. Yet, libraries also had opportunities and challenges different from those of museums. Most libraries, for example, have public funding and so have a broader service mission than most museums, leading them down a different path.

I co-led a project with my colleagues, Abimbola Asojo and Virajita Singh, in which we helped a county library system redesign its service delivery during and after the pandemic. At the height of the infection, we showed how furniture, computers, and circulation paths could be rearranged to keep patrons socially distanced and safe, but with the post-pandemic world in mind, we also looked at how libraries might double as county service centers with digital and in-person navigators to help people access the services they need.

That reflected a larger rethinking of service delivery, partly triggered by the pandemic. While most organizations that shifted to remote work during the pandemic saw employee productivity improve by 5%, [13] they also saw the effectiveness of delivering services to people rather than expecting people to come to them to be served.[14] That has led some governments to think of their service delivery in the same way, meeting their diverse populations where they are, with in-person interactions an option for those who lack digital connections in "walk-ups of last resort" as our county colleagues called them. Our project focused on shrinking the footprint of the county's administrative offices and expanding the delivery of services closer to where people live and work, in their local libraries.

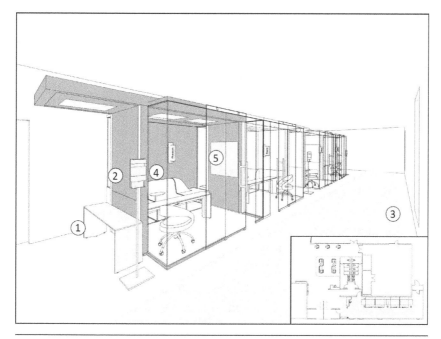

Figure 9.3 Library service centers will allow digital access (1, 2) and confidential meetings (3–5).

The pandemic also accelerated a trend toward re-imagining libraries as information and community centers as much as places to access printed materials and gain knowledge.[15] The shift to online resource access increased significantly during the pandemic, with digital checkouts up 33%,[16] e-book usage up 40%, and e-book checkouts up 52% from the same point the previous year.[17] That led many libraries to look more critically at the use of their facilities, de-accessioning rarely used books, moving others to long-term storage, and replacing some book stacks with spaces for a wider range of activities, including classrooms for adult learning, sound studios for podcasting, and maker spaces for small-scale fabricating.[18] As is happening with museums, libraries in the post-pandemic era will become "people-centered not collections centered," as the architects at Gensler put it.[19]

Decentralizing the Collection

That may take a somewhat different form in libraries than in museums. While the latter might decolonize their collections and recontextualize artifacts, libraries have the opportunity to decentralize their services and to reach out to people wherever they are. That might mean returning to some old ideas, like bookmobiles and book fairs, and experimenting with some new ones, like pop-up book stands and temporary occupations of empty storefronts. Libraries have also become tech hubs in many schools and communities, in which access to digital technology draws people to the library, where they may then also access physical books.[20] That trend, already under way before the pandemic, shows how the rebalancing of the digital and physical worlds may unfold in the post-pandemic era, with digital access as the main factor in deciding what to do where, and with physical space and resources playing more of a supporting part.

Libraries have a different role than museums in terms of equity as well. Many in the museum world have acknowledged that they have traditionally served as "white spaces" not just physically in terms of their white-walled exhibition spaces, but also culturally in terms of who feels comfortable being there and who does not.[21] But given their role in also preserving and protecting valuable and often delicate objects, museums face certain limits in terms of how much they can make their collections accessible; they will likely remain places in which we can see and hear about art works or artifacts, but rarely touch them.

Not so libraries. They have a long tradition of getting their collection into people's hands and encouraging as diverse a range of patrons as possible to utilize their space and resources. While they, too, need to preserve and protect their collections, libraries also have an opportunity to give everyone access to their resources and to make everyone feel comfortable there. Some libraries, especially in urban areas, have partnered with the social-work community to provide services for those experiencing homelessness or other personal challenges who sometimes occupy the library as the only place for them to go during the day.[22] And as homelessness has become an ever larger issue because of pandemic-related evictions and job loss, libraries have become shelters for those experiencing homelessness, as the one place in most cities that will not kick people out.[23]

In the post-pandemic era, library spaces – especially for those who lack a space of their own – will become ever more important not only because of the social interactions they offer, but also because of the compensatory qualities they have. As libraries have increasingly become the home, during the day or evening, for people who have none, these public institutions have, like the private office, become more home-like, with a variety of furnishings and a range of spaces for people of all ages, from children to the elderly, each with their own areas in order to meet their various needs. And libraries have also become places where people can connect not just to books and other media, but also to each other in gathering places and café settings frequently found in these facilities.

Libraries and Public Health

Pandemics heighten our awareness of public health and that will continue to affect libraries as well. How much indoor air quality and social distancing will remain a factor in the operation of libraries remains a question. If nothing else, large indoor spaces with highly diverse populations, like libraries, will need to accommodate those who worry about infection or illness, even if just from a cold or the flu.[24]

We will likely see in most public settings the widespread use of contactless operations such as motion-detecting lighting, hands-free door openers, and automatic revolving doors; non-porous materials like anti-microbial wood or quartz surfaces and ceramic or linoleum flooring; and increased air movement from operable windows, portable air cleaners, and larger ventilating systems. Pandemics often prompt permanent changes to building interiors, whether the widespread adoption of indoor plumbing after the cholera pandemic and the increased use of easily cleaned surfaces like ceramic, metal and linoleum after the flu pandemic. Interiors after COVID-19 will likely see the same, as public buildings especially become more automated, anti-microbial, and easily cleaned.[25]

Interior space use in libraries may see a permanent change as well. While the tradition of large, open reading rooms may continue to occur, we might see a greater variety of places in which people want to work in libraries, for reasons ranging from a desire for social distancing to a need for quiet space. Companies have responded with an array of products that lie somewhere between furniture and rooms, including glass-enclosed, micro meeting pods; semi-enclosed, high-back single seating areas; and phone-booth-sized, one-person workstations. Although mainly intended for open offices, this space-enclosing furniture also serves the needs of library patrons, who increasingly use such facilities as their workplace.

The Library as the Future Workplace

That is especially true of academic libraries.[26] Unlike public libraries, which have to accommodate a broad swath of the population of all ages, college and university libraries serve a somewhat narrower group in terms of age and skill, and as such, they come closer to mimicking the future workplace. The higher-education consulting firm Brightspot sees four characteristics of today's college student that will likely define the future workforce: "purpose seekers," who want work that aligns with their values; "makers," who learn by doing and making; "teamers," who prefer working with others on projects; and "flexers," who can work almost anywhere with anyone.

In terms of academic libraries, those qualities suggest a variety of spaces much greater than the tripartite tradition of book stacks, reading rooms, and circulation-desk areas. At North Carolina State University's Hunt Library, whose architect – Snøhetta – I took part in selecting, it has those traditional elements along with a range of other spaces: group study rooms, data visualization spaces, recording studios, gaming labs, makerspaces, cafés, and lounges.[27] Recognizing the various roles libraries must play in the future helped Snøhetta get the commission: during a weekend workshop, as other competing firms drew buildings, Snøhetta's team made rough drawings and models stuffed with a variety of colored shapes representing the mix of uses that the library would have to house, along with the flexibility to accommodate uses we cannot even imagine.

Building Hybrids

That openness to a future we do not yet know may characterize the future not just of libraries and museums, but almost every other type of building as well. Pandemics initially blur distinctions that existed prior to the event. Just as the outhouse moved in-house after the cholera pandemics and the trolley car became a lot of cars after the 1918 flu pandemic, hybrids like the home–office, home–school, and library maker space have become more common after COVID-19. Eventually, those hybrids become more common and widely embraced, with new policies to address them. Many of the building types we inherited from the past began this way: museums and libraries that originated as private collections in patron's homes, department stores that began as assemblages of small specialty shops, and shopping malls that started as hybrids of urban pedestrian streets and suburban shopping centers.

In the post-pandemic era, that hybridization has occurred not just among building types, but also among digital and physical environments. Museums and libraries may be out ahead of other building types in the sense that many of their leadership and staff have already embraced digital versions of their physical resources and worked to make both as accessible and diverse as possible. Both have moved toward a future in which some of what they have will remain within their walls and much of what they and others have will be without walls or within many walls. And both have realized that what their physical space has to offer must differ substantially from what their digital presence provides, with their buildings now needing to accommodate a much wider range of activities and to create experiences that people can only get by being there.

This suggests that museums and libraries may have a somewhat different geography in the post-pandemic era as well. Although these institutions have long had a responsibility to those who come through their doors to expose them to the larger world of art and learning, most museums and libraries remain very much rooted in the communities in which they stand, with a responsibility to local artists and writers as well as to the local knowledge of the people of those places: showing locally produced work, hosting conversations with local creatives, and documenting the local art and literary scene, among many other possibilities. Such localism does not have to lead to provincialism or parochialism; it can instead encourage the local producers of creative work and build an audience for it.

Moreover, paying attention to the local may be one of the most effective ways in which the physical world can compete with the

Figure 9.4 Museums and libraries will have many walls and, in a hybrid future, no walls too.

digital one. While there is much that the Internet has to offer the consumers of knowledge and information, both important and not, the digital environment cannot compete with people communicating and sharing in a physical enclosure. In this, museums and libraries in the post-pandemic era may not only greatly expand their cultural breadth and their geographical reach, but also rediscover their original, local roles as spaces where a number of people in a particular place can go to study and to muse. That would be a good outcome and one for which we have the pandemic, at least partly, to thank.

Notes

1 "New Survey Suggests 15 Percent of US Museums Could Close Permanently," *Art Forum*, June 2, 2021. www.artforum.com/news/new-survey-suggests-15-percent-of-us-museums-could-shut-down-86047

2 Jason Farago, "10 Ways for Museums to Survive and Thrive in a Post-COVID World," *New York Times*, May 24, 2021. www.nytimes.com/2021/05/21/arts/pandemic-museums-ideas.html

3 Andrew McLuhan, "Understanding Understanding Media," *Medium*, February 1, 2019. https://medium.com/@andrewmcluhan/understanding-understanding-media-8cdd40d46908

4 Aaron Betsky, "Is the Era of Big Museums Over?" *Architect*, October 10, 2014. www.architectmagazine.com/design/buildings/aaron-betsky-asks-is-the-era-of-big-museums-over_o

5 André Malraux, *The Voices of Silence: Man and His Art* (Princeton: Princeton University Press, 1979).

6 Derek Allen, "Has André Malraux's imaginary museum come into its own?" *Apollo*, April 2, 2020. www.apollo-magazine.com/andre-malraux-museum-without-walls/

7 "Museum," Online Etymology Dictionary. www.etymonline.com/search?q=-museum

8 Amy Lonetree, *Decolonizing Museums: Representing Native America in National and Tribal Museums* (Chapel Hill: University of North Carolina Press, 2012).

9 Adam Hochschild, "The Fight to Decolonize the Museum," *Atlantic*, January 2020. www.theatlantic.com/magazine/archive/2020/01/when-museums-have-ugly-pasts/603133/

10 Haitham Eid, "Time to Accelerate Decolonization," *Museums Association*, June 17, 2020. www.museumsassociation.org/museums-journal/opinion/2020/06/time-to-accelerate-decolonisation/#

11 Sarah Boxer, "Snubbing Chronology as a Guiding Force in Art," *New York Times*, September 2, 2000. www.nytimes.com/2000/09/02/arts/snubbing-chronology-as-a-guiding-force-in-art.html

12 "ArtLens Wall," Cleveland Museum of Art. www.clevelandart.org/artlens-gallery/artlens-wall

13 Enda Curran, "Work from Home to Lift Productivity by 5% in Post-Pandemic US," *Bloomberg*, April 22, 2021. www.bloomberg.com/news/articles/2021-04-22/yes-working-from-home-makes-you-more-productive-study-finds

14 Melissa Repko, "As Coronavirus Pandemic Pushes More Grocery Shoppers Online, Stores Struggle to Keep up with Demand," CNBC, August 14, 2020. www.cnbc.com/2020/05/01/as-coronavirus-pushes-more-grocery-shoppers-online-stores-struggle-with-demand.html

15 Amy L. Knapp, "Pandemic Forces Area Libraries to Go Digital, Rethink Services," *The Independent*, January 26, 2021. www.indeonline.com/story/news/2021/01/26/libraries-use-pandemic-reinvent-rethink-way-they-serve-patrons/6699646002/

16 "33% Growth for Digital Books from Public Libraries and Schools in 2020 Sets Records," *Overdrive*, January 7, 2021. www.prnewswire.com/news-releases/33-growth-for-digital-books-from-public-libraries-and-schools-in-2020-sets-records-301202452.html#:~:text=Multimedia%20%26%20Internet-,33%25%20Growth%20for%20Digital%20Books%20from%20Public%20Libraries,-Schools%20in%202020%20Sets%20Records

17 Aarian Marshall, "Publishers Worry as Ebooks Fly off Libraries' Virtual Shelves," *Wired*, October 1, 2020. www.wired.com/story/publishers-worry-ebooks-libraries-virtual-shelves/

18 Ellen Rosen, "Beyond the Pandemic, Libraries Look Toward a New Era," *New York Times*, September 24, 2020. www.nytimes.com/2020/09/24/business/libraries-pandemic-future.html

19 Allison Marshall, Sara Rothholz Weiner, "Design Ideas for the Post-Pandemic Public Library," Gensler, July 28, 2020. www.gensler.com/blog/design-ideas-for-the-post-pandemic-public-library?q=libraries

20 Chris Berdik, "Come for the Computers, Stay For the Books," *Slate*, June 21, 2017. https://slate.com/technology/2017/06/libraries-are-becoming-tech-hubs-for-schools.html

21 Ivan O'Garro, "Disrupting White Supremacy in Museum Architecture," Smith Group, April 19, 2021. www.smithgroup.com/perspectives/2021/disrupting-white-supremacy-in-museum-architecture

22 Tracy M. Soska, Adria Navarro, "Social Workers and Public Libraries," *Advances in Social Work*, September 10, 2020. https://journals.iupui.edu/index.php/advancesinsocialwork/article/view/23690
23 Scott Shafer, "Urban Libraries Become De Facto Homeless Shelters," National Public Radio, April 23, 2014. www.npr.org/2014/04/23/306102523/san-francisco-library-hires-social-worker-to-help-homeless-patrons
24 Lloyd Alter, "Interior Design Lessons From the Coronavirus," *Treehugger*, July 7, 2020. www.treehugger.com/interior-design-lessons-coronavirus-4847976
25 "Reopening: Guidance for Libraries," American Industrial Hygiene Association, December 8, 2020. https://aiha-assets.sfo2.digitaloceanspaces.com/AIHA/resources/Reopening-Guidance-for-Libraries_GuidanceDocument.pdf
26 "Today's Library Is Tomorrow's Workplace," Brightspot, February 5, 2019. www.brightspotstrategy.com/academic-library-design-student-services/
27 "Our Library of the Future," NC State University Libraries. www.lib.ncsu.edu/huntlibrary

PART 3
POST-PANDEMIC INFRASTRUCTURE AND OPEN SPACE

10
CITIES

Pandemics often prompt people to evacuate cities, where epidemic diseases typically first begin to spread. We can see the results of a pandemic-related evacuation of a city in the 1748 map of Rome, drawn by the artist Giambattista Nolli.[1] While long admired and still studied because of its depiction of the public and semi-public spaces of that city, Nolli's map also showed the effects of the "second plague pandemic" that swept Europe from the 14th to the 18th century.[2] So many people either fled – or died in – Rome because of the bubonic plague that, as Nolli's map showed, farms and pastures had arisen within the ancient walls of that formerly high-density city.

Such plague-driven depopulations of cities have happened repeatedly throughout history. When the bubonic plague struck London in 1665, Henry Foe, the uncle of the novelist Daniel Defoe, kept a record of it, which served as the basis of his nephew's 1722 fictionalized version of the events in *A Journal of the Plague Year*.[3] In his novel, Defoe writes that, while many people fled London, many more stayed and endured the great suffering that resulted from the disease. And land uses in London changed as a result. For example, prior to the plague, people were often buried in churchyards in the city, but the sheer number of deaths that resulted from the 1665 infection forced

DOI: 10.4324/9781003198192-13

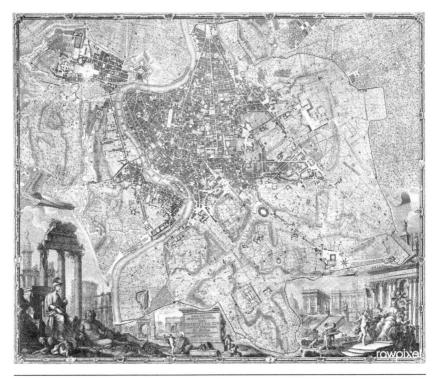

Figure 10.1 Nolli's 1748 map of Rome showed how prior pandemics had partly depopulated it.

the digging of mass graves on the outskirts of London, creating cemeteries that, by the 19th century, had become common in cities around much of the world. That pandemic depopulated the city of the dead as well as the living.

Most cities repopulate to varying degrees after a pandemic, but most also do so in ways different from what came before. The attention paid to clean water and sanitation after the cholera pandemics of the 19th century led to the densification of cities, as more people could live more safely closer to their places of employment and to the opportunities that density affords. And the concern about social distancing after the 1918 flu pandemic led to the suburbanization of cities, as more people could live farther from their places of employment and still enjoy what cities have to offer via technologies like the automobile and infrastructure like freeways.

The COVID-19 pandemic had a somewhat different impact on cities.[4] While some of the largest and most expensive cities in which to live in the U.S. – New York City and San Francisco, for example – saw significant out migration of people, smaller cities like Austin, Tampa, and Tucson saw increases in population during the pandemic. COVID-19 seemed to accelerate trends already under way as people, able to work more remotely, had been moving to less expensive cities and away from cities that have not built enough affordable housing. Cities did not depopulate during and after the recent pandemic so much as see residents move from larger to smaller ones.

Suburbanization also continued apace. Suburbs saw a dramatic uptick in population not just in 2020, but over the previous four to five years, suggesting that, again, the pandemic accelerated a trend already under way. That on-going suburbanization makes sense for at least a couple of reasons. The COVID-19 pandemic, like the Flu pandemic of 1918, arose from a highly contagious, respiratory disease, where social distancing and avoidance of shared interior environments – as occurs in low-density, single-family residential suburbs – can reduce viral spread. At the same time, the real estate industry has seen a demand on the part of many people, particularly among the millennial generation, for the larger houses often found in suburbs to accommodate a future in which more work will be done out of one's home and where commuting into work will be less frequent and not necessarily on a 9-to-5 schedule.[5]

Digitizing Cities

Those urban and suburban trends, however, do not tell the real story about the COVID-19 pandemic's long-term effect on cities. People continued to move from one city to another or from a more urban to a more suburban one, as they have done in the U.S. for 150 years or more. What the recent pandemic wrought was not so much the urbanization or suburbanization of cities, but their accelerated digitization. The digitization of cities is not a new phenomenon. Bill Mitchell wrote about the urban implications of digitization as early as 1995, forecasting the effect of miniaturized electronics and mobile devices on how we occupy and move about the built environments in which we live and work.[6]

Since then, a sizable number of books about "smart cities" have appeared, tracking the rise of information technologies that enable cities to operate more efficiently, deliver services more effectively, and support their residents more equitably than in the analog past.[7] Those books document the rise of digital technology as an essential component to almost every aspect of modern life. Many of the books have a celebratory character, looking at the potential of digital technology to make cities more equitable and sustainable, although some have a somewhat darker flavor, such as Anthony Townsend's look at "civic hackers" intent on subverting the systems upon which so many people and organizations depend.[8] Given the growing threat of cyberwarfare and the likelihood that one or more cities will be subjected to a "Chernobyl-like" cyberattack, as Townsend describes it, cities and the systems that support them have become the new battlefield, with their citizens the unknowing enlistees in this digital warfare.

The COVID-19 pandemic accelerated this digitization in ways that affect the daily lives of people, at least in the most developed countries of the world. While many people had digital tools like smart phones, digital tablets, and laptop computers prior to the pandemic, the events of 2020 showed how much those tools can change how we live, for good and bad. Pervasive digitization allowed us to bring most of what we need to our door, rather than our having to venture out to find what we need, which represents a profound a shift in human existence. Ever since our hunter-and-gatherer origins, we humans have had to seek out what we need and that peripatetic nature has not changed much over the millennia, other than the distance and the means by which we travel, now by car, plane, or transit as much as by foot.

The digitization of daily life can now bring the world to us. Many people, of course, have long had goods shipped to their home or services rendered over the phone or a computer. But those remained relatively minor in comparison to the massive amount of travel most people still did in order to get what they needed in life. When home delivery and remote access became the dominant way of being for

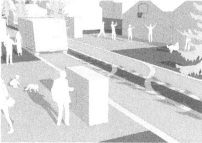

Figure 10.2 Alleys may have secure lockers for packages as well as recycling and trash bins.

people around the globe as we quarantined in our houses, the digital environment became the place in which we looked for things and our residential environment, the place in which we received them. Never has this been done before, at this scale, as most of humanity experienced a digital version of a hunter–gatherer existence.

The digital environment, of course, can be as hazardous to high-tech hunters and gatherers as the physical one was for our ancestors. In addition to our ability to access almost anything via the Internet, for instance, we also had to endure increasingly frequent and costly cyberattacks.[9] In just one month, May 2021, cyber criminals halted production at the world's largest meat process company, operation of the largest fuel pipeline in the U.S., operation of the water system serving 85% of Norwegians, and the proceedings of the Belgium parliament. But fighting this war involved not just national resolve to go after the digital bandits, but also, as Townsend said after one of his talks, "people having better passwords and not opening attachments from people they don't know."

Nor are cyberattacks limited to criminal networks. Bullying, trolling, and intentionally misinforming behavior on the part of some people against others has forced some national governments to take a stand and fight against it.[10] Collectively, that behavior represented digital tribalism, where political parties or activist groups looked upon their opponents not as worthy competitors in the marketplace of ideas, but as untrustworthy adversaries who must be foiled or defeated by any and all means.[11] Some protection against such behavior can happen nationally and globally, but the real protection happens locally and individually, in the decisions each of us makes to secure our personal information and to ignore scam artists and self-serving ideologues.

That mix of the global and the local characterizes other aspects of our digitized, post-pandemic lives as well, as it did post-pandemic periods in the past. After the cholera pandemics of the 19th century and the growth of large, industrial cities, people increasingly made things locally for global markets, and they often lived near the offices and factories that supplied goods for other parts of the world. And after the flu pandemic of 1918 and the growth of sprawling suburbs, that mix of local production for global consumption continued, along with the use of time rather than space as a measure of efficiency and productivity. As people commuted to work, for instance, they increasingly used the time it takes to get to a destination rather than the distance to it, as the basis for deciding if or when to travel.

The digitization of daily life after the COVID-19 pandemic altered those calculations again. As people shop online, telecommute to a meeting, or log into a class, physical distance matters hardly at all; online, many people may have no idea where the others logged in are located. The time zone a person occupies, especially for synchronous meetings or classes, means much more, sometimes determining when a session can be held in order to prevent it from falling in the middle of someone's night. Temporal location matters, as does the coordination of temporal zones, much more than spatial proximity in the digital world.

Rethinking Density

The impact of the recent pandemic, however, goes beyond the receding importance of space and the growing importance of time. Space and time have also become dependent upon the scale at which they occur: globally or locally. The digitization of post-pandemic life has seen the emergence of simultaneous global and local ways of living. Many people can now live globally in ways never possible before, connecting instantly to friends, family, and colleagues – as well as bad actors – anywhere in the world, at a very low cost, through various platforms. At that global scale, spatial distance recedes to a point of irrelevance while time-zone differences loom every larger. Meanwhile, many people can increasingly live locally, meeting most of our daily needs – if not necessarily our travel bug – without having to leave our homes if we so choose, using the same low-cost, digital platforms that facilitate our global connections. At the local level, spatial proximity to those with whom we share common interests or experiences matter much more than time.

We all now exist, in other words, in two simultaneous realities: locally in space and globally in time. And the pandemic showed how those two realities interact. The coronavirus moved quickly from a local epidemic in Wuhan, China, to a global pandemic spreading rapidly around the world. Because it arose in a city and the first wave of infections occurred in cities, some saw this as reason to leave the places where spatial proximity can spread infectious disease more readily. But most large cities are also tied to the global economy of goods, services, and ideas, where people can recover more quickly, both medically, with often the most up-to-date hospitals, and

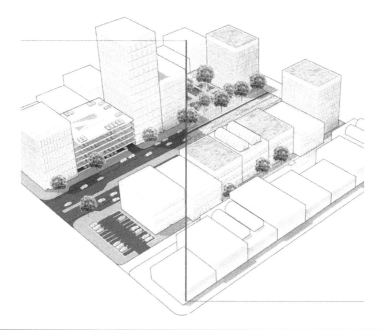

Figure 10.3 Cities after pandemics come back healthier and greener, with more opportunities.

economically, with the greatest concentrations of businesses and financial institutions.

As the physicist, Geoffrey West argues in his scalar analysis of cities, the larger the human settlement, the more efficient it is, for both good and bad.[12] Bigger cities produce more patents as well as more pollution, more creative innovations as well as more criminal activity. And so, while some people flee cities to avoid the concentration of illness brought on by a pandemic, they also often return to cities because such places offer the greatest chance of surviving the infection and a faster acceleration into the future after the pandemic has ended.

Those who blame cities – or fear them – because of pandemics also need to make a distinction in terms of what kind of density we are talking about. The United States, for example, has six times more people than South Korea, and yet had 27 times more coronavirus cases at the same point in the COVID-19 pandemic.[13] Meanwhile, South Korea is 15 times more dense than the U.S.[14] And although the U.S. spends 3.5 times more per person on healthcare than South Korea, the U.S. also has less than one quarter the number of hospital beds per 1,000 people than South Korea.[15] When it comes to density, in other words, it matters what kind we are talking about: In a pandemic, the density of hospital beds matters much more than the density of people or buildings.

A distinction between the density of a city and its size also helps. In a study of over 900 U.S. metropolitan areas, COVID-19 infection rates correlated more to how big a city was rather than to its density.[16] That may have to do with how pandemics often arrive, via travelers who frequently arrive at large city airports – or ports – before they go to smaller settlements. And while the size of the city matters more than its density in terms of infection rates, density matters more when it comes to lower death rates, perhaps the result, say the researchers, of the availability of better or more prevalent healthcare.

That hasn't stopped some from prophesizing the decline of cities in the wake of the COVID-19 pandemic.[17] Decline, of course, is different from change. Pandemics do change cities, but unless one sees any change as a *decline* from what went before, pandemics actually *incline* us to become more open to new ideas and ways of doing things, and incline people to move to other cities where the costs are lower and opportunities just as great. The real question is not whether cities will decline or not, but instead: How will cities change after the pandemic and what does that mean for the lives of people who live there?

People, for example, may not feel comfortable in crowded, indoor spaces, at least for a while after a plague has passed. Pandemics that result from viral respiratory disease, like COVID-19, can lead us to fear proximity to and physical contact with others, and such apprehensions do not suddenly end with a drop in the number of illnesses or deaths. For instance, Dr. Anthony Fauci, who oversaw the U.S. response to the COVID-19 pandemic, predicts that mask wearing may become a common seasonal practice to avoid respiratory infections, be it COVID-19, influenza, or just the common cold, now that we have seen how effective masks can be in keeping people healthy.[18]

Urban Transit

But what about spatial practices, like the use of public transit? While transit use grew after the COVID-19 pandemic, some experts saw a change in how we use and operate transit, with the contactless paying of fares using cards rather than coins, and an increased focus on cleanliness and physical separation among riders, all of which can improve the quality as well as the healthfulness of the experience of taking a bus or train.[19] As often happens after pandemics, a greater attention paid to public health ends up enhancing the public realm and the infrastructure that supports it.

What the public sector invests in also matters a lot. Let's look at transit again. In the U.S., during the COVID-19 pandemic, transit ridership fell between 60 and 80%,[20] but if we again compare the U.S. and South Korea, transit had little to do with the spread of the coronavirus. Although transit use in U.S. cities has increased 33% in the last two decades, approximately 45% of the population has no access to transit.[21] That reflected an under-investment in public transportation compared to other developed countries, with a $90 billion maintenance backlog in U.S. transit services and a continual shortfall in funding, with only 45% of transit costs paid through fares.[22] In Seoul,

South Korea, over 70% of the population uses transit daily, most live within 500 yards of a station, pay less than half of what transit riders pay in New York, and consider the maintenance of the system to be excellent.[23]

South Korea has the world's fifth largest auto industry, so they are not anti-car, but they have had much better results than the U.S. from their expenditures in both healthcare and transportation. The South Koreans have recognized that density can lead to resilience, evident in the number of beds available during emergencies, and that density can also lead to efficiency, obvious in the effectiveness of the transit system. The fact that they also kept their infection rates low during the pandemic suggests that what matters, in the end, is the willingness of the public sector to invest in infrastructure that benefits public health.

Inequality in Metropolitan Regions

One paradox of the suburbanization of metropolitan areas in countries like the U.S. is that, while that settlement pattern arose, in part, out of a concern for better health through greater social distancing, lower crime, and less pollution, the rise of sprawl has also led to a lot of ill health in the form of rising rates of obesity and heart disease related to increasingly sedentary lifestyles. Had we tried, we could not have designed a physical environment more effective in producing poor health than the one that the U.S. government subsidized over the last century.

And we could not have devised a more unequal environment as well. I teach courses in urban design at my school, and we focus on how to create diverse, thriving, and resilient communities that are socially equitable, physically accessible, economically affordable, and environmentally sustainable. The lack of those qualities in many communities around the world drives many of our conversations in class. For the last century or more, many cities, at least in the U.S., have evolved in ways that segregate people by income and ethnicity, that generate extreme inequality when it comes to opportunity, and that demand a lot of fossil fuel to operate, producing a lot of waste and pollution in the process.

Prior to the pandemic, the market forces and governmental regulations driving the form of American cities seemed unstoppable or at least largely undeterred by the visions of urban designers. But who would have thought that a microscopic virus could disrupt what seemed invincible just a few years ago, stopping the global marketplace in its tracks and altering so profoundly how we occupy the cities, suburbs, and towns where most people live? Changes that looked like they might take generations to achieve prior to the pandemic happened out of necessity in a matter of weeks and months, without having to change regulations or enact a law. People did what they had to in order to survive, and cities changed profoundly as a result.

Urban Air

Cities, for example, that had terrible air quality prior to the pandemic all of a sudden discovered what it takes to have cleaner air, as many people stopped driving. Greenhouse gas emissions and air pollution in China, for instance, were down 25%, according to some accounts, because of dramatic reductions in the number of people commuting.[24] This reveals one of the paradoxical aspects of pandemics. As we became healthier, epidemiologically, by getting vaccinated against the infection, the residents of large and highly polluted cities became even healthier by not breathing the polluted air and not getting in cars to drive to work or shop. Like the herd immunity against the virus that a mostly vaccinated population can achieve, we need an injection of longer-term thinking in order to achieve the necessary herd immunity against our addiction to fossil fuels and the continual growth they enable.

To see what such a vaccine might be like, consider the old television series *The Twilight Zone*, whose very first episode was called "Where is Everybody?"[25] The story follows a fighter pilot who finds himself alone in a town, with the lights on, the radios playing, food cooking on stoves, and no one there. After looking for people with an increasing sense of hysteria, he pushes a call button, which is really a panic button that alerts the military officials who had been watching him, having placed him in an isolation booth that simulated the virtual town in order to see his fitness for being alone in space. Rod Serling – the

Figure 10.4 Low-carbon, post-pandemic life will have cleaner air, safer streets, and vegetation.

writer, producer, and narrator of *The Twilight Zone* – ends the episode with this comment: "The barrier of loneliness: The palpable, desperate need of the human animal to be with his fellow man."[26]

During the pandemic and its resultant lockdowns, many people around the world felt some of what that fighter pilot experienced. We occupied places that looked the same, physically: The buildings and cars, trees and lawns, streets and sidewalks were all still as they were prior to the pandemic. But the people were gone, locked in the isolation of our own homes, as our neighborhoods became what Serling described as The Twilight Zone: "the middle ground … between the pit of man's fears, and the summit of his knowledge."

And like that fighter pilot, we were also victims of governmental experiments. Some, like Sweden, tried to push herd immunity by not locking down, while most other countries tried various levels of social control, some of them in very organized ways, like New Zealand and South Korea, and others, like the U.S. and Brazil, in chaotic and self-contradictory ways, denying the virulence or prevalence of the disease even as the infection and death rates said otherwise. If we see the lockdowns during the pandemic as measuring our fitness for being alone in space, we did not do much better than that fighter pilot. People hit the panic button as they saw their food supplies and bank accounts dwindle and government officials, at least in some countries, intervened, opening up facilities prematurely and watching the COVID-19 infections and its viral variants spread.

Global Localization

The irony of this is that we have never had more physical separation in most parts of our cities than now. Many metropolitan areas have a lot of redundant and under-utilized space because of single-use zoning, which has left whole areas of our cities and suburbs nearly empty at different times of the day or week. This represents not just an enormous expenditure of carbon to construct buildings that sit empty much of the time, but it also necessitates an expensive and carbon-intensive transportation and parking infrastructure to accommodate the moving and storage of vehicles.

With the delivery economy moving goods rather than many people, we now face the question: What we will do with all of the infrastructure – the surface parking lots, expansive highways, and widened streets – that we thought we needed to handle a volume of vehicles we may never see again? All of the empty parking lots could become green spaces and recreational fields; structured parking could become emergency shelter or low-cost housing; and residential and commercial districts could become diverse places in which to live and work, shop and play, study and worship – all within the same buildings and blocks. Ultimately, we need to not only "think globally, act locally," as the popular phrase from the environmental movement puts it, but also to live simultaneously at both scales, physically and spatially at the local scale and digitally and temporally at the global scale.

Some cultures may deal with such simultaneity easier than others. Japanese culture, for example, has a word "dochakuka," which means global localization, to capture the idea of learning best practices from across the world and then applying that knowledge to problems occurring locally. In English, the term "glocalization" first appeared in the late 1980s to convey the idea that businesses needed to operate at a global level in terms of supply chains and to respond to local needs with products and services that can respond to community differences.[27] In the post-pandemic era, it isn't just multinational businesses that exist glocally; we all now do, and we – and the world – may be better off because of it.

Notes

1 The Nolli Map Website. http://nolli.uoregon.edu
2 John Firth, "The History of Plague – Part 1: The Three Great Pandemics," *Journal of Military and Veteran's Health*, 20(2). https://jmvh.org/article/the-history-of-plague-part-1-the-three-great-pandemics/
3 Daniel Defoe, *A Journal of the Plague Year* (EBook #376, April 3, 2020). www.gutenberg.org/files/376/376-h/376-h.htm
4 William H. Frey, "America's largest cities saw the sharpest population losses during the pandemic, new census data shows," Brookings, June 8, 2021. www.brookings.edu/research/the-largest-cities-saw-the-sharpest-population-losses-during-the-pandemic-new-census-data-shows/
5 Daniel Bortz, "How the Pandemic Is Persuading Millennials to Leave the City and Make Living in the Suburbs … Cool," *Money*, August 18, 2020. https://money.com/coronavirus-millennials-homebuying-suburbs/
6 William J. Mitchell, *City of Bits: Space, Place, and the Infobahn* (Cambridge: MIT Press, 1995). https://mitpress.mit.edu/books/city-bits
7 Andrew M. Mwenda, Alexander Stubb, Richard Florida, Sangita Reddy, et al., "100 Best-Selling Smart Cities Books of All Time," *Book Authority*, https://bookauthority.org/books/best-selling-smart-cities-books.
8 Anthony M. Townsend, *Smart Cities: Big Data, Civic Hackers, and the Quest for a New Utopia* (New York: Norton, 2014). https://wwnorton.com/books/smart-cities/about-the-book/product-details
9 "Significant Cyber Incidents," Center for Strategic and International Studies. www.csis.org/programs/strategic-technologies-program/significant-cyber-incidents
10 "Rapid Evidence Assessment: The Prevalence and Impact of Online Trolling," Center for Strategy & Evaluation Services. https://assets.publishing.service.gov.uk/government/uploads/system/uploads/attachment_data/file/973971/DCMS_REA_Online_trolling__V2.pdf
11 Tom Wheeler, "Technology, tribalism, and truth," Brookings, February 7, 2020. www.brookings.edu/blog/techtank/2020/02/07/technology-tribalism-and-truth/
12 Geoffrey West, *Scale: The Universal Laws of Life, Growth, and Death in Organisms, Cities, and Companies* (New York: Penguin, 2018).
13 Emilo Parodi, Stephen Jewkes, Sangmi Cha, Ju-min Park, "Special Report: Italy and South Korea virus outbreaks reveal disparity in deaths and tactics," Reuters, March 12, 2020. www.reuters.com/article/us-health-coronavirus-response-specialre/special-report-italy-and-south-korea-virus-outbreaks-reveal-disparity-in-deaths-and-tactics-idUSKBN20Z27P
14 "Country comparison, South Korea vs United States," Country Economy. https://countryeconomy.com/countries/compare/south-korea/usa?sc=XE92
15 Niall McCarthy, "How US Healthcare Spending Per Capita Compares with Other Countries," *Forbes*, August 8, 2019. www.forbes.com/sites/niallmccarthy/2019/08/08/how-us-healthcare-spending-per-capita-compares-with-other-countries-infographic/?sh=62936bdb575d

16 "Study: Urban Density not Linked to Coronavirus Infection Rates – and Is Linked to Lower COVID-10 Death Rates," John Hopkins, June 18, 2020. www.jhsph.edu/news/news-releases/2020/urban-density-not-linked-to-higher-coronavirus-infection-rates-and-is-linked-to-lower-covid-19-death-rates.html

17 Emily Badger, "Covid Didn't Kill Cities. Why Was That Prophecy So Alluring?" *New York Times*, July 12, 2021. www.nytimes.com/2021/07/12/upshot/covid-cities-predictions-wrong.html

18 Paulina Villegas, "Fauci Says Wearing Masks Could Become Seasonal Following the Pandemic," *Washington Post*, May 9, 2021. www.washingtonpost.com/health/2021/05/09/fauci-covid-masks-seasonal-pandemic/

19 Skip Descant, "As Transit Reopens, Long-Term Impacts of COVID-19 Unknown," *Government Technology*, June 8, 2020. www.govtech.com/fs/transportation/as-transit-re-opens-long-term-impacts-of-covid-19-unknown.html

20 "The Impact of the COVID-19 Pandemic on Public Transit Funding Needs in the U.S.," American Public Transportation Association, January 27, 2021. www.apta.com/wp-content/uploads/APTA-COVID-19-Funding-Impact-2021-01-27.pdf

21 "Frequency of Public Transit Use in the United States 2017," *Statista*, June 26, 2019. www.statista.com/statistics/893384/frequency-of-public-transit-use-in-the-united-states/

22 "Transit," *Infrastructure Report Card*, 2017. www.infrastructurereportcard.org/wp-content/uploads/2017/01/Transit-Final.pdf

23 Brian Peteritas, "Seoul's Transit System Service as a Model for America," *Governing*, November 29, 2012. www.governing.com/columns/transportation-and-infrastructure/col-seoul-subway-offers-lesson-in-transportation.html

24 Matt McGrath, "Coronavirus: Air Pollution and CO_2 Fall Rapidly as Virus Spreads," BBC, March 19, 2020. www.bbc.com/news/science-environment-51944780

25 "Where Is Everybody?" *Twilight Zone*, October 2, 1959. www.imdb.com/title/tt0734692/

26 Don Presnell, Marty McGee, *A Critical History of Television's The Twilight Zone, 1959–1964* (Jefferson, NC: McFarland, 2008).

27 Victor Roudometof, *Glocalization: A Critical Introduction* (New York: Routledge, 2016).

11
STREETS

Of all the effects of the COVID-19 pandemic, one of the most immediate and visible had to do with how people used streets differently, as quarantines dramatically decreased the amount of vehicular traffic. In the street outside of my house, for example, people walked in the road to socially distance while still socializing with their neighbors, the neighborhood youth set up a portable basketball backstop-and-hoop and played pick-up games in the street, and new parents a couple of houses away held a roadside celebration of their new-born child, setting up tables and chairs in the parking lane in front of their house as friends and family drove by to offer their congratulations.

Although most streets and sidewalks have since returned to their primary role of moving traffic or people, the experience during the pandemic will invariably change the way in which we see and use the public realm going forward. My neighbors did not go entirely back to their old ways. Many still walk and run in the streets, the basketball backstop is still there, and drivers seem to drive more slowly through the neighborhood than before. People took to the streets during the pandemic and seem to have taken back the streets, to some extent, since then.

Evidence of that change in how people now use the public realm lies in the recommendations of the leading street-standards organization

DOI: 10.4324/9781003198192-14

Figure 11.1 The pandemic increased the use of streets by pedestrians, bikes, and scooters.

in the U.S., the National Association of City Transportation Officials or NACTO. During the pandemic, they released a document entitled *Streets for Pandemic Response and Recovery*, which urged cities and suburbs to prioritize the ability of people to social distance; to provide space in the street not just for bikes, but also for pedestrians; and to see our streets as critical to the health, safety, and equity of the communities through which they run.[1] And the policies and design guidelines they recommended read like a tactical urbanism manifesto: encouraging pop-up parks, sidewalk expansions into former parking or travel lanes, and outright street closures.

In cities like New York people realized how much more livable the city had become during the pandemic, with streets closed to vehicles and devoted to pedestrians and other non-motorized vehicles like bikes and scooters.[2] Noise, pollution, and accidents went way down, and neighbors rediscovered the joys of walking not just along, but also in the streets. While prompted by a desire to social distance and avoid COVID-19 contamination, those behavioral changes also revealed the role that streets once played as places for people to gather as well as paths through which to move.

Letting people take back their streets did not just have psychological and epidemiological benefits. It had economic value as well. In research by a former graduate student of mine, Jessica Horstkotte, she showed how Minneapolis, which has alleys as well as streets serving most properties, could close hundreds of lane miles of side streets and turn that right-of-way over to the people and property owners along it. This happened several decades ago in the city, when it gave a street, Milwaukee Avenue, to the property owners to own and maintain. That led a once-declining area of small houses into one of the most pleasant and desirable residential districts in the city. With shared parking areas for visitors and alleys for the residents, the former street now has a planted center strip, with one narrow sidewalk and another wider one to accommodate emergency vehicles. Milwaukee Avenue showed what post-pandemic streets could be like, with pedestrians and bicyclists, parents and children, neighbors and friends able to interact without having to worry about getting run over, along the rights-of-way where they live, work, and play.

When one neighborhood heard about Jessica's research, they approached the city to turn one of their side streets into another Milwaukee Avenue, but the city said no, for a peculiar reason. Because cities receive state funding based on the number of lane miles they own, officials worried that they would lose some of that aid by turning redundant or little-used streets over to neighborhoods to maintain. The city, though, did not account for the savings it would achieve in the form of reduced road repair, replacement, sweeping, and plowing, which would compensate for the losses in state aid. With local governments already struggling to care for the 77% of the roads in the U.S. that they own, and with deferred maintenance in the U.S. at an estimated $170 billion annually, reducing the number of lane miles seems like one way to reduce the public sector's financial burden and increase the public health of their residents at the same time.[3]

Yet, as we learned during the pandemic, public health benefits too often go unmeasured. Enabling people to use streets for more than just the movement of vehicles lets neighbors get to know each other and it builds social networks that have myriad advantages when it comes to mutual aid. Another street in Minneapolis, 4th Street in the

Towerside Innovation District, offers one example of what that might look like.⁴ Although designed to accommodate cars and trucks, the street has a tree-shaded, level surface, with street furniture – including swings, tables, platforms, and steps – that encourage people to gather, linger, and inhabit both the sidewalk area as well as, when closed to traffic, the street itself. The pandemic showed how much shared streets encourage people to see the public right-of-way as theirs to care for and take care of as much as the public works department. And if cities want to empower citizens and extend their tax dollars, they should stop putting up road blocks and help residents take back their streets.

Places of Protest

Which has begun to happen anyway, whether cities cooperate or not. I live not far from where George Floyd was killed in the street by police officers.⁵ The intersection where Floyd died, 38th Street and Chicago Avenue, almost immediately became a memorial in his memory and for all of the black and brown men and women who have died at the hands of the police. The street became festooned with flowers, a mural went up above where Floyd died, and a sculptural black hand raised in protest occupied the intersection. Renamed George Floyd Square, that four-block area showed how much two otherwise ordinary streets can take on new meaning and become a destination – even a pilgrimage site – for many who cared about the events that transpired there. While the city eventually re-opened the streets, against the wishes of many people, George Floyd Square showed how the post-pandemic street can also serve as a place of remembrance as much as a place of movement.

The protests that Floyd's death triggered also occurred mainly in streets, as people occupied major traffic routes and highways around the world as an expression of their frustration against the institutionalized racism and police brutality that has existed for far too long. Some streets lent themselves to protests more than others. While straightness and width of streets helped accommodate the enormous crowds that formed during these marches, their location and destination appeared to matter more. Streets that connected or led to government buildings or those that began or ended in public gathering places seemed to attract the most attention and better serve the purposes of protesters. Thinking about streets in the post-pandemic world as primary places of protest, able to be closed off, with alternative routes for vehicular traffic, may be one of the most important changes we can make to ensure the public realm remains a place of political expression as much as one of personal transportation.

Healthy Streets

The post-pandemic street may be a place of physical activity and personal growth as well. A street called Discovery Walk,[6] in Rochester, Minnesota, has reinforced that city's identity of as "America's City for Health."[7] The street's design calls for a series of trellis structures that accept exercise-related attachments, benches that encourage people to occupy them in various ways, jet-pools that prompt children and adults to play, and a tree canopy that shades those out for a walk between the Mayo Clinic's core buildings and the new research buildings in Discovery Square. Discovery Walk accommodates cars, but they recede in importance as pedestrians and bicyclists become the street's dominant occupants. If we want to improve public health in the post-pandemic era, streets need to serve many forms of movement, encouraging people to not just sit in a vehicle, but also walk, run, roll, jump, and swing.

Such streets don't happen without a lot of interaction with community members and negotiation on the part of those in control of our public realm: the staff and public officials at various levels of

Figure 11.2 Post-pandemic streets will be safer, with more diverse uses and travel modes.

government. In Egypt, the Cairo Lab for Urban Studies, Training & Environmental Research (CLUSTER) has shown how much the streets and alleys of the future require community engagement of myriad types.[8] In their creation of the Kodak Passageway, CLUSTER re-imagined two, mostly paved, pedestrian routes through downtown Cairo as a green space with shade trees, planted raingardens, benches that double as light fixtures, and pavers that let water infiltrate into the soil below.[9] To help achieve that installation, they held a design workshop, involving a diversity of people who used the passageways or who lived or worked along them, out of which came the idea of thinking of these narrow streets as pedestrian parks. Turning that design idea into a physical reality took a lot of negotiation with city officials who, for example, did not want the benches, for fear of loitering, but who finally accepted them when redefined as street lighting. Projects like this show how the very act of creating streets can build community, suggesting that in the post-pandemic era, street design may be as much as about process as the final product, as much about the trip as the destination.

In the process, we need to learn – or relearn – what makes some streets more appealing than others, urging us to walk and talk rather than ride and drive. The Chinese scholar, Zhehao Zhang, has delved into the reasons why some streets are more walkable than others, based on a number of factors.[10] It turns out that the greater the density of the population and access to public transportation, the greater the number of intersections and destinations within a half mile distance, and the greater the amount of street furniture and other amenities along the way, the more likely we will walk rather than get in a car. While these factors have long favored walkability, the pandemic fueled some of them in ways that might not have seemed possible before COVID-19. For example, as the pandemic prevented people from gathering indoors, many people brought chairs and tables outside in order to socialize. That increase in the amount of street furniture drew more people to want to use it, which increased the chances of seeing and interacting with others and the likelihood that other indoor activities made their way outdoors in a kind of virtuous cycle.

While some of that activity returned indoors, especially with changes in the seasons, the idea of human occupation of streets formerly devoted exclusively to cars, trucks, and buses, will remain to some extent, in part because it makes economic as well as societal sense. Consider the impact that Walk Score has had on how we see and value the physical world.[11] Walk Score ranks houses and apartments in over 10,000 neighborhoods in over 2,800 cities in the U.S., Canada, and Australia according to the accessibility of public transit, the proximity of essential services, and the availability of sidewalks and other pedestrian and bike infrastructure. The scores do not address qualitative issues that can affect our desire to walk; we might not walk, for example, up a high hill or down a busy road or along an unlit street at night, even if our destination remains relatively close. Still, research has shown that Walk Score increases the value of real estate in almost all of the cities studied.[12] By ranking the walkability of communities, this metric helps justify investments in more pedestrian and bike facilities on the part of the public sector as a way to increase the value of private property and with it, property taxes.

Autonomous Vehicle Streets

The automation that has affected how we work in the post-pandemic era will also affect our streets. As computer-controlled machines take over boring, repetitive, and dangerous jobs that most people are neither good at nor eager to do, this includes the driving of vehicles, a boring, repetitive, and dangerous task if there ever was one. Driverless cars or autonomous vehicles will transform our transportation system and with it, the public right-of-way. At the Minnesota Design Center, we have studied the impact of autonomous vehicles on our streets and roadways as part of a three-year National Science Foundation grant.[13] Roughly 94% of car accidents happen as a result of driver errors: 41% of which stem from recognition errors, 33% from decision errors, 11% from performance errors, and 7% from simply falling asleep at the wheel.[14] Those errors arise from the lethargy, inattentiveness, or riskiness that driving can induce in even the most careful drivers.

A little more than one hundred years ago, we took an animal out of our transportation system – horses – and replaced them with the much greater horsepower of automobiles and trucks, which were safer than dealing with horses, cheaper than stabling horses, and cleaner at least in terms of the pollution that horse manure created. A hundred years later, we are in the process of removing another animal from our transportation system – us – for much the same reason. Self-driving or autonomous vehicles are safer, cheaper, and cleaner than what we drive now and they will become a major part of how most of us move around in the post-pandemic world.

Safer than current cars and trucks, autonomous vehicles utilize systems – radar, lidar, and other sensors – long used in the aerospace industry. These technologies have evolved to such an extent that they are now very effective in preventing collisions, as we know from airline accidents, which are almost always the result of pilot error during takeoff or landing. With well over 90% of car accidents caused by driver error, bringing these aerospace technologies into ground-based vehicles will greatly reduce injuries and deaths on our roads.

Cheaper than owning a car or truck, autonomous vehicles are also part of a shift in the auto industry toward the provision of mobility services, where companies will make vehicles and instead of selling them to us, will offer us mobility on-demand. It remains to be seen whether mobility services follow a fee-for-service model like the current ride-sharing companies, or a subscriber-based model as some car companies have begun to do, or an advertiser-based model, which would make the ride itself free. But whatever model becomes most common, all would offer mobility at a much lower cost than what it takes to own and operate a car or truck now.

Cleaner than most of the cars and trucks we drive, autonomous vehicles will also be powered by electricity or fuel cells, which will

Figure 11.3 Shared autonomous vehicles will transform every street, alley, and parking lot.

greatly reduce air and noise pollution. And the reason for this is simple. If the car companies are going to own and operate the vehicles as part of their mobility services, they want technology that is inexpensively operated and easily maintained, which is the case for electric cars and trucks.

While many people speak of their love of cars – as many people did their horses a hundred years ago – the fact that autonomous vehicles offer greater safety and efficiency at a much lower cost to consumers makes the economics of the driverless, mobility service revolution in our transportation system unstoppable. This does not mean that driven vehicles will disappear. Like the riding of horses, the driving of automobiles will continue to occur, mostly in rural areas for reasons of safety and liability. Driving cars will also become what it once was at the beginning of the 20th century: an expensive hobby. The expense will come largely from high insurance rates, which increase as the insured pool of high-risk drivers shrinks as more people switch to mobility services. And like stabling horses, storing cars will typically happen outside of urban and suburban areas. Eventually, drivers will be banned from metropolitan areas except for the police and other emergency personnel, who will be able to continue driving vehicles in the city, just as they are allowed to ride horses there.

The transition from a horse-drawn transportation system to a horse-powered one took roughly two decades in the early 20th century, where old photos show almost no cars on urban streets in the early 1900s and almost no horse-drawn vehicles there by the early 1920s. The transition from driven vehicles to autonomous vehicles may take that long, or less time, given the greater speed with which the 21st-century economy operates and the significant profits that car companies will realize as they shift from being primarily goods-producing to service-providing businesses.

Changing Infrastructure

What changed in the early 20th century was not just the type of vehicles on our roads, but the nature of the roads themselves. As cities, suburbs, and small towns went from accommodating horses and horse-drawn vehicles to accommodating drivers and driven vehicles, most roads went from having a dirt and gravel surface to having a surface of pavers – cobbles or paving bricks – and eventually continuous pavement of concrete or asphalt. The hydrology of our road system also changed in the transition from horses to cars, as we went from pervious surfaces, with swales or ditches handling major rain events, to impervious surfaces, with curbs and gutters channeling stormwater to below-grade sewers and eventually to our waterways.

Autonomous vehicles will involve an equally dramatic change in our roadway infrastructure. Unlike drivers who tend to wander within their lanes as they drive and so require a continuously paved road surface to accommodate that movement, driverless cars maintain the same path, with little or no wander as they move down a roadway. Research has shown that the precision of their movement leads to repetitive wear on the road surface, rutting softer materials like gravel or asphalt relatively quickly, which suggests that autonomous vehicles will require a different kind of road surface than that required by driven vehicles.[15]

Autonomous-vehicle-ready streets will likely combine aspects of both the horse-drawn carriage road, with its pervious surface, and the horse-powered car or truck road, with its impervious surface. To handle the repetitive wear of precisely guided autonomous vehicles, roadways will need wear-resistant tracks or grade beams with high-strength concrete to ensure greater longevity. Those tracks will enable the remainder of the road surface to be pervious, allowing ground cover to grow and stormwater to percolate into the road bed and recharge the aquifers below.

This may, in turn, allow cities to abandon their expensive and environmentally damaging stormwater sewer system, a savings that could be used to help pay for the new infrastructure. For large storm events, former surface parking lots – many of which will no longer be needed as the demand for parking greatly diminishes in a mobility service future – can become constructed wetlands and retention ponds that can hold large amounts of rainwater when necessary.

The narrowing and greening of autonomous vehicle streets will enable them to accommodate a much wider range of activities than what most streets now allow on much wider sidewalks and bike lanes.

Activities like play grounds, community gardens, and pop-up retail, that we typically do not think of as street friendly because of the danger drivers present to pedestrians and bicyclists, will likely emerge as a result of this transformation in our transportation system. The pandemic gave us a taste of what those uses of the street might be like, as the economic shutdown largely cleared street of cars and enabled those other activities to occur. The vastly safer performance of autonomous vehicles suggests that such non-transportation-related functions will begin to repopulate our streets as the post-pandemic era continues to evolve. Revolutions often begin in the streets, and the revolution in how we use streets has already begun.

Parking Prospects

A revolution in parking has also already begun. Vehicles spend over 90% of the time parked and as one of the more expensive possessions in most households, it makes no sense to have such high-cost assets remaining unused for so long. It also makes no sense to devote so

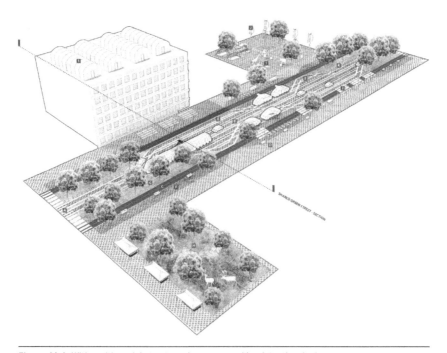

Figure 11.4 With multi-model streets and no more parking lots, the city becomes greener.

much valuable real estate to storing those assets. At least in the U.S., parking takes up an enormous amount of land, by some estimates, equivalent to the size of states like Connecticut and Vermont,[16] with some cities giving roughly 25% of their downtown land area over to surface parking.[17]

Mobility services will drastically reduce the need for such wasteful land use, as people get dropped off and picked up where they are rather than needing to park their own cars within walking distance of their destinations. What cities do with that amount of land becoming available for other uses remains one of the questions – and opportunities – of the post-pandemic city. Most surface parking lots occur on private property, often zoned for commercial or industrial uses, and so cities will need to incentivize the owners to seek higher and better uses for that land. Some places have started to use tax strategies to motivate that change, creating an incentive for landowners to optimize their property's value.[18] But cities can also use zoning policies to encourage property owners to use land once used for parking to meet other unmet needs of a municipality, from wetlands that can handle major rain events to affordable housing that can address the shortage of low-cost shelter in so many communities.

Parking lots can also help meet the increasing demand for curb space, since in a mobility service future, people will want to be picked up and dropped off close to where they want to go – or where they want their packages to go. Instead of repetitive striping across a continuously paved surface, former parking lots might provide undulating curbs, like the fingers in a hand, to maximize the curb's perimeter and to enable people to walk unimpeded to and from their destinations. This will require much less surface area than parking does now, which will provide ample space for green space, which will have not just environmental benefits, but social and psychological ones as well, as we substitute parks for parked cars.

Start-Up Streets

We may also see former parking lots take on old tasks in new ways. Parking lots prior to the pandemic often hosted pop-up markets for everything from farmers produce in the summer to Christmas trees in the winter, but the cooler and greener versions of those spaces may play an even more central economic role. The economist, Tyler Cowen, wrote about the "walking dead" businesses that he saw during the pandemic, "doomed by COVID-19."[19] He observed that "according to one estimate, about half of small businesses will be out of cash within a month, and many of them will close," as a result of "the disappearance of ... ghost capital," which helped explain why "42 percent of recent layoffs will result in permanent job loss," according to a University of Chicago report, affecting about 14 million people whose previous places of employment either went out of business or permanently downsized their staff.[20] The economic ghosts produced by the pandemic will haunt us all for years – maybe decades – to come.

Cowen predicted that "Civic spaces will repopulate as commercial ones depopulate, giving urban landscapes a confusing feel" – or a hopeful one, depending upon one's perspective. Cowen was right: most commercial districts and downtown areas had fewer stores after the pandemic, but what about the repopulation of civic spaces that Cowen described? In many parts of the world, commerce occurs not just in rented storefronts or retail establishments, but also in the streets, along sidewalks, and across public open spaces, with people bantering and bargaining as they shop. Such things rarely occur in the U.S., in part because the public sector frequently equates that with loitering and panhandling, with laws enacted to prohibit it. But with many people still unemployed after the pandemic and whose only hope for work will be what they can create for themselves, governments need to rethink their prohibitions against pop-up commerce and allow the repopulation of civic spaces with small-scale entrepreneurial activity. Repurposed parking lots provide ideal places for such activity, providing space for people trying to restart their lives and to avoid becoming one of the economy's walking dead.

Blue Zone Streets

Post-pandemic streets and parking lots may also aid our physical as much as our social and economic health, becoming "blue zones" as much as green ones. Dan Buettner, the health writer, coined the term to describe places around the world in which people live longer, happier, and healthier lives.[21] Buettner has identified five factors that he sees as key to longevity: having purpose, eating a mostly plant-based diet, being in the "right community" and the "right tribe," and moving "naturally." Some of those factors seem obvious, like having a reason to live, being able to follow a passion, and leading a physically active life, including a lot of walking as part of daily routines. And for vegetarians, Buettner's plea to eat a mostly plant-based diet has environmental benefits as well as physical and ethical ones.

But the part about the "right community" and "right tribe" appears less evident and less obviously something that we can each achieve. By "right community," he means living in a place that is "pro-social," "pro-pedestrian," and "pro-plants": places that encourage walking, enable casual conversations with neighbors, and welcome gardening and growing food as a part of the everyday landscape. And by "right tribe," he means having friends and family who are "engaged," "active," and "dependable." Where and how we live and who we live with or near, in other words, matters in terms of how long – and how well – we live. This seems particularly pertinent to a post-pandemic era. Pandemics reveal weaknesses in our public health system, but they also sensitize us to the importance of taking care of our own health and that of those we care about.

Buettner is a committed bicyclist – every time I have met with him, he came by bike – and the provision of connected bike lanes and wider sidewalks in post-pandemic streets could help foster the "pro-social" and "pro-pedestrian" ethic that will help us all have a better chance of leading longer lives. And the added green space in former parking lots could help advance Buettner's "pro-plants" point. In addition to hosting farmers markets, such open spaces could become places for serious urban agriculture and considerable community gardening. Growing food not just in rural areas, but also in our cities and suburbs can improve the quality of locally available food and, as Buettner observes, also slow down our heart rate as we watch nature take its course and speed up our socializing as we chat with those who grow what we eat.

Which leads to what may be the most important aspect of leading a good life: being in the "right tribe," as Buettner puts it. Tribalism, as behavioral scientist Stevan E. Hobfoll notes, has become a pernicious problem in today's socially mediated world, where people can pick their "tribes" based on their prejudices toward any number of subjects.[22] But Buettner recognizes that dark side of tribalism by emphasizing the word "right." Picking the right tribe, versus the wrong one, makes all the difference, something that we have all seen in the protests around the world that have occurred since George Floyd's murder by the Minneapolis police. In the wake of that event, the right tribes – the active, engaged, and dependable ones – took part in peaceful protests in the streets, mainly during the day and mostly within with the legal limits placed on them. The wrong tribes mostly came out at night to burn buildings, loot stores, and torch cars. Being a part of the "right tribe," means doing right, as much as possible, for the greatest number of others – humans and non-humans alike – and in the post-pandemic world, that means engaging in as much healthy personal and social behavior as possible.

Rethinking Highways

The opportunities to do so extend even beyond streets and parking lots. Highways, too, will get reconsidered and possibly removed as a result of autonomous vehicles and mobility services. Highway construction through poorer sections of cities and suburbs, often dividing communities of color, represented one of the great atrocities of 20th-century planning in the U.S. and other countries as well. In my city, interstate highway 94, mostly funded by the Federal government, took out over 100 blocks of residential and commercial real estate, running right through St. Paul's predominantly African American Rondo neighborhood, which had long thrived despite its residents' struggles to gain access to capital because of redlining on the part of banks.

The construction of I-94, dividing the Rondo neighborhood, happened despite the urging of St. Paul's city planner, George Herrold, who, as early as 1945, proposed routing the highway on an elevated path over existing railroad lines to prevent the disruption of neighborhoods.[23] Many decades later, I-94 now needs major repairs, presenting drivers with the prospect of years of delay and even greater traffic congestion as that road work occurs, which suggests that we might want to revisit proposals like those of George Herrold. The public sector could save people years of sitting in traffic by taking up Herrold's idea of building an autonomous-vehicle-ready highway, elevated above the railyards, and then filling in the old I-94 highway trench, selling the land to partly pay for the new road, and enabling the creation of the parks and recreational fields, the affordable housing, and business opportunities that the community wants and needs.

Similar opportunities exist in cities across the U.S. and the time has come to rethink the decisions on the part of city leaders and highway engineers in the post-World War II era. We need to do so, not only as part of the reckoning with racism that prompted some of those decisions, but also as our transportation system moves to mobility services. Because highways are often some of the most congested roads in a region, autonomous vehicles tend to avoid them, able to move much more efficiently through urban and suburban side streets with technology that lets the vehicles know where open roads exist.[24] Which suggests that, rather than retain existing highways or even build new ones, we might ask if we need them anymore, and given the negative impacts that they have on those who live near them, if we want them either.

Figure 11.5 Covering highways creates opportunities for parks and affordable housing.

Rewilding Streets

And we might think about more than just the people who live near highways. During the pandemic, my neighborhood saw not only people take to the streets, but other animals as well, from wild turkeys strutting down the road during the day to foxes, racoons, and rabbits darting across the street at night. Watching those animals reminded me of Alan Weisman's book, *The World Without Us*, which invited readers to ask: What would happen if people suddenly vanished from the planet?[25] Weisman's thought experiment had some surprising results, such as the speed with which buildings and highways crumble when not maintained and the degree to which cities disappear under the onslaught of nature.

When I first read Weisman's book, I wondered: What might create the conditions that Weisman imagined? I thought of the neutron bomb, a weapon that can release enough radiation to kill people without the blast to level buildings. I did not think, at the time, that a virus could have the same effect, at least in the short term: clearing the streets of cars and letting animals repopulate what was once theirs. Weisman's book reminded me of how fragile we are as a species and how ephemeral are the products of our civilizations, and it makes a convincing case for how well the world will do without us: how many plant and animal communities would recover and thrive along our former streets. While the coronavirus offered us a lesson in public health, it also provided us with a lesson in humility, one that we humans have long needed to learn.

Notes

1 "Streets for Pandemic Response & Recovery," National Association of City Transportation Officials. https://nacto.org/publication/streets-for-pandemic-response-recovery/

2 Winnie Hu, Nate Schweber, "Will Cars Rule the Roads in Post-Pandemic New York?" *New York Times*, August 10, 2020. www.nytimes.com/2020/08/10/nyregion/nyc-streets-parking-dining-busways.html

3 R. Richard Geddes, Thomas J. Madison, Jr. "Fixing America's Roads & Bridges: The Path Forward," Committee for Economic Development of The Conference Board. www.ced.org/pdf/TCB-CED-Fixing-Americas-Roads-and-Bridges.pdf

4 Thomas Fisher, "At the Corner of 4th and Innovation," *Star Tribune*, December 19, 2015. www.startribune.com/streetscapes-at-the-corner-of-4th-and-innovation/362944451/

5 Dara Moskowitz Grumdahl, "38th and Chicago: Holy Ground," *MSP Magazine*, August 23, 2020. https://mspmag.com/arts-and-culture/38th-and-chicago/

6 "Discovery Walk," Coen + Partners. www.coenpartners.com/discovery-walk

7 Destination Medical Center. https://dmc.mn/

8 Cairo Lab for Urban Studies, Training & Environmental Research. https://clustercairo.org/

9 Ibid. https://clustercairo.org/2014/08/03/kodak_passageway/

10 Zhehao Zhang, Thomas Fisher, Fang Feng, "Assessing the Rationality and Walkability of Campus Layouts," *Sustainability*, 12(23), December 2020. www.mdpi.com/2071-1050/12/23/10116

11 Walk Score. www.walkscore.com/

12 Joe Cortright, "Walking the Walk, How Walkability Raises Home Values in U.S. Cities," *CEOs for Cities*, August 2009. https://nacto.org/docs/usdg/walking_the_walk_cortright.pdf

13 "Smart and Connected Communities," National Science Foundation. www.nsf.gov/funding/pgm_summ.jsp?pims_id=505364

14 Traffic Safety Facts," U.S. Department of Transportation, National Highway Traffic Safety Administration. https://crashstats.nhtsa.dot.gov/Api/Public/ViewPublication/812115

15 WSB & Associates, AECOM, "MnDOT Autonomous Bus Pilot Project, Testing and Demonstration Summary," Minnesota Department of Transportation, June 2018. www.dot.state.mn.us/automated/bus/finalreport.pdf

16 Michael Kimmelman, "Paved, but Still Alive," *New York Times*, January 6, 2012. www.nytimes.com/2012/01/08/arts/design/taking-parking-lots-seriously-as-public-spaces.html

17 Charlie Gardner, "We Are the 25%: Looking at Street Area Percentages and Surface Parking," *Old Urbanist*, December 12, 2011. https://oldurbanist.blogspot.com/2011/12/we-are-25-looking-at-street-area.html

18 Todd Litman, "Parking Taxes," Victoria Transport Policy Institute, August 29, 2013. www.vtpi.org/parking_tax.pdf

19 Tyler Cowen, "We're Surrounded by the Walking Dead," *Bloomberg*, May 22, 2020. www.startribune.com/we-re-surrounded-by-the-walking-dead/570706852/

20 Terina Allen, "3 Bitter Truths about the Coronavirus Job Losses and the Economy, *Forbes*, May 10, 2020. www.forbes.com/sites/terinaallen/2020/05/10/3-bitter-truths-about-the-coronavirus-job-losses-and-the-economy/?sh=6ffbfb567f92

21 Blue Zones. www.bluezones.com/

22 Stevan E. Hobfoll, *Tribalism: The Evolutionary Origins of Fear Politics* (New York: Macmillan, 2018).

23 Matt Reicher, "The Birth of a Metro Highway (Interstate 94)" *Reconnect Rondo*, September 10, 2013. https://reconnectrondo.com/the-birth-of-a-metro-highway-interstate-94/

24 Sam Lubell, "Here's How Self-Driving Cars Will Transform your City," *Wired*, October 21, 2016. www.wired.com/2016/10/heres-self-driving-cars-will-transform-city/

25 Alan Weisman, *The World Without Us* (New York: St. Martin Press, 2007).

12
COMMUNITIES

Pandemics force us to ask some fundamental questions about our relationships: Who should I quarantine with? Who can I depend on if I need help? Who can I trust in order to remain safe? Plagues, in other words, confront us not only with our own mortality, but also with the question of who constitutes our community, be they family or friends. Pandemics also force us to ask equally basic questions about what matters most to us: What do I need while quarantining? What don't I need and did I ever really need it? What can I live without? Pandemics are heavy events that weigh on us and worry us, but they are also opportunities for us to lighten our load, so to speak, and live more intentionally with who and what we really care about.

That came to mind as I watched the movie *Nomadland* in the middle of the COVID-19 pandemic. It won an Academy Award for the best picture of 2020, with its lead character, Francis McDormand, winning for best actress, and its director, Chloé Zhao, for best director.[1] The movie revolves around the life of a recently widowed woman, Fern, and her experiences as she escapes her past and finds a new community among people who live nomadically out of their vans.

That existence may seem strange to many of those who saw the movie or who read Jessica Bruder's 2017 book by that same name.[2] Most people do not live in vans in mobile communities, although

DOI: 10.4324/9781003198192-15

during the pandemic, sales of recreational vehicles and camping equipment grew rapidly, as many people saw this as a way to have a socially distanced holiday.[3] But the life depicted in *Nomadland* recalls not just an odd, but also a very old way of life and one that might become more common for more people in a post-pandemic era of social, economic, and environmental disruptions.

To get a sense of how ancient Fern's nomadic life really is, consider this: If I stretch out my arms, a span of about 70 inches, and if that distance equals the roughly 200,000-year existence of human beings as a species on this planet, then the length of my two arms and shoulders would equal the amount of time humanity lived nomadically, in small communities occupying temporary or mobile shelter. The length of my index finger would equal the roughly 10,000 years that people have lived in permanent settlements, and the very tip of the finger, the few hundred years that people have occupied modern cities.

In other words, the way in which many people live, in permanent buildings, in cities, suburbs or towns, with varying degrees of access to modern technology, is a very recent phenomenon in human history. For 95% of our time as a species on this planet, humanity lived more

Figure 12.1 A digitally enabled life is a nomadic one, recalling how we lived most of our history.

like Fern, moving in relatively small caravans of people, in search of sustenance, livelihood, and land. Nomadic humans mostly lived with those who they cared for and who cared about them, and they kept only the things that mattered the most to them, needing to travel lightly as they moved from place to place. This was not an easy life, as the caravan community in *Nomadland* demonstrates, but it is also a life that is increasingly possible because of modern communication and transportation technology. Digital connectedness has enabled physical freedom as never before.

Not that many people will choose to live like Fern. Many, perhaps most, will choose to remain rooted in a place, in permanent buildings, filled with personal possessions. But some people will make – or be forced to make – a different choice, and live more lightly and even nomadically, with the aid of mobile digital devices, wireless internet connections, and diverse forms of transportation and shelter. In the post-pandemic era, we have moved into a new hybrid form of human existence, in other words, in which many people now have a choice of living as humanity did for the last 10,000 years or as our ancestors did for the previous 190,000 years.

While the enabling technology to make that possible has evolved over many decades, it took the pandemic to drive home the profound change this represents. As most of the human population quarantined to varying degrees in different parts of the world, we experienced what it means to have a choice of staying in place or taking to the road. Pandemics, in a sense, represent what ecologists Stephen Jay Gould and Niles Eldridge first called "punctuated equilibrium," in which periods of relative statis give way to rapid, even sudden, changes, often the result of a major external event or an inherited genetic trait that prompts the change.[4]

The COVID-19 pandemic provided such a prompt. While companies had developed lightweight, widely accessible, mobile, digital technology for many decades prior to the pandemic, such technology remained something that we mostly used inside the fixed-in-place buildings and permanent settlements that most people occupied at various points of the day or week: homes, offices, schools, stores, and the like. That disjunction between mobile technology being used in immobile settings did not bother most people or even strike most of us as odd. After all, the history of technology is full of examples – from electric lights that initially looked like gas lanterns to cars that at first mimicked horse-drawn buggies – of new inventions fitting into what is already familiar to us. The user interface in a lot of digital technology did the same, with virtual files, folders, and trashcans echoing their physical equivalents in the standard office.

The pandemic helped us reconcile those digital and physical realities. As most of us quarantined at home, we experienced the truly radical implications of mobile, digital technology. We saw how much could get done – and get delivered – from almost anywhere, as long as we had a digital device and a decent Internet connection; and while most of us remained in place during the pandemic, we could at least see how to lead a nomadic life, able to live almost anywhere and take what we needed with us, and how little physical stuff we actually needed. That might help explain why *Nomadland* had so much resonance for so many people during the pandemic. We could see ourselves as Fern, if only in our imagination.

The New Nomads

To those of us who live in houses and who have a lot of possessions, a technology driven version of an ancient, nomadic existence may seem odd or even outlandish. But plenty of data suggests otherwise. For instance, the business world has seen the rise of "career nomads," people with marketable skills who move from job to job or even from one industry to another with great frequency.[5] That once required that employees physically move, which dampened the desire to make such shifts in the past. But in the era of remote work, where an employee's physical location matters very little, the ability of people to change jobs without having to change locations makes career nomadism much more appealing, at least to those who have some of the character traits that define nomads: tolerance for ambiguity, curiosity, and openness to differences.

Many people, of course, cannot live and work remotely. But the enormous differences among housing prices in various parts of the world have made remote work more appealing – or for some, a necessity. In part because of the slowdown in residential construction and building-material production as a result of the pandemic, the demand for housing in the post-pandemic era – especially affordable housing – has rarely been greater.[6] Some of this stems from pent-up demand that built up during the pandemic, when the real estate market went into quarantine along with most buyers and sellers, but some of it also comes from the realization on the part of many people that they need more living space or a different kind of space if they are also going to be working, at least part of the week, at home. Having a house or apartment, fixed in place and that we can call our own, remains something that most people prize.

At the same time, the number of people giving up living in a house or apartment and, like Fran in *Nomadland*, living in vans or recreational vehicles has also grown. Some estimates put the number of Americans living that way at 1 million prior to the pandemic, [7] and the number has almost certainly grown, given the growth in recreational-vehicle use during and after the recent plague, with some suppliers reporting a 40% increase in sales over the previous year.[8] An even larger number of people call themselves "digital nomads," who live lightly and carry few possessions with them. Some estimates put that number at 4.8 million with as many as 17 million people reporting they would want to live that way someday.[9] And an even larger number – almost 80 million worldwide – live nomadically and mostly involuntarily as refugees, escaping conflicts in their native lands and moving to other countries in search for safety and a better life.[10]

There is surely some overlap among these types of nomads. Some digital nomads no doubt live in their own vehicles and as the book *Nomadland* documents, some van-dwellers work remotely. Still others have taken to the road to escape difficult situations at home, as they try to survive in America in the 21st century, as the subtitle of the book puts it. However, there seems to be as much diversity among modern nomads as we can find in other housing markets. Vehicle dwellers, for obvious reasons, almost never cross an ocean, while digital nomads tend to move among global cities, evident in the ratings of various urban locations as the best places for a mobile workforce to live.[11]

Meanwhile, refugees have few possessions and little technology, with one exception: one study found that, among global refugees, over 70% have cellphones.[12] But unlike other nomads, those escaping to other countries for political, economic, or environmental reasons, often have little choice as to where they will go, dependent as they are upon government resettlement policies.[13]

That mix of reasons aligns with the long history of human nomadism. Nomads have traditionally moved to new territory for at least three reasons: seeking new pasture for the animals they shepherd, pursuing markets for the crafts they produce, or following the movement of animal herds that they hunted.[14] In many ways, the new nomads have similar reasons. Recreational nomads search for greener pastures, digital nomads seek productive activities, and political and environmental refugees hunt for a better life.

While many people will continue to live in houses and residential buildings for the foreseeable future, the rise of technology supported nomadic living suggests that people will have more choice in how and where they live than in the past. Prior to the pandemic, many people tended to describe anyone who did not occupy permanent shelter as "homeless," reflecting the assumption of many of those who live in houses and apartments that everyone else should have – and want – the same for themselves. This is particularly hypocritical when urban and suburban communities either ignore or prohibit camping on the part of people who are experiencing homelessness, even as those same community members may go camping on the weekends themselves.

The post-pandemic era may flip those assumptions on their head. The rise of the sharing economy, in which two-fifths of the American workforce, for example, receives all or part of its income from non-full-time jobs, suggests that a sizable number of people will be looking for more flexible or temporary living arrangements, with the ability to move at almost a moment's notice.[15] Traditional home ownership or long-term leases are increasingly at odds with how a growing number of people may want to live, and communities that outlaw short-term or other unconventional ways of living may find themselves at a real competitive disadvantage.

The barriers that many communities have raised against those who want to live in ways out of the norm also recalls the redlining that occurred in many U.S. cities in the 20th century. No longer allowed to discriminate based on race, religion, ethnicity, or sexual orientation, many communities now use zoning codes to keep out people they do not want in their city. The requirements for permanent foundations and the minimum unit sizes, heights, and setbacks described in these codes are all ways of excluding people who do not fit some norm, although this has also backfired on communities, who have made it difficult for all residents to have access to affordable housing. The "missing middle" of housing has largely disappeared in many municipalities as a result.[16]

Zoning, at least in the U.S., did not start this way. The earliest zoning codes in the 20th century focused more on ensuring that buildings did not block sunlight from reaching the streets, in the case of New York City, or in the case of Los Angles, that industrial activities remained safely separate from all the other land uses, which had very few other constraints placed upon them.[17] Zoning in the U.S. once had the character that zoning still has today in Japan, where municipalities typically separate nuisance uses like heavy industry into their own area, but then allow almost everything else to occur everywhere else, in a rich mix of residential, commercial, retail, and institutional uses.[18] Nor do most Japanese codes specify minimum unit sizes or the mix of uses inside buildings, making property rights real and not just empty political rhetoric.

Japan's inclusive zoning will serve it well in the post-pandemic era. It allows people to live and work how they want and largely where they want, and it has created a lot more affordable choices for people than the exclusionary practices in countries like the U.S. In an era in which living lightly, minimally, and affordably has become a more popular choice for many people, the exclusionary zoning practices in many American cities will only send a signal to especially younger people that they are not welcome, which is not a strategy for success.

Such exclusionary practices also pit urban communities against rural ones. Take camping, for example. People can readily do it in rural areas of the U.S., with whole industries aimed at supplying their equipment and accommodating their needs. But when the same activity happens in urban or suburban locations, it becomes illegal and is viewed by many regulators as a threat to public health and safety, despite the much greater access in cities to restrooms, showers, transportation, and the like. And the same happens with other forms of housing, like recreational vehicles, where people can stay as much as they want in rural or remote areas, but face fines for staying in such vehicles in many cities and towns.

In the post-pandemic world, Not-In-My-Backyard (NIMBY) prejudices become increasingly self-defeating. Now that the pandemic has proven that many people can live and work almost anywhere, the more a place puts up exclusionary barriers to people, the more people will simply go somewhere else. NIMBY may become No-one In My Backyard Anymore as people evacuate places with such attitudes, which seem fine for those who seem not to like living near other people – until they have to pay for municipal services with a shrinking tax base. Maybe then, a more inclusionary approach to zoning and more accepting view of diverse ways of living will finally become preferable to rising taxes and declining populations.

That shift in attitude has already begun to happen in some places. For several years, my colleagues and I had worked to get municipalities

Figure 12.2 People will have more choice in how and where to live and what to live with.

in our region to address the needs of people experiencing homelessness within their boundaries, something that a surprising number of community leaders, especially in the suburbs, would not even recognize as a problem. For too many, homelessness is a big-city problem and a county, state, or federal responsibility, in what can only be called municipal NIMBYism. The more comfortably housed people may be, the more uncomfortable some of them seem to be about those who are not. Nomads, for some reason, make some people mad.

So we started to look elsewhere for partners who might be interested in ending homelessness. As we worked with people living in tents, vehicles, and other forms of shelter, we learned a lot. We learned, for example, how much homelessness involved not just the lack of shelter, but also the loss of family or friend networks beyond those who they lived with on the streets. While the dominant housing-first approach to homelessness does get people into housing so that they can then work on their other challenges, simply putting a person in a housing unit can isolate them from their community and do little to improve their long-term prospects. So we started to take a "community first" approach to the problem, creating housing clusters that enable people who have experienced homelessness to live in communities with others who they care about and who care about them.[19]

Community First! Village, in Austin, Texas, first modeled the community first approach to extremely affordable housing, but its large scale, with hundreds of units, changed the nature of what constitutes a community. Our work showed that people living on the streets had a much smaller group of friends they considered to be their community, and so we decided to focus on micro versions of this approach, scaled to the size of the communities in which most people felt connected. We also learned that those who have experienced homelessness do not necessarily want conventional apartments, where they often get placed by well-meaning housing agencies. Instead, most talked about wanting simpler things: a bed, a chair, and a table; a lockable door and a storage space for their few belongings; a flexible unit that could accommodate single people as well as couples; and a community space that could house the kitchen, baths, showers, and dining hall, where the members of the community can gather.

They also wanted outdoor space that was private and safe, without feeling fenced in, with a design that would fit in with the neighborhood and not broadcast its difference from what stood around it.

We also learned that many people experiencing homelessness had had numerous encounters with the justice and healthcare systems, having been arrested for loitering or occupying public property or having been injured as a result of spending so much time on the streets and in vulnerable settings. Many in this population were also surprisingly religious, perhaps in part because having faith that things will get better is all that some of them have. With that in mind, we began to work with the health and faith communities. Both had strong reasons to address the needs of this population, one for medical and financial reasons and the other for moral and spiritual ones, and both responded enthusiastically to the idea of our working together.

Our partnership with the health community included staff from the largest public hospital in the region, an architectural firm, a local housing non-profit, and colleagues in my center and in the school where I teach. The effort we launched, called "Envision Community," revolved around the recognition that what those who lack a permanent home need is not just housing, but a group of people who they know and trust.[20] We worked with Street Voices of Change, an organization comprised of people who had experienced homelessness, and developed a community design that consisted of flexible two-room housing units around a central courtyard, with a common house in the front containing kitchen, dining, laundry, and shower facilities. The housing units are portable so that the entire community could move if they wanted to, a possibility that appealed to those who had been on the move for much of their adult lives.

The development's design violated many of Minneapolis's zoning restrictions, and so the city asked us to write a new section of the zoning code for "intentional communities," which it approved just prior to the pandemic.[21] While intended largely for people who have been chronically homeless, the ordinance would also benefit those who lost their homes during the pandemic and found themselves living on the streets, many for the first time. The pandemic showed how quickly a population can face housing instability and how quickly the public sector needs to act in order to help people who have become unwilling refugees in their own communities. And as we learned from those who have experienced chronic homelessness, people can also quickly become nomadic, moving to places where there are better conditions and opportunities. If cities want to keep their residents, rethinking what constitutes residency is a good place to start.

In the neighboring city of St. Paul and in its suburbs, we took the community first approach in another direction, working with the faith community in an effort called "Settled."[22] Most faith communities recognize their historic role in offering shelter to those who have nowhere else to go. In the U.S., faith communities have the added advantage of having the protection of the Federal "Religious Land Use and Institutionalized Persons Act" (RLUIPA), which lets faith communities sidestep zoning restrictions in order to fulfill their mission.[23] While enacted to protect churches whose buildings and properties might not comply with zoning requirements, RLUIPA also allows them to add extremely affordable housing that also may not comply with local codes.

Settled also takes a community first approach in the creation of intentional communities that it calls "sacred settlements," comprising six to eight tiny homes on land owned by religious groups, with the community able to use the kitchen, common rooms, and bathrooms in the nearby church or temple. Through the process of building the tiny homes in these settlements, with volunteer labor from the congregations, using both donated and purchased materials, Settled also builds community among different faith groups. Liberal and conservative congregations from a variety of religions have stepped forward to participate in Settled, and however much they might disagree theologically or even politically, they have come together to make homes for those in need.

While protected by a Federal-government law, these faith communities do not take government funding. That constraint, along with the relatively unskilled, volunteer labor involved in the construction, meant that the tiny homes had to be simple, low cost, and easily built, so even a small congregation and a few donors could afford to participate. The freedom from government restrictions also allowed the sacred settlements to accommodate a diversity of occupants, not just people who have been chronically homeless, but also "missionals": people who have lived in permanent housing and who choose to live among those who have not.

The missionals show that a life led with few possessions and a lot of community connections can be something we choose to do rather than something forced upon us. As people have toured the tiny homes that Settled have made, some visitors have said as much: that if they had a choice, the simple life, free of debt, would be what they would choose. Wishful thinking, perhaps, but resonant of the life our ancestors lived before humanity embarked on the experiment of living in permanent settlements.

That resonance took an ever-greater variety of forms during and after the pandemic. Data indicated that post-COVID leisure travel went up 5% over pre-pandemic levels, camping up 6%, and the interest in camping up 10%, suggesting that the pandemic led many people to consider a camping vacation who would not have done so otherwise.[24] Research also showed a significant increase in the popularity of posh forms of camping called "glamping," as people of means sought forms of recreation where they could socially distance.[25]

One example of that arose in New York City's harbor. Called Collective Governors Island, people can pay – for a substantial fee – to stay overnight in tents of various sizes and levels of luxury.[26] Although camping is illegal in New York City's parks, the Governors Island campground shows that the prohibitions against urban camping have as much to do with class prejudices as public-health or safety concerns. The more you can pay, the more you can play, at least in cities and suburbs, even though the people most in need of being able to camp are those without the income to afford places like the Governors Island campground.

The sharing economy version of glamping in the form of Airbnb has had equally perverse effects.[27] On one hand, the ability to camp out in someone else's bed and bedroom enables us to use the excess capacity that we have in the built environment more efficiently and to access a greater variety of accommodations, often at lower prices than conventional hotels. And renting out an unused bedroom can provide financial aid for people struggling to pay their own mortgages or rents. On the other hand, research shows that short-term rentals like Airbnb can drive up rental rates, housing costs, and property prices. Airbnb has become, in some sense, just another form of glamping, in which the well-off can crash where they want – be it a fancy tent or a short-term apartment – while municipalities make it ever harder for the poor to do so. It appears that many places do not mind nomads as long as they come with money.

But nomads, with a lot of money or little, mind such places, and they will avoid or move on from places where they feel unwelcome. In the post-pandemic era, no community has a lock on its residents and it will not thrive unless it creates choices for people, regardless of their income, and unless it remains open to the greater variety of ways in which people will be living and working in the future. Those communities that perpetuate inequality through zoning might look at data from past pandemics to see the consequences of that. While the poor suffer the most during pandemics, as the COVID-19 pandemic showed, inequality tends to drop, often dramatically, afterward.[28] In the hundred years after the Black Death, the amount of wealth held by the top 10% of the population dropped from 65% to under 50%, and in the roughly 50 years after the 1918 pandemic, it dropped from 90% to under 60%.

Pandemics, in other words, not only expose widespread inequality; they can also decrease it for a variety of reasons, from markets responding to post-pandemic labor shortages to governments responding to demands to rectify the inequities the pandemic revealed. If communities want workers and if municipalities want residents, one of the first things they can do is to drop arbitrary prohibitions against diverse forms of housing and a diversity of people. That is especially true in the wake of COVID-19, when people have never had more ability and more of an incentive, when facing inequality, to simply move on.

Notes

1 Brooks Barnes, Nicole Sperling, "'Nomadland' Makes History, and Anthony Hopkins, in Upset, Wins Best Actor," *New York Times*, April 25, 2021. www.nytimes.com/2021/04/25/movies/academy-awards-oscars.html

2 Jessica Bruder, *Nomadland: Surviving America in the 21st Century* (New York: Norton, 2017).

3 Dale Bowman, "Camping Gone Wild: Surge Keeps Going in RVs and Camping During the Pandemic," *Chicago Sun Times*, September 19, 2020. https://chicago.suntimes.com/2020/9/19/21446485/camping-gone-wild-surge-keeps-going-rvs-camping-during-pandemic

4 Stephen Jay Gould, Niles Eldridge, "Punctuated Equilibria: An Alternative to Phyletic Gradualism," *Models in Paleobiology* (San Francisco: Freeman Cooper, 1972), pp. 82–115.

5 "Career Nomads, More than a Temporary Asset," Korn Ferry Institute. www.kornferry.com/content/dam/kornferry/docs/article-migration/career-nomads-more-than-a-temporary-asset-v2.pdf

6 Derek Thompson, "Why You Should Wait Out the Wild Housing Market," *Atlantic*, May 2021. www.theatlantic.com/ideas/archive/2021/05/us-housing-market-records/619029/

7 "RV Statistics 2020–2021," Condor Ferries. www.condorferries.co.uk/rv-statistics

8 Lawrence Banton, "RV Sales 'Through the Roof' During COVID Pandemic," *Cheddar News*, December 30, 2020. https://cheddar.com/media/rv-sales-through-the-roof-during-covid-pandemic

9 "Digital Nomads: A Rising Workforce Trend," MBO Partners. www.mbopartners.com/state-of-independence/research-trends-digital-nomads/

10 "Figures at a Glance," UNNHCR, The UN Refugee Agency. www.unhcr.org/en-us/figures-at-a-glance.html

11 "Go Nomad," *Nomadist*. https://nomadlist.com/

12 Markus Balazs Goransson, Lotta Hultin, Magnus Mahring, "The Phone Means Everything,' Mobile Phones, Livelihoods and Social Capital among Syrian Refugees in Informal Tented Settlements in Lebanon," *Migration and Development*, April 14, 2020. www.tandfonline.com/doi/full/10.1080/21632324.2020.1746029

13 "Resettlement Services," Office of Refugee Resettlement. www.acf.hhs.gov/orr/programs/refugees

14 "Nomads – The Facts," *New Internationalist*, April 5, 1995. https://newint.org/features/1995/04/05/facts

15 Arun Sundarajan, "How the Sharing Economy Could Transform the US Housing Market," Freddie Mac. June 2018. www.borroweroffthefuture.com/content/pdfs/how-sharing-economy-could-transform-us-housing-market.pdf

16 "Missing Middle Housing," Missing Middle Housing. https://missingmiddlehousing.com/

17 Amanda Erickson, "The Birth of Zoning Codes: A History," *Bloomberg City Lab*, June 19, 2012. https://devonzuegel.com/post/north-american-vs-japanese-zoning

18 Devon Zuegel, "North American vs Japanese Zoning," *Order without Design*, May 30, 2018. https://devonzuegel.com/post/north-american-vs-japanese-zoning

19 Gabrielle Clowdus et al., "Remote Care Communities: Healthcare Housing for The Chronically Homeless," *Housing and Society*, March 2018. www.researchgate.net/publication/323530283_Remote_care_communities_healthcare_housing_for_the_chronically_homeless

20 Envision Community. https://envisioncommunitymn.org/

21 "Intentional Community Ordinance," City of Minneapolis. www.thedmna.org/wp-content/uploads/2016/05/Intentional-Community-FAQs.pdf

22 Settled. https://settled.org/

23 "Religious Land Use and Institutionalized Persons Act," United States Department of Justice. www.justice.gov/crt/religious-land-use-and-institutionalized-persons-act

24 David Lange, "Share of Camping Leisure Trips Before and After the Coronavirus (COVID-19) Pandemic in North America as of April 2020, by Traveler Type," *Statista*, April 6, 2021. www.statista.com/statistics/1155347/change-in-share-of-camping-trips-coronavirus/

25 Alex Ledsom, "The Boom in Posh Camping. People Want Wilderness Combined with Creature Comforts," *Forbes*, September 9, 2019. www.forbes.com/sites/alexledsom/2019/09/09/the-boom-in-posh-camping-people-want-wilderness-combined-with-creature-comforts/?sh=6b9c925a1c8f

26 Collective Governors Island. www.collectiveretreats.com/retreat/collective-governors-island/

27 Harriet Sherwood, "How Airbnb Took Over the World," *Guardian*, May 5, 2019. www.theguardian.com/technology/2019/may/05/airbnb-homelessness-renting-housing-accommodation-social-policy-cities-travel-leisure

28 Lizzie Wade, "From Black Death to Fatal Flu, Past Pandemics Show Why People on the Margins Suffer Most," *Science*, May 14, 2020. www.sciencemag.org/news/2020/05/black-death-fatal-flu-past-pandemics-show-why-people-margins-suffer-most

13
LANDSCAPES

One of the changes in human behavior during the pandemic involved our relationship to the landscape and to nature. People went outdoors more, in part because it offered a safer place to interact with and socially distance from others, and in part because it provided relief from our isolation during the pandemic-induced quarantines. One study found that use of parks increased over 63% with the onset of the pandemic.[1] Meanwhile, home gardening grew at record rates, with one seed company reporting a 270% increase in sales during the pandemic.[2]

With that came a change in how individuals and organizations used open space. Because of prohibitions against indoor gatherings, in just my neighborhood I saw churches holding services in parks, schools using parking lots as classrooms, and restaurants turning adjacent sidewalks and alleys into dining rooms. Outdoor space, in other words, became not just an interlude as we move from building to building, but also a destination in which we engage in activities typically conducted inside buildings. The pandemic forced us to re-imagine the role of nature in our lives and to re-visit the role the landscape once played and might play again in the future.

Maybe we need periodic reminders of this for our own good. Many years ago, I attended a conference on humanity's relationship to the

DOI: 10.4324/9781003198192-16

natural world, when one speaker, who argued that we humans were the primary predator on the planet, was corrected by another, who said: "Humans do not occupy the top of nature's pyramid. Viruses do." The recent pandemic brought that point home. Humanity may be the most powerful species on the planet because of our technology, but we also remain prey to the real predators on the planet, novel coronaviruses like COVID-19.

Had we understood the extent to which viruses prey upon us, we might have better prepared ourselves for what descended upon the world in 2020. We might have had the medical equipment, testing capacity, and vaccine production needed for an outbreak of this scale, and we might have altered our behavior and the built environment to make it easier for us to avoid the transmission of the virus once it appeared. Other species have developed protective measures against their predators as part of how they have evolved, and we might see such public health measures as the same. The sooner we stop thinking of ourselves as invincible, the sooner we will also become less vulnerable.

In this, we have much to learn not only from other species, but from indigenous human communities. While indigenous populations did not have modern medicine to protect them against novel disease, they did live in more physically active ways, in less polluted natural environments, and among those who shared their immunities. Indeed, many of the activities that we now do indoors – working, learning, and worshipping, for example – occurred outdoors, in nature, for most indigenous communities, most of the time. While doing such things in buildings has certainly increased human comfort, privacy, and security, the pandemic reminded us of the infection risks that can occur when sharing indoor space with other people. Nature may be the source of zoonotic disease, but it is also offers some of the best protection against it.

Many indigenous languages have that idea embedded in them. I have worked with two colleagues, Jessica Hellman and Ekene Ijeoma, on a proposal for a district undergoing redevelopment near my university. We proposed using Dakota words to identify the streets and buildings in the district, in recognition of the Dakota land upon which it stands. The project emerged out of a conviction that we have much to learn from indigenous people about their relationship with the natural world, an especially urgent lesson, given the dire consequence of climate change and the need to re-imagine modern society's treatment of nature. We intend to work with the Dakota community in this renaming effort, not only to increase interest in the Dakota language, but also to show how that language conveys a worldview that seems particularly pertinent now.

The Dakota people view the natural world as something sacred, that should be approached with reverence and treated with respect. As a result, many Dakota names for people and places identify their relationship to the land or to natural features of the landscape. In Dakota, for example, Mnisota – the origin of the name of Minnesota – means "cloudy or sky-tinted water."[3] The language drew upon nature not just for names, but also as a way to connect its tribal members to the landscapes they occupied. Understanding and appreciating a language, though, is one thing; living the life enabled by that language is something entirely different and much more difficult.

Which is why we should not waste what we have had a taste of during the pandemic. It forced us to live in more indigenous ways, so to speak: to spend much more time living and working, recreating and relaxing, and worshipping and learning in nature. And now, in the wake of the pandemic, we need to ask: What would it take for us to continue to do so? How might more outdoor living, in a more symbiotic relationship with nature, become the norm rather than a short-term response to a black-swan event? To answer such questions, let's engage in a thought experiment.

Several years ago, I attended a conference near where the French explorer, Samuel de Champlain, landed in 1604 in what was then called Acadia, now Nova Scotia, in Canada.[4] I went to that French landing site, having also visited the location where the English established their first settlement in Jamestown in 1607, and where the Spanish created St. Augustine in 1565. All three places marked the location where Europeans invaded a continent already occupied by a wide range of indigenous people, with not just exploration, but also the exploitation of land and the extraction of resources in mind.[5]

Yet, of the three invading nations – the French, English, and Spanish – each acted differently, at least initially, toward the land and its people.

Historians continue to parse those differences: private interests largely paid for and led the English invasion, for example, while the French and Spanish governments sponsored their invasions. But those nations sorted out in another way when it came to how they interacted with the indigenous people and how they viewed the landscape. The English and, to a somewhat lesser extent, the Spanish sought to control territory, oppressing or eradicating the indigenous populations in the process, through a variety of means, from armed conflict to biological warfare. They sought not to learn from native cultures, but to dominate or convert them.

The French, at first, took a different approach. While they, too, invaded native territories and built settlements there, the French mainly focused on extracting the furs of animals through trade with indigenous people, which required establishing a market relationship with them. This, too, had its dark sides: the French got involved in conflicts among tribal communities, such as the Iroquois Wars,[6] and their pursuit of beaver and other furs led to dramatic decreases in the populations of many animals.[7] But the fur trade did demand a degree of trust and reciprocity between the French and native people and a degree of land stewardship, at least enough so that the flow of animal furs would keep coming.

With that in mind, let's imagine for a moment how things might be different had the French way of working with the native population prevailed over that of the English and Spanish? What if, instead of taking the land, those of European descent had respected indigenous rights and continued to trade with native people, who maintained their tribal lands? Such questions may seem pointless, since that obviously did not happen, but we can learn a lot from such thought experiments. If nothing else, they – like the pandemic – allow us to imagine another way of being in the world.

A thought experiment can also identify possible solutions to some of our most difficult, unsolved problems. Take our water shortages, for example. If we look at a watershed map of North America, for example, and the map of pre-contact tribal nations, there is a lot of

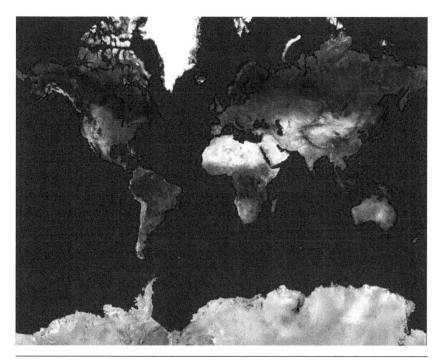

Figure 13.1 The world as it might look, were we all to live according to radical indigenism.

overlap.[8] The territory of many tribes roughly followed the watersheds upon which they depended, with the multiple watersheds along the Atlantic and Pacific coasts having the greatest diversity of tribal cultures, and the larger inland watersheds of the Mississippi basin supporting fewer tribes with more extensive land.

The modern equivalent might be the watershed management organizations tasked with protecting water quality in each of the regions, but those organizations rarely line up with political boundaries and have little relationship to the diversity of people and cultures who now occupy watersheds. Meanwhile, the frequently arbitrary borders that people of European descent established between nations and among states and provinces cut across watersheds, which has not helped in the recent water wars between American states like Georgia and Florida or Texas and New Mexico.[9] We don't steward our water resources; we squabble over them. A more reasonable organization would be to align political boundaries with the continent's watersheds, which might well have happened had indigenous people remained in charge.

Re-imagining North America's political structure along indigenous lines might also help address the problem of atmospheric carbon accumulation and of climate change more broadly. North America has 15 ecological regions defined by the types of forests, plains, or deserts they represent.[10] Prior to the European invasions, indigenous communities evolved in accordance with those ecosystems and lived in harmony with them, although not entirely. Archeologists have calculated that the indigenous community of Cahokia, for example, cut roughly 1 million trees immediately surrounding a settlement of just 25,000 people, eventually clearing a 9-mile swath of forest, although many experts do not think deforestation led to the community's decline.[11]

Indigenous land stewardship, however, was far better than current agricultural and development patterns, which destroys about 10 billion trees annually, leading to an estimated 46% drop in the number of trees that existed on the planet prior to human civilization.[12] Were indigenous practices to still prevail, according to our thought experiment, we would be planting trees as fast as we cut them.

There are some modest efforts in that direction, such as the Trillion Trees Initiative, which has the goal of planting 1 trillion trees by 2050.[13] That is a worthy effort, but an insufficient one: a trillion trees is not nearly enough to absorb 48 billion tons of carbon annually, and the carbon sequestration of those trees is needed now, not just by 2050.[14] To absorb that much carbon, assuming an average of 290 trees per acre, it would require nearly 7 billion acres or over 90% of the roughly 12 million square miles of arable land on the planet, leaving very little land to farm.

In other words, we cannot tree-plant our way out of the problem of climate change; we have to live our way out of it, which takes us back to our thought experiment. To stop appreciably adding to the amount of carbon already accumulated in the atmosphere, we need to live low-carbon lives, dramatically reducing or eliminating carbon-emitting activities and technologies as fast as possible. While that would not end climate change, it would slow it down and avoid the predicted 6°C increase in global temperatures, an increase that would be suicidal, given the extreme heat, more powerful storms, and increased flooding that just a 1°C increase has brought.[15]

The pandemic gave us all a taste of what it would be like to lead a low-carbon life. Most people drove and flew much less or not at all, and most of us lived more outdoors than we did before, which reduced heating and cooling demand. And most of us saw how easy it is to get what we need delivered to us and to connect to others through digital platforms and devices, making travel largely unnecessary. We might call that experience a high-tech version of indigenous living, as we quarantined with those who we were closest to, while turning to the natural world for relief and solace.

We might also call it a low-tech – or "Lo-TEK"– life, as designer Julia Watson calls it in her book by that name.[16] In it, she documents what she calls "radical indigenism" among native people across the globe, where they have developed highly sophisticated ways of meeting their needs and adapting to their environments using the materials they have available from the land they occupy. That indigenous – and highly ingenious – technology often gets portrayed as primitive or backward, when in fact it involves a high level of skill and a remarkable resourcefulness that few modern people can match.

For our thought experiment, we would probably need both high-tech and low-TEK strategies: high-tech ways of connecting to other people and sharing information and ideas from afar and low-tech ways of living using local resources and evolving techniques that allow us to live as lightly on the land as indigenous cultures have long known how to do. Both involve the digital – the digital computer and the digits of our fingers – and both entail a level of sophistication that most modern technology cannot match.

While such a future may seem far out or at least far off, the pandemic showed how quickly the future can become present. I helped co-found the International Geodesign Collaboration or IGC, an organization consisting of over 200 universities in over 60 countries, that looks at how modern societies might move in more environmentally resilient and socially just directions by the years 2035 and 2050.[17] The IGC member institutions try to make the future present in the policies and decision making of governments around the world, recognizing that we have little time to act before the stakes in not acting become too great.

To show the cost of non-action, the IGC universities look at the early, late, or non-adoption of environmentally friendly development strategies, and measure the outcomes of those strategies according to the United Nations' Sustainable Development Goals and the carbon sequestration benchmarks of the Trillion Trees initiative. In almost all cases, the IGC research shows that the non-adopter option – a path followed by many governments unwilling to disrupt the carbon economy – leads to extraordinary costs and extreme environmental disruption by 2050.

Those outcomes reinforce the argument made at the beginning of this book, which is that the 400-year Ponzi Scheme of exploiting people, extracting resources, and extinguishing species is not only morally and ethically objectionable, but also environmentally and economically unsustainable. In one IGC project after another, the non-adoption strategy condemns people to a future that is "solitary, poor, nasty, brutish, and short," to use Thomas Hobbes's phrase.[18] Some parts of the world will become too hot, others too flooded, and still others too dry to inhabit.[19] While keeping things as they are may seem like the most prudent response to the not yet fully known effects of climate change, it is also the riskiest and most irresponsible course.

The late adopter scenarios in most IGC projects might be called the political realist options, in which humanity begins to move in a positive direction after a lot of denial, damage, and outright resistance to change. In one nation after another, the IGC member universities grapple with the unwillingness among many people and their leaders to give up not just the carbon-based economy, but also the idea that humanity can – and should – command and control nature. By 2035 in many of the late adopter scenarios, the impacts of climate disruption become increasingly massive as millions of people flee coastal areas or hot zones, as food systems become disrupted and scarcities become common, as political polarization and gang violence increase, and as pandemics become more common as zoonotic diseases erupt with little warning or preparedness on the part of governments.

Given the cost and chaos of that scenario, many of the IGC universities see late adopters getting to a point where they have had enough and cannot afford to deny the impact of climate change any longer. As a result, people begin to reduce consumption by sharing goods and services, to embrace a range of environmental and equity goals, and to move development in a more sustainable and resilient direction. The late adopters, in other words, start to do the right thing after they have done the opposite, eventually getting to a better place by 2050 after taking a somewhat circuitous and tumultuous path to get there. The late adopter scenarios in the IGC projects may be the most realistic, given the current level of denial that remains a factor in so many discussions about climate change, but they cannot compare to what the early adopter scenarios have to offer.

In most of the IGC projects, the early adopters must act in the face of a lot of uncertainty and a considerable number of unknowns as climate change continues to have impacts that not even the most pessimistic scientists predicted. And yet, while acting with incomplete information has its risks, it also offers the greatest opportunities. Our thought experiment on an indigenous North America represents one such early adopter scenario. In an embrace of indigenous practices regarding the landscape and the natural world, early adopters might initiate a massive reforestation and native replanting of the continent, greatly expanding habitat for native species and concentrating agriculture in solar-powered, hydroponic farms able to feed the human population in a much smaller physical and ecological footprint.

At a local level, the early adopter scenarios might also see, by 2035, a more mobile, pop-up approach on the part of many businesses and institutions, where they deliver goods and services or set up shop in structures that are temporary, lightweight, and easily portable, leaving no trace of human occupation behind. Meanwhile, open spaces might become more varied, with parks serving a much wider range of activities and with connected habitat corridors emerging across the landscape. That early adopter scenario is also a very old one, as we know from indigenous communities that wisely recognized how much we are part of the natural world rather than foolishly thinking we are better and smarter than it.

The pandemic certainly made the foolishness newly apparent. Consider what it revealed about our food system, based on the massive slaughter of animals that goes on every day, out of sight and out of mind for most of us. The pandemic brought that to everyone's attention when animal processing plants began to close during the plague as large numbers of employees, working in close quarters, became sickened by COVID-19, closing the assembly line of meat to American food markets.

We learned that just one closed plant processed 20,000 hogs a day, or 5,200,000 hogs a year. And globally, the amount of human slaughter of animals seemed almost incomprehensible: with more than 200 million animals slaughtered in the world every day and, when adding wild animals and fish, the daily kill comes close to 3 billion or 72 billion land animals and 1.2 trillion sea creatures every year.[20] That would be the equivalent of killing the entire human population of 7.8 billion people in a little more than two-and-a-half days, or the equivalent of every person on the planet killing 163 animals a year, or approximately one animal every other day, all year long.

Most people did not see this killing field, only its meat products, neatly wrapped and sorted in grocery stores. Hiding the process by which this food came to us kept people from questioning the ethics of this butchery of animals who, as fellow sentient beings, feel fear and pain as much as we do. It doesn't take much imagination to picture how we would respond if another creature raised us for slaughter, crowding us into pens and feeding us as much as possible to fatten us up fast for their food. Would any of us accept this as our just fate? Compared to the carnage that we inflict upon other animals, COVID-19 was forgiving: 4 million victims worldwide as I write this. We kill that many animals every half hour, every day. Maybe the pandemic was nature's way of warning us that unless we stop the mass slaughter of other animals, one day a virus will jump from animals to humans capable of slaughtering us too.

By 2050, the early adopter scenario of our thought experiment has had a transformative effect on North America. I did a study with a graduate student, Lingxiao Shu, in which we extended the idea of the ecologist, E.O. Wilson in his "Half-Earth Project."[21] Wilson argued that we need to conserve half the earth for species other than humans if we hope to preserve the biodiversity that we depend upon. If there was ever a modern, indigenous way of thinking about nature, that was it. What we did in our study was take that one step further to see how much more of the earth's land and seas we could preserve by concentrating the human population on as small a footprint as possible.

Using the infographic developed by the designer and writer Tim De Chant, we imagined the entire human population living at the density of Paris, in roughly six-story high buildings along active, pedestrian-oriented streets.[22] We also imagined the human population, forced by extreme climate change, having to move to the one place in the world with enough fresh water to sustain us: North America's Great Lakes. In our study, we looked at how much land it would take if humanity lived in a Paris-like city along the roughly 9,700-mile shoreline of those lakes. With rooftop greenhouses capable of feeding the people in the buildings below and with solar powered cladding capable of powering each building without a centralized power source, we calculated that a city about 8.5 miles wide along that entire perimeter could accommodate every person currently alive. We also calculated that the Great Lakes, alone, had a many thousand-year supply of fresh water to meet the drinking, bathing, and food-producing needs of the human population.

While the idea of the entire human population living in one, continuous, low-rise city might seem outlandish, it was a thought experiment in order to show how little land humanity actually needed in order to survive, and how easily we could let the rest of the planet

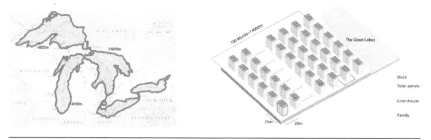

Figure 13.2 Climate change forcing humanity north, to fresh water, letting the planet recover.

recover from the impact that humanity has had on it. This was not a "half earth" scenario, but a 99.99% one. Such a scenario would obviously demand a transformation in how human beings relate not just to the natural world, but also to each other, socially, culturally, and politically. But it is a thought experiment that might guide us in the post-pandemic, post-Ponzi Scheme world in which we have now entered.

The COVID-19 pandemic did not just affect us all in myriad ways in the short term, over the next few decades. It also represented nature's shot across the bow, so to speak, where we saw what lies in store for humanity if we do not change our ways. For all of its challenging and tragic impacts in the short term, the recent pandemic paled in comparison to some that have come before, like the Black Death, [23] which killed an estimated 50% of Europe's population, or the 1918 flu pandemic that infected an estimated 500 million people worldwide.[24] But there are other viral diseases, such as viral hemorrhagic fevers like Ebola, that have a much higher mortality rate than COVID-19 and that are one plane flight away from infecting the global population if we do not greatly improve our readiness to stop such an event from ever happening.

But the challenge that the pandemic put at our feet is more than epidemiological. It involves almost every aspect of modern life and of our individual lives as well. We can continue to participate in the Ponzi Scheme that has brought us to the point of collapse or we can create a better way of being, one modeled more on the ways humanity lived for most of our history as a species and that we have only relatively recently forsaken. The thought experiment of imagining our living in more indigenous ways was not just to value the ways of native people, but also to remind ourselves that we were all, once, native people, occupying the planet in ways that coexisted with each other and all of the other species on the planet.

Remembering that – and rediscovering what that means in a modern context – remains the real opportunity that the pandemic has created for us. This is not about going backward to some imagined primitive way of life, but instead going forward to a more just and sustainable world that is high-tech and low-tech at the same time, using both our digital devices and the digits of our hands to create a better future for everyone on this planet, human and non-human alike. It stems from an abundance mentality, rather than a scarcity one, and it arises from a desire to learn from nature and native people rather than to exploit them. Finally, it comes from the recognition that a good life means being good to all of life, to that of other species as well as to our own.

Notes

1 Zoe M. Volenec, Joel O. Abraham, Alexander D. Becker, Andy P. Dobson, "Public Parks and the Pandemic: How Park Usage Has Been Affected by COVID-19 Policies," *Plos One*, May 19, 2021. https://journals.plos.org/plosone/article?id=10.1371/journal.pone.0251799#:~:text=We%20find%20that%20park%20visitation,to%20experience%20elevated%20visitation%20levels.
2 Don Kinzler, "The Pandemic Propelled Gardening to New Heights. Will the Trend Last?" *Ag Week*, December 26, 2020. www.agweek.com/lifestyle/home-and-garden/6813622-The-pandemic-propelled-gardening-to-new-heights.-Will-the-trend-last
3 "Origin of 'Minnesota'," State Symbols USA. https://statesymbolsusa.org/symbol-official-item/minnesota/state-name-origin/origin-minnesota
4 Thomas Fisher, "Seeing the World Whole," *Journal of Architectural Education*, 64(2), March 2012. www.jaeonline.org/issues/beginning-design#/page2/
5 Francis Jennings, *The Invasion of America: Indians, Colonialism, and the Cant of Conquest* (Chapel Hill: University of North Carolina Press, 2010)
6 Zach Parrott, Tabitha Marshall, "Iroquois Wars," *The Canadian Encyclopedia*, July 31, 2019. www.thecanadianencyclopedia.ca/en/article/iroquois-wars
7 Rachel B. Juen, Michael S. Nassaney, "The Fur Trade," Fort St. Joseph Archaeological Project, Western Michigan University, 2012. https://scholarworks.wmich.edu/cgi/viewcontent.cgi?article=1009&context=fortstjoseph
8 "Native American Tribes and Nations," *History on the Net, Salem Media*, August 18, 2021. www.historyonthenet.com/native-american-tribes-nations
9 Robert Glennon, "Interstate Water Wars Are Heating Up Along With the Climate," *The Conversation*, April 19, 2021. https://theconversation.com/interstate-water-wars-are-heating-up-along-with-the-climate-159092
10 "Ecoregions of North America," United States Environmental Protection Agency. www.epa.gov/eco-research/ecoregions-north-america
11 Meilan Solly, "Why Did Cahokia, One of North America's Largest Pre-Hispanic Cities, Collapse?" *Smithsonian*, April 16, 2021. www.smithsonianmag.com/smart-news/why-did-cahokia-one-largest-pre-hispanic-cities-north-america-collapse-180977528/
12 Elizabeth Pennisi, "Earth Home to 3 Trillion Trees, Half as Many as When Human Civilization Arose," *Science*, September 2, 2015. www.sciencemag.org/news/2015/09/earth-home-3-trillion-trees-half-many-when-human-civilization-arose
13 Trillion Trees Initiative. https://trilliontrees.org/
14 "Tons of CO_2 Emitted into the Atmosphere Globally, This Year," *The World Counts*, 2021. www.theworldcounts.com/challenges/climate-change/global-warming/global-co2-emissions/story

15 Richard B. Rood, "If We Stopped Emitting Greenhouse Gases Right Now, Would We Stop Climate Change?" *The Conversation*, July 7, 2017. https://theconversation.com/if-we-stopped-emitting-greenhouse-gases-right-now-would-we-stop-climate-change-78882

16 Julia Watson, *Lo-TEK: Design by Radical Indigenism* (New York: Taschen, 2021).

17 International Geodesign Collaboration. www.igc-geodesign.org/

18 Thomas Hobbes, Ian Shapiro, editor. *Leviathan: Or the Matter, Form, and Power of a Commonwealth Ecclesiastical and Civil* (New Haven: Yale University Press, 2010).

19 Al Shaw, Abrahm Lustgarten, "Climate Maps Show a Transformed United States," ProPublica, September 15, 2020. https://projects.propublica.org/climate-migration/

20 Matthew Zampa, "How Many Animals Are Killed for Food Every Day?" *Sentient Media*, September 16, 2018. https://sentientmedia.org/how-many-animals-are-killed-for-food-every-day/

21 Half-Earth Project. www.half-earthproject.org/

22 John Pavlus, "Inforgraphic: If 7 Billion People Lived in One City, How Big Would It Be?" *Fast Company*, October 31, 2011. www.fastcompany.com/1665327/infographic-if-7-billion-people-lived-in-one-city-how-big-would-it-be

23 Sharon N. DeWitte, "Mortality Risk and Survival in the Aftermath of the Medieval Black Death," *Plos One*, May 7, 2014. www.ncbi.nlm.nih.gov/pmc/articles/PMC4013036/

24 "1918 Pandemic (H1N1 Virus), Centers for Disease Control and Prevention. www.cdc.gov/flu/pandemic-resources/1918-pandemic-h1n1.html?web=1&-wdLOR=c42A30F1A-0190–8A46-B7A0-B0EECAD9AE95

Figure Credits

1.1 Luigi Tiriticco, Flickr CC BY 2.0.

1.2 Rawpixel Ltd, Flickr CC BY 2.0.

1.3 John Snow.

1.4 Tomi Knuutila, Flickr CC BY 2.0.

1.5 Elvert Barnes, Flickr CC BY-SA 2.0.

2.1 Flickr CC BY 2.0.

2.2 Sydney Ulrich, Baonhia Xiong.

2.3 James Pettinari.

2.4 Emily Stover.

3.1 Rawpixel Ltd, Flickr CC BY 2.0.

3.2 Key West Wedding Photography Flickr CC BY 2.0.

3.3 Cityswift Flickr CC BY 2.0.

3.4 Chad Davis, Flickr CC BY 2.0.

4.1 Dan Gaken, Flickr CC BY-SA 2.0.

4.2 Ivan Radic, Flickr CC BY 2.0.

4.3 Georgia National Guard, Flickr CC BY 2.0.

4.4 Jonathan Rolande, Flickr CC BY 2.0.

5.1 Paul Wicks, Flickr CC BY 2.0.

5.2 New York National Guard, Flickr CC BY 2.0.

5.3 Ron Cogswell, Flickr CC BY 2.0.

5.4 Insomnia Cured Here, Flickr CC BY-SA 2.0.

6.1 Joseph Hang, Java Nyamjav, Chon Fai Kuok, Hoyoung Lee, Julia Luke, Brian Smith.

6.2 Joseph Hang, Java Nyamjav, Chon Fai Kuok, Hoyoung Lee, Julia Luke, Brian Smith.

6.3 Joseph Hang, Java Nyamjav, Chon Fai Kuok, Hoyoung Lee, Julia Luke, Brian Smith.

6.4 Joseph Hang, Java Nyamjav, Chon Fai Kuok, Hoyoung Lee, Julia Luke, Brian Smith.

7.1 Joseph Hang, Java Nyamjav, Chon Fai Kuok, Hoyoung Lee, Julia Luke, Brian Smith.

7.2 Joseph Hang, Java Nyamjav, Chon Fai Kuok, Hoyoung Lee, Julia Luke, Brian Smith.

7.3 Joseph Hang, Java Nyamjav, Chon Fai Kuok, Hoyoung Lee, Julia Luke, Brian Smith.

7.4 Joseph Hang, Java Nyamjav, Chon Fai Kuok, Hoyoung Lee, Julia Luke, Brian Smith.

8.1 Joseph Hang, Java Nyamjav, Chon Fai Kuok, Hoyoung Lee, Julia Luke, Brian Smith.

8.2 Joseph Hang, Java Nyamjav, Chon Fai Kuok, Hoyoung Lee, Julia Luke, Brian Smith.

8.3 Joseph Hang, Java Nyamjav, Chon Fai Kuok, Hoyoung Lee, Julia Luke, Brian Smith.

8.4 Joseph Hang, Java Nyamjav, Chon Fai Kuok, Hoyoung Lee, Julia Luke, Brian Smith.

9.1 Joseph Hang, Java Nyamjav.

9.2 Joseph Hang, Java Nyamjav.

9.3 Jamie Piatt, Vera Dong.

9.4 Joseph Hang, Java Nyamjav.

10.1 Giambattista Nolli, Rawpixel Flickr CC BY 4.0.

10.2 Joseph Hang, Java Nyamjav.

10.3 Joseph Hang, Java Nyamjav.

10.4 Joseph Hang, Java Nyamjav.

11.1 Joseph Hang, Java Nyamjav.

11.2 Joseph Hang, Java Nyamjav.

11.3 Joseph Hang, Java Nyamjav.

11.4 Joseph Hang, Java Nyamjav.

11.5 Joseph Hang, Java Nyamjav.

12.1 Joseph Hang, Java Nyamjav.

12.2 Joseph Hang, Java Nyamjav, Chon Fai Kuok, Hoyoung Lee, Julia Luke, Brian Smith.

13.1 NASA.

13.2 Lingxiao Shu.

INDEX

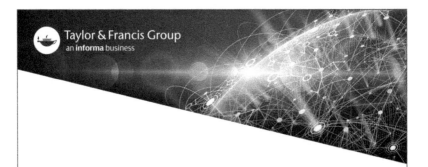

Printed in the USA
CPSIA information can be obtained
at www.ICGtesting.com
LVHW021607290424
778795LV00009B/199

9 781032 055817